# LT. BILL FARROW

# LT. BILL FARROW
## DOOLITTLE RAIDER

### JOHN CHANDLER GRIFFIN

*4/7/07*

*Coy—*
*My very Best!*

*John Griffin*

**PELICAN PUBLISHING COMPANY**
GRETNA 2007

*The word "Pelican" and the depiction of a pelican are trademarks
of Pelican Publishing Company, Inc., and are registered in the
U.S. Patent and Trademark Office.*

**Library of Congress Cataloging-in-Publication Data**

Griffin, John Chandler, 1936-
  Lt. Bill Farrow : Doolittle raider / John Chandler Griffin ; foreword
by Charles Duke.
    p. cm.
  Includes index.
  ISBN-13: 978-1-58980-422-7 (alk. paper)
  1. Farrow, William Glover, 1918-1942. 2. World War, 1939-1945—
Prisoners and prisons, Japanese. 3. World War, 1939-1945—Aerial
operations, American. 4. World War, 1939-1945—Camaigns—Pacific
Area. 5. Prisoners of war—United States—Biography. 6. Prisoners of
war—Japan—Biography. 7. Air pilots, Military—United States—
Biography. I. Title. II. Title: Lieutenant Bill Farrow.
  D805.J3F375 2006
  940.54'252092—dc22
  [B]

                                      2006025314

Printed in the United States of America

Published by Pelican Publishing Company, Inc.
1000 Burmaster Street, Gretna, Louisiana 70053

This little volume is humbly dedicated to all those fine young airmen who so selflessly volunteered for Lt. Col. Jimmy Doolittle's raid on Tokyo back in April of 1942, one of the most memorable events of World War II. Some lived, some died. In our memories they will all live forever.

# Contents

# Foreword

Several years ago I had the distinct privilege and honor to be a speaker at a reunion of the Doolittle Raiders in Columbia, South Carolina. At this dinner-banquet, a video recorded by the first President Bush was shown. In the video he recalled as a young man how the Raiders were his heroes. As I spoke, I said that I was a young boy of six when the Raiders flew their daring mission. The Raiders also became my heroes. In the eyes of a little boy these men were like Superman. I wanted to emulate them and so daydreamed that I was a pilot flying similar missions. Little did I realize that one day as an Air Force pilot and astronaut, I would have the pleasure of meeting some of my boyhood heroes, including Gen. James Doolittle.

Of course I never met Bill Farrow, but his story, as told here, still inspires me. It is a story of a small town boy from South Carolina who volunteered to serve his country and who found himself participating in one of the most dramatic and daring missions of World War II. His story like so many others helps me understand what it is to be a man of courage and faith. Ignoring all the risks, he volunteered for this most dangerous mission knowing the probability of returning home safely was very small. This is a story of self-sacrifice and heroism far above the call of duty. Had all gone according to plan, successful recovery in China was doubtful, but when the launch came early and added almost four hundred miles to the trip, the odds fell almost to zero. Yet no one backed out. They were determined to take the war to Japan.

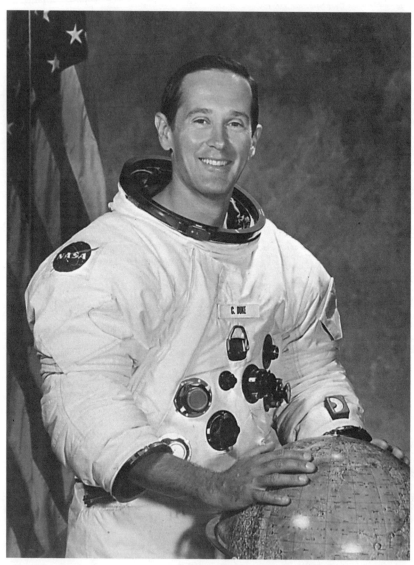

*A native of Lancaster, SC, Gen. Charles Duke graduated from the US Naval Academy in 1957, received an advanced degree from MIT in 1964, and was accepted into NASA's astronaut program in 1966. In 1972 he achieved immortality when he piloted* Apollo 16 *to the moon, becoming only the tenth man ever to walk on the lunar surface. In 1973 he was named South Carolina's Man of the Year, and was inducted into the South Carolina Hall of Fame that same year. His identical twin, Dr. Bill Duke, a noted physician, is a resident of Lancaster.* (Photo courtesy of Gen. Charles Duke)

How does one find the strength and courage to carry on in the face of such seemingly insurmountable odds? In Bill Farrow's case, it was his faith in God and a sure knowledge that he was doing the right thing. The Scriptures state that God is with us and that He is an ever-present help in times of trouble. Bill Farrow knew this and trusted in his Creator. Even in the face of all his cruel and terrible ordeals, and finally a Japanese firing squad, his faith never wavered. He held fast in the face of humiliation, deprivation, and death.

This story and countless others from World War II need to be told and retold and preserved for future generations. Just as this story motivated me and my generation in the Vietnam War and instilled in us a feeling of patriotism and the courage to serve, it will, I believe, also inspire our children and grandchildren to serve if called upon. Indeed, as long as our people remember the heroism and sacrifices of these men, we will continue to stand in the gap when needed.

I thank God for men like Bill Farrow and all the Doolittle Raiders who gave so much that we may enjoy our freedom.

Charlie Duke
*Apollo 16* Astronaut
March 14, 2006

# Preface

On the evening of October 14, 1942, the eve of Bill Farrow's execution, the Japanese allowed him to write last letters to his loved ones in America. These letters were to be turned over to the International Red Cross for immediate delivery, but the Japanese never delivered the letters. To the contrary, they were discovered by American authorities at war's end in August 1945. Farrow wrote one of these letters to Lt. Ivan Ferguson, his old friend and flying mate back at Pendleton Air Base in Oregon. Following receipt of this letter in September 1945, Ferguson sent the following message to Farrow's mother, Jessie Stem Farrow, in Darlington, South Carolina:

> Dear Mrs. Farrow:
>
> You can be sure that Bill was himself right to the last, and displayed that courage which was always an outstanding characteristic of his. He was a fine friend, and one who possessed the courage to live out his ideals. Certainly no one died more gloriously in this war than Lt. William G. Farrow. He was a true hero until the last, and I consider him an outstanding example of American manhood and American ideals. He had completed the rise above himself which made it easier for him to give his life. He was able to do this through his faith in God, and the realization he had lived a good life even though short. If all of us would live as he did, war on this planet would be impossible and unknown.
>
> To me he is not dead and will never die.

This letter expresses well the sentiments of everyone who ever knew William Glover Farrow, a true American hero.

13

# Acknowledgments

Jimmy Doolittle's raid on Tokyo in April 1942 will go down in history as one of the most famous events in the annals of American warfare. And of course this work deals with that great event, but only to a certain extent. More, it is intended to stand as a humble tribute to the memory of Lt. William Glover Farrow, a member of that heroic team of patriotic American flyers. He was a native of Darlington, South Carolina, and a young man who personified all that is good in our society. But then, on a black day in October 1942, his life was needlessly snuffed out by a cruel foreign enemy.

Obviously I never knew Bill Farrow, and have learned about him only through the experiences of others. There was his Aunt Margaret Stem, for example, whom I interviewed on several occasions after she had become a resident in a retirement home in Florence, South Carolina. I was working on a magazine article about Farrow at that time, and Margaret Stem was a storehouse of knowledge. She had been like a second mother to Bill during his growing-up years in Darlington, and she probably knew him better than anyone else. She kept my pen flying as she related detail after detail of his life and activities between 1918 and 1942. On my last visit with her she opened a trunk and took out a book titled *Tall and Free as Meant by God*. It was a very poignant book that Margaret herself had written years following Farrow's death, a beautifully written memorial of sorts, which presents a fine picture of Bill up until his becoming a participant in Doolittle's famous raid on Tokyo. This work also provides an inside look at how his family survived over a thousand days of sorrow and worry during the war, until they finally received official confirmation that the Japanese had executed Bill. Margaret was kind enough to autograph and present a copy of her book to me, which I will treasure forever.

Of course Bill Farrow did not live in a vacuum but was constantly surrounded by others. This was especially true once he had become a member of Doolittle's Raiders, living, eating, and sleeping twenty-four hours a day with his courageous comrades. Certainly those brave men also claim a place in this work. An invaluable source of information here was C. V. Glines's work *Four Came Home,* the story of those eight Raiders who had the misfortune to fall into the hands of the Japanese immediately following the raid on Tokyo. Their terrible experiences were common to all, but I tried to relate them to the reader through the eyes of Bill Farrow.

I would also like to mention the help given me by Tom Gaskins, president of the Darlington County Historical Society. Tom and his associates planned a Bill Farrow Day in Darlington, and he has avidly supported this work about Farrow as though it were his own.

And many thanks to those very devoted women, Doris Gandy and Kay Williamson, who manage the Darlington County Museum where the Bill Farrow papers are housed. Both take their work very seriously and seem to know exactly where to find anything I ever asked for. Indeed, the museum has numerous boxes of Farrow material, including mounds of printed material written by Farrow himself, as well as dozens of rare photographs, newspaper articles, and letters.

Also I would like to express my gratitude to Bill Farrow's sister, Mrs. Marjorie Farrow Maus of Ft. Jones, California, who most graciously spoke to me any time I called. After the passage of sixty years she continues to find it extremely painful to recall those cruel days of World War II. Still, she bravely answered my questions as best she could.

And there are so many others, elderly residents of Darlington

County mainly, who came forward with invaluable bits of information. My deepest gratitude to them also.

Closer to home, I would like to thank our dean at USC-Lancaster, Dr. John Catalano, for his continued support of my projects, both moral and financial. And the same is true for our academic dean at USC-Lancaster, Dr. Ron Cox.

And I also want to mention my wife Betty King Griffin, my daughter Alexis, and my three granddaughters, Kori, Emmalee Grace, and Serrah Roxanne. They are my toughest critics, and I appreciate their dedication and unending efforts to help me devise a perfect, error-free work some day.

As for Farrow's comrades, those dauntless Raiders who survived three years and four months in various Japanese prison camps, I feel the utmost admiration for those fellows. As of this writing, three of them are still living. They are:

Jake DeShazer and wife Florence of Salem, Oregon; Bob Hite and wife Dorothy of Camden, Arkansas; and Chase Nielsen and wife Phyllis of Brigham City, Utah. These are wonderful people, and once I explained to them that I was writing this book as a memorial to Bill Farrow, they responded most graciously. Not only did they answer my repeated questions, but on several occasions they even sent me personal photographs and other materials which have proven invaluable.

It seems safe to predict that these brave men will one day take their place alongside Nathan Hale and Colin Kelly as among America's all-time greatest heroes. May they live forever.

# Introduction

It was just after 3:00 P.M. on October 15, 1942, a cold overcast afternoon with dark storm clouds hanging low in the sky over Shanghai, China. There, in cell #6 in Kiangwa Military Prison, young Bill Farrow and his two companions waited nervously for the clock to strike the fatal hour of their execution. Meanwhile, a squad of Japanese soldiers was sent to the outskirts of Shanghai to Public Cemetery #1, where they cut down the tall weeds and cleared away the trash that littered the area. They then erected three small wooden crosses, each three feet high, placing them ten feet apart. A few hours later the three American airmen, Lt. Bill Farrow, Lt. Dean Hallmark, and Cpl. Harold Spatz, captured members of Lt. Col. James Doolittle's raid on Tokyo and all convicted in a kangaroo court of committing war crimes against the Japanese people, would be forced to kneel here and their arms tied to the crosses. They would then suffer the consequences of their terrible crimes.

Now, standing by the three crosses, facing to the front, the Japanese soldiers stepped off twenty paces. On this spot, at exactly 4:00 P.M., the firing squad, armed with high-powered military rifles, would take their positions. To the rear of the firing squad the Japanese counted off another ten feet. Here they placed a long polished table and six chairs. This was the ceremonial altar where the Knights of the Bushido, high-ranking Japanese officers who would serve as the formal execution committee, would sit

19

and observe the executions to make sure that everything was done according to time-honored ritual.

At that very moment, back in their filthy jail cell, Bill Farrow and Harold Spatz realized that Dean Hallmark, the heroic pilot of the *Green Hornet,* was only semi-conscious, too ill to understand that in the coming hours he would be breathing his last. Watching over Hallmark, Harold Spatz, the young gunner aboard Farrow's plane, the *Bat Out of Hell,* was coping with his impending death calmly and with self-control. At twenty-four, Bill Farrow was three years his senior and college educated. Spatz admired the deeply religious and well-educated Bill Farrow and trusted him without question. It seems most likely that Farrow and Spatz discussed spiritual matters during their final hours to ease their nerves and prepare themselves for the ordeal to come.

At 3:30 P.M. they were startled out of their contemplation. Their cell door was jerked open and Farrow and Spatz were hauled to their feet by four burly guards, then they were hand-cuffed, blindfolded, and shoved from the cell. Moving too slowly for their gleeful guards, the two prisoners were prodded with the sharp tips of their bayonets. Behind Farrow and Spatz, Dean Hallmark was rolled onto a stretcher and carried to the black 1938 Ford truck waiting to bring them to the cemetery.

According to official Japanese documents, the three con-demned American airmen arrived at the cemetery at precisely 4:00 P.M. The truck came to a halt, and the flyers were dragged to the ground. Extremely apprehensive now, they stood quietly, waiting for further orders. A sergeant spoke gruffly, and a guard quickly removed their blindfolds and handcuffs.

Farrow and Spatz looked at one another. Attempting an escape crossed their minds, but after six months of starvation and cruel tortures they were so weak that they could hardly stand, much less run away. Farrow was chagrined to realize that his body was visibly quivering with fear and anxiety.

At a command, the guards grabbed the prisoners' arms and led them up a small hill to the three crosses in the execution area. Each was positioned before a cross and forced to kneel down, Farrow positioned between Spatz and Hallmark. The guards tied their wrists to the crossbars, then looped a length of rope around their necks to force their heads to remain upright.

At that point Lt. Goro Tashida led a nine-man rifle squad to the area. Three of the soldiers were posted as security guards around the site. The other six were marched in double ranks to a point twenty feet to the front of the helpless prisoners. Two riflemen were assigned to each American. The second marksman, standing to the rear, would fire only if the primary marksman missed or suffered a misfire.

Now, with thunder appropriately rumbling overhead, four high-ranking Japanese officers, the Knights of the Bushido, accompanied by an interpreter and a medical officer, took their places behind the altar to the rear of the firing squad. The leader of the Knights of the Bushido, Maj. Itsuro Hata, who had prosecuted the airmen at their mock trial, lit incense and directed his fellow officers to remove their caps. As Major Hata later testified at the War Crimes Trial in 1946, he then read a brief statement in English to the airmen "to make them feel more easy about their coming death."

Then, at a signal from Major Hata, Capt. Sotojiro Tatsuta, the prison's warden, approached the kneeling airmen and told them, as he would later testify at the War Crimes Trial, "You have lived as heroes. Now it is time to die as heroes."

At that point Farrow raised his eyes to the warden and said, "Captain, would you see to it that our loved ones back home are told that we died bravely?"

"And I am happy to state," testified Tatsuta to the court, "that they all met death as only true warriors can do."

Following the executions, the medical officer stepped forward and verified that the men were indeed dead. Their bodies were placed in three crude wooden coffins, which were laid side by side before the altar. The Japanese officers standing behind the table, in the tradition of the Bushido, stood with heads bowed, praying silently for the souls of the slain airmen. They then replaced their caps, and everyone departed the area.

The entire procedure had taken just half an hour, and the Japanese High Command at last had their revenge.

The bodies of these three heroes were immediately placed in the back of a truck and driven to the Japanese Residents'

Association Crematorium in Shanghai. Within the hour their bodies had been cremated and their ashes placed in urns. The Japanese had promised that their ashes, along with their last letters home, would be returned to America via the International Red Cross. But it was not until war's end some three years later that American authorities would discover the urns containing their remains at the International Funeral Home in downtown Shanghai, where they had been hidden by frightened Japanese warlords who feared reprisals from American investigators.

It was not until then, in September 1945, that anyone learned the fate of these three airmen. Their families had prayed and sent them packages via the Red Cross throughout the long months and years of the war. Now they were crushed to learn that their hopes and prayers had come to nothing, due to the cruelty of their Japanese enemies.

# LT. BILL FARROW

# CHAPTER 1

# Events Are Set in Motion

Bill Farrow, who enjoyed only a brief stay here on earth thanks to a cruel and unforgiving enemy, is without question one of America's all-time greatest heroes. Indeed, he was a most intelligent and deserving young man, a dedicated scholar and Christian, who should have lived to become a leader among men in his home state of South Carolina. Truly, his story is unusually inspirational.

Who knows? Should his illustrious life have continued as it had been for the first twenty years, he might well have become governor of the state some day. Certainly no one in his rural hometown of Darlington would have been in the least surprised. In fact, many of his friends and relatives confidently predicted that the day would come when young Bill Farrow would become known throughout the nation as Gov. William Glover Farrow.

But thanks to fate or destiny or God, forces ultimately beyond Farrow's control, such was not to be. Instead of graduating from the state university and eventually taking his place among the upper echelons of South Carolina's most outstanding citizens, he decided at the age of twenty-two to withdraw from the university and become an Air Corps pilot. Then, only two years later, after a series of strange and harrowing adventures, a squad of merciless Japanese soldiers would lead this country boy from Darlington, South Carolina, to an ancient cemetery on the outskirts of Shanghai, China, where he would be bound to a cross and brutally executed.

And now one can only ponder the strange enigma of Bill Farrow. How could such a deserving young man, a young man who should have lived to a ripe old age, honored and feted by all who knew him, wind up at the age of twenty-four in an ancient cemetery, halfway around the world from family and friends, in Shanghai, China, of all places, where his life would be so cruelly snuffed out?

As though his untimely death was not tragic enough, his remains were then cremated and his ashes hidden away in a Japanese mortuary until found by American authorities at war's end three years later. Not until then did his family learn that he was dead.

Most of us, if we are so inclined, can look back over our lives and easily determine what events led us from Point A to Point B. In all likelihood, the events we trace seem fairly commonplace and rational in nature—college, marriage, a promising job, or the purchase of a new home perhaps. But such was not the case with Bill Farrow.

Indeed, it seems that his very existence was dominated by a series of unlikely events and bizarre occurrences that would lead him inevitably from the warmth and comfort of his family in Darlington to that deserted cemetery in Shanghai, China. Truly, it is almost as though we can actually see the hand of fate manipulating events in his young life.

## Bill Farrow's Birth and Early Life

Bill Farrow's mother, Jessie Stem Farrow, was one of the luckiest girls in Darlington. Her father was the prominent and prosperous Fred Stem, owner of several tobacco warehouses. He was a man widely respected for both his intelligence and his honesty, and served several terms as mayor of Darlington. As for his very attractive and charming daughter, Jessie, she was raised in a beautiful home at 141 Cashua Avenue, in the most well-to-do section of Darlington. Growing up, it is said, she never lacked or wanted for anything. Fred Stem's pocketbook was always open to the needs of his wife and daughters.

She was born in 1897 and dreamed of some day meeting the man of her dreams, a man very much like her wonderful father. In 1917, just after America entered World War I, the "war to end all wars," that man came along. His name was Isaac Glover Farrow, and he was a prosperous tobacco buyer for a major cigarette company in Raleigh, North Carolina. They met while he was in Darlington to purchase tobacco from her father. After several months of courtship, he asked her to marry him, and she accepted.

Newspapers in Darlington and surrounding cities carried the news of their engagement and wedding. It was billed as the social event of the year. Jessie Stem, the daughter of Fred Stem, was married on June 17, 1917. The wedding took place at her home on Cashua Avenue, and more than two hundred guests were in attendance. As for their big honeymoon, Isaac cautioned her that with the war in full swing they should not be too ostentatious. Instead of a two-week trip to Florida, he suggested softly, perhaps three days in nearby Florence would be in order. After all, Florence was some twelve miles from Darlington and had a population of more than three thousand citizens. Certainly there would be plenty to see and do in such a city. Jessie very quietly agreed. Fred Stem frowned and pursed his lips. Still, Isaac was her husband, and whatever he said . . .

Some fifteen months later, on September 24, 1918, just forty-eight days prior to the great armistice that would end World War I, William Glover Farrow was born in Morehead City, North Carolina, where the Farrows then made their home. His father was still a tobacco buyer, while his mother Jessie, like most women of that era, remained at home to care for her baby.

Very soon after their marriage, Jessie discovered that Isaac was given to strong drink, fast cars, and perhaps a fast woman or two every now and then. Still, the 1920s was a time of unprecedented prosperity, and the Farrows enjoyed the best of everything. In time, some four years following Bill's arrival, Jessie gave birth to a daughter, Margie Farrow. To the outside world they seemed the perfect family.

As for baby Bill, his white-blond hair and sunny smile gave rise to the nickname Cotton Top. He was described as a beautiful child with a most agreeable disposition. He immediately became

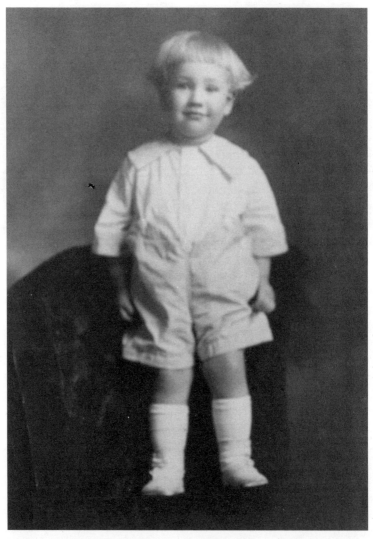

*William Glover Farrow at the age of two in a photo taken in Morehead City, NC. His father, Isaac Glover Farrow, was a prosperous tobacco buyer, while his mother, Jessie Stem Farrow, was a homemaker. In 1929, Jessie, fed up with her husband's errant ways, took her two children and returned home to her parents in Darlington, SC, where she would remain until taking a Federal job in Washington, DC in 1941.* (Photo courtesy of the Darlington County Historical Society)

a favorite with everyone who met him. He was especially doted on by his grandparents, the prominent Stems back in Darlington.

Jessie would later write that as an infant Bill loved animals, and that she purchased a black cat that she called Kitty. "Bill was very good to Kitty, but it took a couple of good spankings for him to learn not to carry Kitty around by the tail. But he learned. And that was the way with everything with Bill. When he was hardly more than a year old, long before he could talk, he could understand what someone else was saying to him. I could say, 'Bill, bring Mommy a magazine off the table,' and he would wobble over to the table and bring me back a magazine. I knew then that he was a most intelligent child. It was almost enough to make you believe in reincarnation."

Later, in 1929, just before the stock market crash, Isaac moved his family to Raleigh, North Carolina. It was then that Jessie experienced another in a long series of unpleasant confrontations with her husband. She had threatened to leave him on numerous occasions, but this time she meant it. Totally distraught and in tears, she phoned her parents. Before the day had ended, the Stems had driven to Raleigh, picked up Jessie and her children, and returned to Darlington.

Jessie's brother, Fred Stem, Jr., was another prominent member of the Darlington community and the owner of several tobacco warehouses, while her uncle, Harold McFall, another prominent member of the community, owned the McFall Hotel, a ritzy establishment where tobacco buyers from across the South stayed while in Darlington. Aware now that Jessie needed work to support herself and her children, Uncle Harold gave her a job as manager of the McFall Hotel. Aware also that she needed a place to live, he gave her a very nice apartment there. She and Bill, now eleven, moved in immediately, while Margie remained with her Stem grandparents. This arrangement would last until Jessie moved to Washington, DC, a decade later.

Following on the heels of this traumatic change in their lives came the Great Depression. It was 1930, and Bill was twelve years old and in the seventh grade at school. Still, despite the breakup of his family, and the fact that he and his mother were living in a

*The McFall Hotel as it looked in 1929. It was destroyed by fire during the 1960s.* (Photo courtesy of the Darlington County Historical Society)

hotel, he continued to impress everyone with his cordial personality and desire to please. More than anything, he always wanted to make his family proud of him. He would walk a mile out of his way not to disappoint them. This was a trait that would follow him throughout his life.

He was somewhat self-conscious, however, because he stood almost a head taller than his classmates, and this unusual height led to a lifelong tendency to scrunch down when standing. Worse, perhaps, he had a near-genius IQ, was a straight-A student in school and a youth leader in his church, and thus was inevitably held up as a model to all the other children. It was a role Bill did not relish but tried to play down. In fact, in order to avoid the goody-goody label, he would often act the daredevil when out with his friends. Several of his old Darlington pals recall that Bill ran afoul of the law on several occasions by waiting for nightfall and then nonchalantly climbing atop the city's two-hundred-foot water tower. Generally, it took threats from the local police to get him down.

Others recall that as a high school student he enjoyed taking his Uncle Fred's new 1934 Buick out on the sandy back roads around Darlington to see just how fast he could traverse all those hairpin curves without winding up in the top of a pine tree. Some of the boys absolutely refused to ride with him.

On Sundays he and his family regularly attended the First Baptist Church of Darlington. Bill and his family were devoutly religious, and it was his deep faith in God that would later sustain him during those terrible six months of starvation and torture in various Japanese prisons.

*Downtown Darlington in 1930. The McFall Hotel is on the left at the far end of the street. The building with the dome is the Darlington County Courthouse. The tall building with the spire is the Darlington Theater. The early stop light in the foreground warns drivers not to turn left.* (Photo courtesy of the Darlington County Historical Society)

Bill's aunt, Margaret Stem, a graduate of Winthrop and Duke Universities, was a teacher, social worker, and former Baptist missionary, who became a second mother to Bill and a tremendous influence in his life. Indeed, it was his Aunt Margaret who lent him financial support in 1938 so that he could attend the University of South Carolina. In 1969 she authored a highly readable biography of Bill (*Tall and Free as Meant by God*) in which she wrote that her greatest contribution was to pass on to Bill her own shining faith in God, "to help him find his own faith in the living God."

Jessie was extremely proud of her son and loved him dearly, but she told him in no uncertain terms that money was tight and thus he would be responsible for earning whatever spending money he might need. As always, Bill understood. And at the age of fourteen he found a job at a local filling station where he washed cars all day on Saturdays, earning five cents per auto. Later, in the tobacco season, during those blistering days of summer, he would earn money working odd jobs and running errands down at his Uncle Fred's big tobacco warehouse in Darlington.

But Bill, a child of the Depression, had already learned that many of the better things in life—hiking, reading books in the library, riding his bike, swimming in the local creek, and engaging in school activities—cost nothing. Those pleasures were absolutely free. Plus he was one of the most popular boys in school and always had a bevy of friends, both male and female.

He and his friends especially looked forward to summer, freedom from school and homework, and going swimming in nearby Black Creek, a fast-running stream of black water that would bring out chill bumps even in July and August. Prior to the advent of air conditioning, Black Creek provided a wonderful way to cool off.

Margie Farrow, Bill's younger sister, recalls that she, Bill, and their numerous Stem cousins loved to visit their grandparents' home on those hot evenings in summer and sit in big lawn chairs in the front yard. "My grandparents would have all their windows open and electric fans going all over the house, but still you could hardly breathe it was so hot. So we'd all go over there, and my mother and grandparents would come out and sit in the yard with us. I remember our favorite topics of conversation concerned asking our grandparents what they did when they were little. And we'd tell little moron jokes, which were popular back then, and tell riddles. Sometimes one of my Stem cousins would bring his guitar, and then we'd all sing songs. My Granny Stem would always make peach ice cream, and we kids would take turns turning the handle of that big churn. The peaches were fresh, grown right there in Granny Stem's backyard. Gosh, that ice cream was good. All in all, it was a wonderful time. This was back during the Depression, and we were poor as church mice, but we were truly happy." (Today Margie Farrow is Marjorie Maus of Ft. Jones, California.)

In 1930, at the age of twelve, Bill joined his local Boy Scout troop, which opened new worlds for him. As always, he took the activities seriously and endeavored to do his Scout work to the

*It was a warm Sunday afternoon in September 1930, and young Bill Farrow and his mother had just returned home from the First Baptist Church of Darlington. Here he rides his bike in front of the McFall Hotel.* (Photo courtesy of the Darlington County Historical Society)

best of his ability. In particular, he enjoyed the long hikes and overnight camping trips. They would set up camp in a wooded area near Black Creek, then each boy would be taught to build his own fire and fry his own bacon and eggs. Later, they would roll up in their blankets and try to sleep. At dawn they would rise and refresh themselves by diving headlong into the cold water of Black Creek.

*Bill Farrow as a lad of sixteen in 1934 taking a refreshing dip in Black Creek, Darlington's favorite swimming hole. By this time the nation was in the grip of the Great Depression, and young people sought entertainment wherever they could find it, as long as it was free. That same year Bill earned his Eagle Scout badge. He already stood two inches over six feet.* (Photo courtesy of the Darlington County Historical Society)

In 1934 he received his Eagle Scout badge. His mother and grandparents could not have been prouder. But this was typical of young Bill Farrow. He always excelled in whatever he attempted.

If he was troubled by his parents' divorce, he refused to show it. He was surrounded by loving family members and friends, and his pastor at the First Baptist Church, Wirt Davis, recognizing Bill's deep spiritual concerns, went out of his way to keep him headed in the right direction.

When Bill was fourteen he entered the ninth grade at St. John's High School in Darlington. In the afternoons he enjoyed visiting the Darlington County Library. It seems that earlier in his school career he had promised his mother that by the time he finished

high school he would be familiar with the world's greatest literature. And there at the library he could accomplish that goal. And
do it for free. He was blessed with a natural curiosity about himself and the world he lived in, and he knew that the answers to his
questions could be found in those great books that rested on
shelves there in the library.

Indeed, Bill truly loved to read, and he once told his Aunt
Margaret that he would stroll into that library, look around at the
thousands of books surrounding him, and realize that no matter
how hard he tried, he could never get even a small percentage of
those books read. For young Bill this was a frustrating realization.
Still, he tried to read them all, and his free afternoons and
evenings were often spent reading the great authors, historians,
and philosophers of the Western World. His sister recalls that he
particularly liked adventure novels such as *Huckleberry Finn,* and
the short stories of Jack London. Later, when he entered the
University of South Carolina, he was considered one of the best
read students in the freshman class.

Yet he was by no means a reclusive bookworm. His old friends
remember that they had only to drop by his apartment at the
McFall Hotel, and Bill would toss aside whatever he was reading
at the moment, grab his leather jacket, and they would be off
downtown to see friends who might be drinking Cokes down at
the local drugstore.

By his junior year in high school, girls were beginning to play
an increasingly important role in his life, and it seems that he had
a special girlfriend for each of his different activities. By this time
he stood six-two, had pale blond hair, blue eyes, and a lopsided
Gary Cooper-like grin that made him a favorite with the girls of
Darlington. His Aunt Margaret recalls that there was an Emmie,
whom he frequently invited to go on his hiking jaunts. And there
was a Marjorie, whom he would visit at her home to while away the
hours playing casino, everyone's favorite card game at the time.

He once told his mother that he was particularly struck by
Marjorie's home life, the fact that she lived in a real house, with
a real mother and father. He looked forward to the day when he
could marry and have a real home and family of his own such as
Marjorie and his other friends did. He could see then that his

words had saddened his mother, who was struggling to provide the best she could for her children, and he hastened to assure her that she was the best mother in the world and that he appreciated all her efforts. And that was another thing—he was always most sensitive to the feelings of others.

And he had another special girlfriend, a girl named Bess Dargon, whom he would visit at her home. Later, in 1938, while a member of the Civilian Conservation Corps and stationed in Liberty, South Carolina, Bill was saddened to learn that Bess had married another boy.

(In 1945, after Bill's tragic death had been announced to the world, Bess Dargon Barron joined Bill's Aunt Margaret on the reviewing stand at the University of South Carolina where she delivered a speech in honor of Bill's memory to the young men of the university's Air ROTC program. Then the president of the university stood and announced that as of that day the program would be officially known as the Bill Farrow Air ROTC Squadron.)

And his sister Margie recalls that Bill often took a girl named Kitty with him as he climbed atop the city water tower at night. Thus, thanks to Bill's romantic proclivities, the local police then had two teenagers to coax down from that lofty perch instead of just one.

Other old friends recall that with his long limber legs Bill was an excellent dancer and delighted in attending balls and dances in the high school gym or the local country club where the young people would dance to the Big Band music so popular during the 1930s. Often they would scandalize their parents by doing the Jitterbug and the Black Bottom, African-American dances that were sweeping the nation.

In June of 1935 Bill finally walked across the stage to receive his diploma from St. John's High School. This was indeed a proud moment for him, and even more so for his mother and grandparents who had worked so hard for so long to see him take this most important step on the long road to success in life.

Still, he was only sixteen yeas old. But his mother had already told him that once he completed high school he would become responsible for making his way in the world. But what was he to do?

*On June 2, 1935, sixteen-year-old Bill Farrow proudly walked across the stage to receive his graduation diploma from St. John's High School. Suddenly he was on his own. Yet there were no jobs available during those tough Depression days. As for college, he had not two cents to rub together. Thus college was totally out of the question. Indeed, his was a dilemma faced by most young people of that era.* (Photo courtesy of the Darlington County Historical Society)

He wanted more than anything to attend college, but with no money available to pay his tuition, college was out of the question. As for getting a job in 1935, millions of American men, family men with wives and children to support, were struggling with the problem of unemployment. Yet young Bill had been told that he was now responsible for getting a job and supporting himself. Unfortunately, there were no jobs available.

His aunt, Margaret Stem, recalls sitting on her front porch with Bill one June evening, drinking ice tea and discussing the Great Depression. She remembers a very frustrated Bill saying, "Now I'm told to go out and get a job. At a time when there are no jobs. How does a fellow learn overnight to support himself?"

Of course that was the same question that thousands of young men all over the nation were asking. Many hopped freight trains and hoboed their way to the big cities across America in hopes of landing employment. Bill never resorted to riding the rails, but he did stick out his thumb and hitchhike to several nearby towns in hopes of finding work. And of course he pored over newspaper ads and pounded the streets of Darlington.

As the summer of '35 came to a close he saw many of his former classmates and some of his well-to-do Stem cousins leaving Darlington for one college or another—which made young Bill's predicament seem that much worse. But as always he kept his chin up. Surely, if he persevered, something would materialize. God had a way of making good things happen. Of that he was sure.

He continued to attend church every Sunday, and he did continue to search for work, any kind of work, even digging drainage ditches for the city if it paid wages. But days and weeks turned into months, and still nothing materialized. By that time his clothes were worn, and the soles of his shoes had disintegrated. He soon joined others in singing America's favorite Depression-era song, "Brother, Can You Spare a Dime?"

Then, in the spring of 1936, just when he was about to resign himself to a lifetime of bumming off his relatives, he excitedly burst into his aunt's house one afternoon.

"I've found a job," he shouted, delirious with happiness.

His aunt ran and embraced him, then both danced up and down, around and around. It seems that a factory in nearby Hartsville was going to give him a try operating a very complex metal lathe. He had been interviewed by the plant manager who was impressed with his intelligence and air of sincerity and thus decided to give him a chance. And the best part was that he would start at ten cents an hour. He and his aunt did a quick mental calculation. Ten cents an hour times forty-eight hours a week. Why, my goodness, that came to four dollars and eighty cents a week! A princely sum back during the Depression. Certainly better than he had once made washing cars or running errands down at the tobacco markets.

So, beginning the next Monday, Bill would crawl out of bed at 5:00 A.M., six mornings a week, gobble down a big bowl of cream of wheat, and make himself two peanut butter sandwiches and an apple for lunch. Then he would climb into a pair of overalls and a blue work shirt, dash out of the McFall Hotel, and rush out to the highway where he would stick out his thumb and hope for a quick ten-mile ride to Hartsville. It was a tough life, to be sure, but young Bill Farrow never considered that fact. He could only think of all the wonderful things he could do with four dollars and eighty cents a week!

But two weeks later his sweet joy turned to bitter disappointment when his foreman told him not to return. He had no experience operating such a complex machine and was thus too slow in turning out the product. In a word, he was fired.

His aunt recalls that he returned to her home that morning filled with disappointment, harshly reproaching himself for not being able to make his employer happy. Still, his spirit was far from broken, and he resolved to hit the streets again that very afternoon. Come hell or high water, he would find a job. Indeed, the last thing he wanted was to continue as a burden to his poor mother who was struggling just to make ends meet.

It was at that point that he took a fateful step, one that set him along a path that would eventually lead him to that deserted cemetery in Shanghai. He decided to apply to become a member of the Civilian Conservation Corps (the CCC boys as they were called). This was a paramilitary life that appealed deeply to Bill Farrow, and it had a direct bearing on his decision to join the Air Corps in 1940.

Several of his friends had become CCC boys over the past few months. They lived in barracks wherever they were stationed, and were given three free meals a day. Even better, each boy was paid thirty dollars a month, certainly a nice salary during those hard Depression times. Of course not all the money was paid to the boy. Twenty-four dollars of it was sent home to his parents (who could definitely use the money), while the boy himself received six dollars a month to purchase whatever incidentals he might need, things not furnished by the Federal government. Everything considered, the CCC boys sounded like a pretty good proposition to Bill. At least he would no longer be hanging around Darlington for his mother to support.

Thus on a bright spring day in May of 1936 young Bill Farrow cheerfully climbed in the back of a big truck with several other Darlington boys and headed for Columbia, the state headquarters for the Civilian Conservation Corps. Not only were they being given free transportation, but each boy was given a big cheese sandwich and a jar of cold strawberry Kool-Aid. Things were looking up already.

Once they arrived at central headquarters, each boy was assigned to a state camp. Young Bill, still only seventeen years old, was assigned to the Liberty Camp near Greenville, South Carolina.

A week later his mother received a letter from Bill in which he told her that he could hardly write for the big blisters on his hands, the result of using a pick and shovel all week as the boys cut down trees and dug ditches to make way for the new state park they were constructing. They worked six hours a day, Bill said, but their sleeping quarters, a long barracks, was clean and comfortable, and they were fed three nourishing meals a day, and all the guys were "swell fellows." Not a bad proposition, everything considered.

"Bet Uncle Fred would be surprised to see me using these tools so energetically," he joked. He also pointed out that the boys took turns pulling kitchen police (washing pots and pans in the kitchen), and that he was being taught everything about how to keep a home spotless. As a result of such training, he said, he would doubtlessly make somebody an ideal husband some day.

At that same time he also wrote a typical teenage hometown-chauvinist letter to Kitty, his old water tower girlfriend:

> You know, Kitty, Darlington is a swell place. I believe we have more fun than anybody. I don't see how anyone can have more fun than we do. For one thing, Darlington has a swell bunch of

*In May 1936 Bill Farrow became a member of the CCC boys. He was stationed in Liberty, SC, and spent the next year cutting down trees and digging ditches to fashion state parks. Here he is helping keep records for the camp commander.* (Photo courtesy of the Darlington County Historical Society)

young guys and gals who are broad-minded, understanding and carry a feeling of good will toward each other.

He also pointed out to Kitty that he frequently hitchhiked to nearby Greenville to visit with some old Darlington friends now enrolled at Furman University. "I am having fun going to dances. Have seen a lot of Bobby and Herbie—two swell guys."

Bill then went on to describe the Greenville Country Club, using terms far superior to those usually found in teenage essays:

I had a grand time at the dance Saturday night. Met some awfully nice girls. That is a beautiful place at the Country Club. I climbed the tower and enjoyed the scenery. The dance hall had red ceiling lights which were reflected on the water and looked like a gondola with red satin in the bottom. I rode over in a big Buick with a tremendous-sounding horn on it that silenced all the rest. It was pretty in spite of its loud tone—it had a sort of musical wave in it—a solid blast of sound, but a sort of vibration that was pleasing to the ear.

Thanks to the camp commander, the boys were given little idle time to become homesick. And thus in his free time Bill played on the camp basketball and tennis teams. And he continued to read books and write letters.

So the summer of 1936 came and went. Then in mid-September, just days prior to his eighteenth birthday on September 24, he wrote to his mother: "Tell Aunt Marge [Margaret Stem] to be watching out for that gold watch—you know I've only three more years now. I know if I can go eighteen years, I can go three more."

It seems that his Aunt Marge had promised Bill that if he neither drank nor smoked prior to his twenty-first birthday, she would buy him a gold Bulova watch. And so Bill, who lived his spiritual life seven days a week, was reminding her that he had only three more years to go.

Subsequently, on September 24, 1939, Margaret Stem did present Bill with a gold Bulova watch for his twenty-first birthday. In April 1942 it was confiscated by the Imperial Japanese Army. Where it might be today is unclear.

Despite his apparent contentment with life in the CCC camp, he still yearned to attend college. He was acutely aware that he had a brilliant mind, that he was far more intelligent than the average young man of his age, and that he was simply wasting valuable time working with a pick and shovel in a CCC camp. He had studied the histories of this great nation and found that most men who ever amounted to anything had gotten their start through education. At that time he knew not how he would manage it, but he was convinced that a gracious God would somehow present him with an opportunity to continue and refine his education.

In October 1936 he appealed to his mother to help him find a way to attend college:

> I know you have a lot of expenses and have done everything for me possible, but if you'll sacrifice a little for me now, it means as much to me or more than any former sacrifices you have made. This is the only way I see to improve my position to help all three of us.

Then he chastised his mother for worrying over a small amount of money she had somehow misplaced: "As for that little bit of money that was lost—you know the axiom, a man is as big as the thing that annoys him. You shouldn't be so little as to let a thing like that break you up so. You should have learned by now how to take it, after our stormy existence."

As Christmas rolled around, Bill arrived home on a nine-day leave. He proudly showed off the few dollars he had earned pulling KP for the other fellows on the weekends. Over the past several months, it seems, he had very unselfishly given up his own free weekends and worked for the other boys who had duty. He did this to earn extra money with which he wanted to help his mother and grandparents with expenses during the holidays. He also brought home a nice sweater for his little sister, Marjorie, now in the ninth grade at St. John's High School.

Following the holidays he returned to camp to face a cold, grim January. The very weather seemed to make him even more aware of his depressing, dead-end existence. On January 21, 1937, he wrote his mother:

> The days are so dreary and gray—they make a fellow feel despair because the utter colorlessness and loneliness of them exactly coincide with the life we lead here. I can see the trees waving around like stricken souls—bedraggled souls at that!
>
> I am undecided as to whether I should go to business school next year with Uncle Fred's help, or to join the Navy. I might stay on here and wait for the breaks. I believe I am slated for a raise when the company strength is raised. One of the boys is leaving and I may get his job which pays $45. A job on the out-side paying $80 would not compare with it.

In fact, Bill did get that new job, and was taught land surveying. His new boss was married to a Darlington girl and treated young Bill like his own son. More important, surveying alone out in the forest was a job that Bill particularly enjoyed. Each morning he was handed his surveying equipment and a bag lunch, driven to an assigned spot in the forest, then left to his own devices until picked up in the afternoon. For the first time ever, he was his own boss. It gave him an exhilarating sense of freedom. And if there was anything Bill Farrow treasured, it was freedom.

As for his spiritual and moral life, Bill was as firm and unwavering as ever. He wrote to his mother that he frequently saw many of the boys get their money on payday then go out and spend it all on beer and whiskey. That evening they would be brought back to camp dead drunk with not a cent in their pockets.

He wrote: "You asked about Jerry. Well, we aren't so chummy now. He raises too much Cain for me, or talks like he does. I had temperance bred in me, a fact I am thankful for."

Bill continued with the CCC boys until April 1937. At that time he resigned after a Mr. Arthur offered him a job managing his filling station in Hartsville. Of course he still had no transportation, so in order to avoid having to hitchhike back and forth to work every day, he took a room with a Mrs. Newsome, a kindly older lady who operated a boardinghouse that was within easy walking distance of his work. As it turned out, Mrs. Newsome was the aunt of famous major league baseball pitcher Bobo Newsome, a Hartsville native who was billed as the Clown Prince of Baseball. In the evenings she would regale Bill with tales of Bobo's antics, both on and off the field.

But still he wasn't happy. Working in a filling station in 1937 paid very little, nor was the work extremely challenging—at least not for Bill Farrow.

His Aunt Margaret remembers one Sunday afternoon in July of that year, and Bill standing in her living room, staring forlornly out the window.

"Aunt," he said sadly, "I hope I won't have to spend the rest of my life working in a filling station." He shook his head and sighed. "For years now I've yearned to have a big break in life, to be a part of the challenge of my generation. But now my days consist of Fill 'er up, sir? Check that oil, sir? Check those tires, sir? Want me to catch that windshield, sir? There's really not much of a challenge in that."

"Oh, I know that, Bill, and I know just how disappointed you are. With your intellect and ambition, you've always had a drive to become somebody, more than just a face in the crowd."

He turned back to face his aunt. "It's not that I think I'm better than anybody else. It's just that I've always enjoyed responsibility and a feeling that I'm doing something of some value to society. Does that make sense?"

"Bill, I've known since you were twelve years old that you could become governor of this state some day—if you just had the education and training."

Farrow dropped down on Margaret's big couch and stared up at the ceiling. "Oh, Aunt, you don't know what I'd give to go to college. Education is the key; I've always known that. But how can I go to college? I don't have two cents to rub together."

Aunt Margaret sat down beside Bill, took a sip of ice tea, and did some quick mental calculations.

"Okay, you know I'm not a rich woman. But here's what I'm prepared to do—"

"Yes, Aunt?"

"For the next twelve months, until September of 1938, I want you to save every penny you can get your hands on, and I'll do the same. Then, this time next year, I'll match you dollar for dollar towards your college education. But rest assured, you will go to college. You will get a chance."

A look of disbelief on his face, he reached out his hand to her.

She said, "No, don't say anything, Bill. Just start saving every cent you can get your hands on, and I'll do the same."

Overwhelmed with gratitude, Farrow buried his face in his hands for a moment. Then he looked up and said, "Aunt, this is just too good of you. I can't believe you'd do this for me. And don't worry, I won't spend anything I don't have to spend. Not for the next year anyway."

"Fine. That's just what I knew you'd say."

"And believe me, Aunt, I won't disappoint you."

"I know you won't, Bill."

"And if Mr. Arthur will let me work ninety-eight hours a week, I'll take him up on it. Let's see, at ten cents an hour that would be . . . My goodness, nine dollars and eighty cents a week! We'd be rich!"

He and his aunt then laughed uproariously.

She would later write that Bill left her home that afternoon with a smile on his face and a spring in his step that she hadn't seen for several years. No one had to tell her that with just a little help, Bill Farrow would do just fine at the university.

# CHAPTER 2

# The University Beckons

His aunt's word was all the encouragement Bill Farrow needed, and for the next year he refused to purchase anything or even to go out with his friends. Indeed, he began to hoard money like the world's most confirmed skinflint. In December 1937 Bill received a rare phone call from his father in Raleigh asking what his son would like for Christmas. Bill, once he had recovered from his shock, asked his father not to buy him a gift at all but to deposit the money in his savings account for college. And so it went.

And thus in August 1938, with enough money to pay his tuition and room fees, Bill matriculated at the University of South Carolina. He was poor and broke, but so were a great many other students. At last he was supremely happy. Finally, after all those years of dead-end jobs and getting nowhere, there he was, a student at the state university. The sky was the limit.

He began pursuing a degree in civil engineering, but he also delighted in reading history, philosophy, and literature. Too, he was a sociable young man who made friends easily, and soon he pledged the Pi Kappa Alpha fraternity. He never became a member because he lacked the funds. But still he reveled in the good fellowship, and was a regular at the fraternity parties and dances.

When Christmas 1938 rolled around, Bill came home for the holidays. He was now twenty years old, and, according to his mother's own measurements, he stood six-four in his stocking feet. His mother stood back and looked at him. Then she urged him not to grow any more, saying, "You could wind up working in a carnival if you get any taller."

According to his report card for that semester, he had completed fifteen hours' work with a B-plus average. His proud relatives decided that instead of spending money on gifts and celebrations that year, they would pool their money and give it to him to help pay another semester at the university. Truly, his doting mother and her Stem relatives made Bill's university education a family project.

And there was help from other quarters. Indeed, when he began running low on funds during the spring semester of 1939, his Pi Kappa Alpha friends invited him to room at the frat house free of charge, which certainly solved one of his big dilemmas.

It was then that Bill learned that his younger sister Marge had dropped out of school to marry her childhood sweetheart, and his mother was brokenhearted. To her Bill would write:

> Don't feel too badly about it, Mom. Just bear up and be sweet and don't ever give up. We Farrows had a poor start in life but we'll get somewhere yet. We're just ordinary people with ordinary troubles—troubles that happen to everybody every day. When we die we want to feel that our life has been lived as fully as we could have lived it. "To strive, to seek, to find, and not to yield"—that is a good slogan. And don't kid yourself— you're never too old to develop. This old world is controlled by laws—and so is reason. For every action there is a reaction. Set yourself to do something, and if you're strong enough, it will be done.

Always of a spiritual nature, Bill at this time, like many other college freshmen, spent much idle time discussing and debating religion with his friends at the university. They would sit and listen to their atheistic professors in the classroom by day, then gather in their dorm rooms in the evenings to discuss their professors' scornful comments. To hear anyone abuse religion or disparage the Bible was a new and disagreeable experience for young Bill Farrow, a devoted Southern Baptist. And soon he would write his Aunt Margaret that he had been reading Aldous Huxley, who stated, according to Bill, that "blind faith is sheer stupidity, but that the

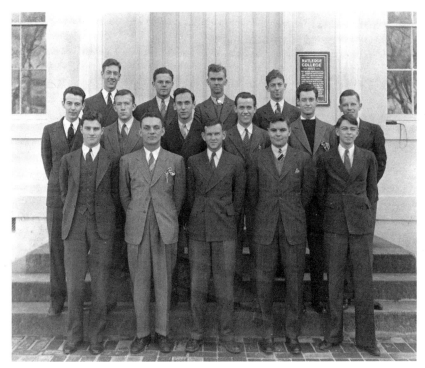

*In the fall of 1938 Bill Farrow at last was able to enroll at the University of South Carolina. An excellent student, he was also outgoing and sociable. Here Bill (top left) poses with other pledges of the Pi Kappa Alpha fraternity on the steps of Rutledge College on the Horseshoe at the university.* (Photo courtesy of the Darlington County Historical Society)

study of natural science fills the yearning for spiritual things—sets the right course for our conduct by knowledge of God's handiwork and the order of the universe." Bill then commented:

> We should all know what kind of laws govern this old world of ours, and how to use these laws to our advantage. Knowledge of these laws shows us the way we must go in order to keep our heads from being cracked. But he is wrong about the blind faith idea, because there are ways to find out things besides the five senses, don't you think? You say you've believed ever since you were a child that there exists a kind of God you'd want if you had a choice.
>
> I am mixed up about religion but what it has to promise is just what I want. I want some one thing I can put all my energy

into. I don't know how to make religion practical, or should it be? You seem to make yours work for you. Why can't I?

Following his exploration of Aldous Huxley, the ever-curious Bill Farrow tackled the works of Matthew Arnold. Nor did modesty prevent him from disagreeing with the great philosophers whenever he felt the urge. To his Aunt Margaret he would write concerning Arnold:

> It seems to me that this very humility that comes from knowing our extreme unimportance would tend to make us work harder, and not be elated or depressed over either success or failure. The good we do is so little that it removes the self-conscious pride in our little accomplishments.
>
> Our focus on life must be the realization that we are just living specks in a mammoth civilization bound in by the tremendous number of years, strenuous effort of mankind to advance itself, the abiding faith of man in a God that created all of this—in the Past and Present—and bound in by a Future that we are pushing into every minute—a Future that perhaps holds pain and trial for us but one that we must continually strive in, do our level best, and then, the end of life here being succeeded by what lies beyond.

A few weeks later, proving that his entire life did not totally revolve around Aldous Huxley and Matthew Arnold, Bill wrote to his Aunt Margaret that he had met a girl named Adeline:

> She is a really true Christian, who told me what a good feeling it is to know that we, being only human, can do wrong sometimes and immediately be forgiven for our sins, and thus can face life with a will to do better. And it's nice to know we can have our lives continue after death, but after a short little life here we can go on where we left off, as a sort of serial.

At this point Bill Farrow had less than four years to live. And it was doubtless his firm belief in God, that higher force determining his path, and an afterlife that enabled him to face death so bravely during his final agonizing moments. His words, as he wrote to his mother the night before his execution, imply that he had no doubt whatsoever that he would pass from this life to heaven in the blink of an eye.

Still, money was an unending problem for young Bill Farrow, and many days, without funds to buy a meal, he went without food at all. But he had earlier had the foresight to bring a box of soda crackers from home back to the university. He told his mother that when he was broke, he would eat a dozen crackers, then drink a big glass of water. Those crackers would expand and fill all the empty spots, he said, so at least his stomach wouldn't growl during class time.

Bill again enrolled at the university in the fall of 1939. Home for Thanksgiving, he related the following story to his Aunt Margie: It seems that in early October of that year he was awakened one morning by a knock at his dorm room door. It was a student messenger from the dean's office. He handed Bill a note. The dean wanted to see him immediately. Feeling somewhat apprehensive, as any sophomore would who had just been called to face the dean, he asked the messenger: "What does the dean want with me?"

The messenger shrugged. "How should I know? The dean doesn't tell me what's in the message; he just sends me to deliver it."

Bill, who did not drink or smoke, knew that he was not guilty of disturbing the peace or breaking any university rules, or anything else he could think of. Still . . .

It was a somber Bill Farrow who entered the dean's office some thirty minutes later. The dean arose with a big smile upon his face, shook hands with Bill, then motioned for him to have a seat across from his desk.

"So you're Bill Farrow," he said without preamble.

"Yes sir," Bill replied, without conviction.

The dean nodded, tapping his pencil on the desk. "Well, Mr. Farrow, I know that you have compiled an outstanding record to date at the university, and you're said to be of excellent character."

Puzzled, Bill sat nodding his head, waiting to hear what great sins he might be guilty of.

"Well, I've worked pretty hard, sir."

The dean nodded his strong agreement. "So it gives me great pleasure to inform you that the Civil Aeronautics Authority in Washington has chosen you as one of three university students to receive pilot's training at government expense. What do you say?"

Bill's jaw dropped. "Well, yes, of course, sir. I mean, I hardly know what to say. But of course I would give anything to receive pilot's training. Especially if the government's paying for it. Yes, definitely."

"Good. I thought you'd agree. You see, Bill, with the war heating up in Europe and the Pacific, the government wants to get as many of our young men trained as quickly as possible. No telling when you'll be needed to defend America."

"Gosh, well, yes, I'll do whatever, sir. Just tell me where and when, and I'll certainly be there. My goodness, this is certainly unexpected."

The dean smiled. "I definitely understand. But I think it would be an excellent opportunity for you to expand your horizons. And at government expense, no less."

"Fine. When do I get started?"

"Representatives from the Civil Aeronautics Authority will soon be in touch. I don't know the details, but I understand that you and the other two fellows will be driven to the civilian airport in Orangeburg three days per week to begin your training from a licensed pilot. And your training will start next week. A fellow named Beverly Howard is president of the Hawthorne School of Aeronautics in Orangeburg, and he will oversee your training."

"Swell, sir, I'll be waiting."

The dean eyed him up and down. "By the way, Bill, how tall are you anyway?"

Bill swallowed nervously. "Well, just a little over six feet the last time I measured."

The dean nodded. "Well, I think you'd have trouble fitting into the cockpit of one of those little fighter planes, but I bet you'd make a heck of a great bomber pilot."

Bill flushed and smiled his agreement.

Then again he and the dean shook hands, and a heady young Bill Farrow made his departure. His steps were light as he practically skipped back to the dorm. Then he immediately phoned his mother with the good news. He was one of only three students from the entire university chosen to receive pilot's training at government expense. It was a tremendous honor. Plus think of all the practical advantages. Perhaps he

*In 1939 Bill Farrow was one of three university students selected by the Civilian Aeronautics Authority to receive pilot's training at government expense, a tremendous honor. He trained under Beverly Howard at the Hawthorne School of Aeronautics in Orangeburg. Here, seated in a biplane trainer, he surveys Orangeburg from the air.* (Photo courtesy of the Darlington County Historical Society)

could become a highly paid commercial pilot. Or maybe even a crop duster with his own business. His mother expressed her deep reservations, but what could she say? He was right—it was indeed a tremendous honor. And certainly there were practical advantages. Plus it was all free. But still, her little boy zooming around all over the country in one of those crazy aeroplanes?

And to a degree Jessie was right. For at the moment Bill Farrow accepted the dean's offer he set into motion a series of events that would lead directly to his execution in a Shanghai cemetery three years later. But how could he know? How can anyone ever know?

Several months after beginning his flight training he wrote to his Aunt Margaret:

> I soloed Sunday, and was I scared! I trembled all over like a leaf the whole time I was up. On my first landing I bounced about eight feet—the tail came down—Wham! The instructor was parked right next to the runway and got a bird's-eye view of the whole thing. Everybody at the airport was watching too, so I said, "Farrow, that was lousy" to myself, and went up two more times, coming down with two perfect three pointers. We take a 100-mile trip alone before long—some fun!

It was also in the fall of 1939 that he met a wonderful girl at the university. Her name was Lib Sims, and she lived with her parents in a very nice home near the campus. Bill wrote his aunt that he had never felt about any other girl the way he did Lib. They would go for long walks around Columbia, visiting the State House and other historic sites. On the cold evenings in winter he would visit her home, and they would sit by the open fire and discuss their plans for the future.

Over the Christmas holidays he brought her home to meet his folks. She and Bill astounded and pleased everyone by announcing that they planned to be married just as soon as they finished college and were able to find good jobs. For the first time ever, Bill Farrow was in love. His folks could not have been more pleased, nor could the future have looked brighter.

In March of 1940 Bill finally received his pilot's license. He wrote his aunt that the other two boys who had also received their

*Bill (left) is pictured at the Pi Kappa Alpha Christmas dance of 1939. The young lady beside Bill is Lib Sims, a university coed. Soon they would plan a wonderful marriage. But then Bill was captured and executed by the Japanese, and all his plans for the future came to a senseless end.* (Photo courtesy of the Darlington County Historical Society)

licenses planned to travel to Pensacola Naval Air Station on June 9 to take their physical examinations for entering the Army Air Corps. "I have also applied," he wrote, "and if they accept my application I'm going down to Pensacola too."

When Aunt Margaret read those words, a little warning bell went off inside her head. Perhaps it was intuition, but she experienced a sudden wave of fear for what the future might hold if Bill withdrew from the university to become an Air Corps pilot. She could sense that the United States was on the verge of entering a great war, and she still harbored vivid memories of the horrors of World War I. Thus she strongly urged Bill to reconsider, but it was no use. The humdrum life of a university student could not compare with the glory and excitement of life as an Air Corps pilot. Plus, pilots were paid very nice salaries, which would be an important consideration to a young man considering marriage.

But his enlistment was still months away.

Bill returned home for summer vacation in early June 1940. His Uncle Fred Stem owned a cottage at Myrtle Beach, and so

Bill, Margie, and their cousin, Peppy Stem, took off almost immediately for a two-week vacation at the beach. After a long cold winter at the university, just lying around on a warm beach, gazing out over that big blue Atlantic Ocean, seemed like heaven to Bill. Yet in the midst of all that beauty, he was aware that just beyond the horizon deadly German U-boats lurked beneath the waves, waiting like hungry gray sharks for any British ship that might have the misfortune to pass within range. By that time Germany and Britain were already at war, and Britain was heavily dependent on the importation of supplies and equipment from the United States, a lifeline that Germany was determined to disrupt.

As for food, whenever Bill felt the least bit hungry, he had only to pick up his towel, then trudge through the sand up to their little cottage where his aunt had a big platter of sandwiches—ham, banana, pimento cheese and pineapple—all laid out very appetizingly on a big glass platter in the kitchen. Plus, there were big bowls of potato salad and sliced tomatoes and cucumbers, and another big bowl of chocolate pudding, just waiting for whatever hungry soul might come along. And Bill Farrow was always one of those hungry souls.

Jimmy Dorsey's "Green Eyes" was the number-one song in America that summer, with Helen O'Connell doing the vocals. It was a song that Bill came to love, and he insisted on whistling it at every opportunity, much to Margie's annoyance. At night he and the others would walk down to the Pavilion and its big beachside dance floor, and there those happy jitterbugs would dance the hours away to the Big Band music of that era—the Dorsey brothers, Kay Kaiser, Les Brown, and Glenn Miller.

The days slipped by all too quickly, and then it was back to Darlington and back to work. Arising before daylight each morning, Bill would quickly slip into a pair of khaki pants and a T-shirt and then jog down to his uncle's big tobacco warehouse to earn expense money for college. The heat in the warehouse was stifling so that by five o'clock Bill and his coworkers were drenched in perspiration. Frequently they would pick up a bar of soap and head for Black Creek to wash off and take a cool swim before heading home. All in all, it was not a bad summer, and with the economy picking up, Bill was making good money.

But not all the news was good news. Indeed, by that time the world was shocked to learn of the Rape of Nanking, as it soon came to be called. There, the commander of the Imperial Japanese Army, in celebration of the capture of that doomed Chinese city, had gleefully informed his soldiers that they had thirty-six hours to roam the streets of the city and the countryside, committing any crimes they might wish against the Chinese people, and to do so without fear of punishment. In other words, for the next thirty-six hours those ruthless Japanese soldiers were free of all legal or moral restraints. They could commit whatever crimes they wished, and do so with impunity.

The world was stunned to learn from neutral newsmen that Japanese soldiers had brutally executed thousands of Chinese prisoners of war. Indeed, Japanese officers all over the city were conducting contests to see who could decapitate the most Chinese prisoners of war in an hour's time. (Newspapers carried photos of the happy winner and his headless victims. He had decapitated 105 Chinese prisoners in a sixty-minute period.)

But even more horrid was the fate of defenseless women and girls throughout the area. When Japanese soldiers could not find them in the streets, they began going door to door. They would break in and drag out any females unfortunate enough to be caught. Later, it was estimated that more than 200,000 women and girls had been brutally gang raped, tortured, and often murdered by these marauding criminals.

Surprisingly enough, it was soon learned that the German ambassador in Nanking, once he learned of the terrible atrocities in progress, had bravely ventured out into the city with trucks (bearing the Nazi swastika) and rescued thousands of Chinese women and girls and had them transported back to the German embassy compound for protection. German or not, he was a most courageous human being.

Soon atrocity stories involving the Imperial Japanese Army were appearing in newspapers throughout the Western World. Totally shocked, citizens were shaking their heads and asking,

"Just what sort of animals are those people anyway?" But from Korea to China, the conquering Japanese Army's first move once they occupied an area was to terrorize the local population, with rape and murder the order of the day. (At war's end Americans were outraged to learn that some 10,000 American and Filipino prisoners of war had died or were murdered by their Japanese guards during the infamous Bataan Death March when the Philippines fell in April 1942.)

Bill Farrow and his friends, like all other Americans, read the current magazines and the daily newspapers and listened to the news on the radio. He was totally aware of the war in progress in Europe and the Pacific, and he suspected that it would not be long before America would be forced to become involved. He particularly liked to discuss the war news with his friends when they were taking their breaks down at the tobacco warehouse. They would all find themselves a place in the shade, drink ice tea, and heatedly discuss the latest Japanese war crimes. They would shake their heads in disbelief at what they had heard and read about the Japanese, then they would describe in graphic detail what they would do if they could ever get their hands on just one of those "damnable savages."

Doubtlessly such war news made Bill Farrow even more eager to become a pilot in the Army Air Corps. He had passed his physical at Pensacola, and now he was waiting to be called up. He told his friends that it was just a matter of time before he might drop a big bomb down the chimney of the emperor's palace in Tokyo.

Little did this tall country boy realize at the time just how accurate his boast would soon become.

On the weekends during that summer of 1940, Bill would hitchhike down to Orangeburg whenever possible, where his flight instructor would let him take a trainer up to zoom around for a while. Following one such outing, he wrote his Aunt Margaret a brief note in which he described his feelings when up in a plane:

> I love the exhilarating feeling—up there in the air, all alone. Your nerves are taut, you think twice as fast as usual. When you're on the ground finally, tingles race up and down your spine as the wheels make contact and she settles down. You

breathe a sigh of great relief—Mother Earth feels mighty good beneath you.

It was just a matter of time. He had followed the path he saw laid out before him, and now fate was drawing the noose tighter and tighter around Bill Farrow's neck.

If only . . . if only . . .

## CHAPTER 3

# Air Corps Cadet to Air Corps Pilot

Instead of returning to the university in the fall of 1940 Bill remained at home, working whatever odd jobs came his way while impatiently awaiting his call from the Air Corps. In the meantime his flight instructor, Beverly Howard, would pick him up on Saturday mornings and drive him to Charleston to refine his flight training.

Then, in November the call he had been awaiting for so long finally came, and he was instructed to report immediately to Love Field in Dallas, Texas, for induction. He would later relate to his family just how his physical examination for the Air Corps proceeded once he reached Love Field. It seems that there was a rule concerning height and weight for Air Corps pilots. So Farrow, fearful that he might wash out on both counts, ate dozens of bananas and drank gallons of water before he went in to be weighed, and he made sure to slump down as far as possible when being measured, since he stood two inches above the six-two height limit.

He said that he approached the army doctor perfectly naked except for a towel knotted around his waist. The doctor look at him, frowned, and gave him a punch in the stomach. "Stand up straight," he ordered brusquely. Then he and Farrow both laughed.

"Okay, you made it, son. You're only six-two. I don't really know how tall you are, but you aren't much over six-two. Besides, the Air Corps is desperate for good pilots."

*It was the fall of 1940, and Cadet Bill Farrow took his Army Air Corps basic training at Love Field in Dallas. He now stood 6-4 and weighed almost 200 pounds. His Japanese captors would later marvel at their giant captive. At this point Farrow's future looked bright ahead.* (Photo courtesy of the Darlington County Historical Society)

Bill took his initial training at Love Field. And, as always, he was totally dedicated to the task at hand. Unlike many of the other boys who spent their spare time sleeping or drinking beer down at the PX, Bill did everything possible to increase his knowledge of airplanes and flying. He wrote his Aunt Margaret that he read constantly, his goal being to "search out current, past and future topics on aviation, and work hard on each day's lessons."

He was particularly impressed with the character of the other young men taking pilot's training with him. They all lived together in a long barracks, and Bill wrote his mother that he could leave money on his desk, be gone for several days, then return to find his money just as he had left it.

On December 23, 1940, the Friday before Christmas, Bill's unit finally received a weekend pass. They had to be back on base at eight o'clock Monday morning, but many of the boys were so eager to see their folks that they went to great lengths to visit home, if only for a few hours. Bill caught a ride with a young cadet from North Carolina who would pass within a few miles of Darlington. Together, they drove all night, taking turns at the wheel, and Bill finally arrived at the McFall Hotel at nine o'clock Saturday morning.

It was Christmas Eve, and his relatives were thrilled to see him walk in the door, especially since his visit was unexpected. They insisted on filling him with their good Christmas food, then loaded him down with fruitcake, candy, nuts, and chocolate fudge to take back to base with him.

They looked at him, all decked out in his new cadet uniform, and marveled at how mature he looked, and how much weight he had gained since leaving home. A laughing Bill informed them that the Air Corps fed its volunteers very well, and that he took advantage of every morsel. In fact, he said, he was now approaching two hundred pounds. He was no longer the skinny scarecrow they all remembered.

Just after sunrise the next morning his friend from North Carolina came by and they began the long drive back to Dallas. It was now Christmas Day, 1940. Certainly Bill had no way of knowing it, but this was the last Christmas he would ever spend with his family. He had just turned twenty-two.

Six weeks later Bill informed his mother that he had completed

*Bill Farrow received both the silver wings of an Air Corps pilot and the gold bar of a second lieutenant at Kelly Field on July 11, 1941. He was then assigned to Camp Pendleton in Oregon where he flew the latest in America's air arsenal, the B-25 medium bomber. He was twenty-two years old.* (Photo courtesy of the Darlington County Historical Society)

*Bill Farrow catches up on his aviation lessons in the barracks at Kelly Field in the fall of 1940. His fellow cadets were young men of character, he said, who would not think of bothering anything that belonged to someone else.* (Photo courtesy of the Darlington County Historical Society)

his training at Love Field and was being assigned to the Air Corps base in San Angelo, Texas, a brand new facility, for more basic training.

He was assigned to Class 41-E, the first class ever to finish at San Angelo. There, in addition to his other duties, he volunteered to write for *The Fledgling*, the class yearbook. Soon, once his officers had read a few of his articles, he was asked to serve as both features editor and associate editor. One article he wrote was titled "To Our Instructor." In it Bill wrote:

> Being an instructor is much like being a sculptor—the students must be molded to the right kind of flying, must conform their habits to the cultivation of precision and never failing accuracy.
>
> "It's just as though he were reading my mind," is a frequent comment. Timid students must be bolder, overconfident ones tamed down.

We found our instructors a businesslike bunch, but, under-
neath the tough exteriors of all of them, lurked that love of flying
that never leaves a man once it is born in him. You momentarily
hated him when he bawled you out for some boner, you were
cheered when he commended you. Together you shared some
beautiful sights—a soft dazzling cloud layer beneath, the sun glis-
tening on graceful wings, cutting through the blue, the breathtak-
ing sight of a plane performing acrobatics.

In the spring of 1941 Bill and his classmates completed their
training at San Angelo and were immediately sent to Kelly Field
for their advanced training. It was make-or-break time for young
Bill Farrow. Indeed, the work was demanding, but the rewards
were great—for those who made it. And Bill made it, finishing
number one in his class.

Thus on Friday, July 11, 1941, he stood with his fellow cadets at
a graduation ceremony. That day he received the silver wings of
an Air Corps pilot and the gold bar of a second lieutenant. He
was more than delighted to learn that henceforth he would be
paid the munificent salary of $245 per month. He did a quick
mental calculation and discovered that $245 per month averaged
out to eight dollars per day, a princely sum for a young man
accustomed to making ten cents an hour pumping gas in a filling
station. Even better, he didn't have to wear dirty work clothes
while earning that money. Nor did he have to hitchhike to work
every morning.

Following graduation, Lt. Bill Farrow and his best friend, Lt.
Ivan Ferguson, a native of Merced, California, were assigned to
the Seventeenth Group, Thirty-fourth Bombardment Squadron,
stationed at Camp Pendleton, Oregon. There, wrote Farrow to his
mother, "We found a dusty, hilly town, the air base a teeming bee-
hive of activity with the building of barracks, roads, and airports."
He also mentioned a visit to Spokane "with all its surrounding
lakes, all crystal clear, all set like blue jewels in rolling mountains."

Farrow's group was assigned to fly the latest weapon in
America's air arsenal, the Mitchell B-25 medium bomber, a sleek
two-engine plane large enough to deliver five five-hundred-
pound bombs on an enemy target, yet small enough and fast
enough to outrun many fighters of that era.

Certainly it had never occurred to anyone at that point, but the B-25 was also small enough and fast enough to take off from the flight deck of an aircraft carrier.

Of course young Farrow had no way of knowing it at the time, but he had just helped forge another link in that immutable chain of cause and effect that would lead inexorably to his death in a Shanghai cemetery just a year later. Had he been assigned to any Air Corps group other than the Seventeenth, or had he been assigned to fly any model plane other than the B-25, he might be alive today. Indeed, it was none other than the Seventeenth Group, flying their brand new B-25 bombers, that Lt. Col. James Doolittle would recruit for his famous raid on Tokyo just a few months down the road.

Of course America still had not entered World War II at that point, but it was obvious to everyone who had ears to hear or eyes to see that it was only a matter of time before the United States would be forced to come to the aid of beleaguered England, France, Russia, or China. Many hoped it would be sooner rather than later.

Farrow's primary duty was to fly submarine patrol out over the Pacific off the coasts of Oregon and Washington. Although the

*The Mitchell B-25 medium bomber. It was large enough to deliver five 500-pound bombs, yet small enough to take off from a carrier deck. It was just the thing Lt. Col. Jimmy Doolittle was looking for.* (Photo courtesy of the U.S. Army Archives)

United States was not at war with Japan, on every flight Farrow prayed that he would spot a Japanese submarine trying to slip through the net. He would zoom down, he said, drop a big bomb on the sub's periscope, and yell, "That one's for Nanking!"

Later he wrote his mother that his unit would soon be partici-pating in the giant maneuvers scheduled throughout the south-eastern states in the late summer of '41. "We're supposed to go to Jackson, Mississippi, and Fort Bragg [North Carolina] for maneu-vers. I'll go as co-pilot, ferrying a new plane from California."

From Jackson, the Seventeenth Group then moved to Augusta, Georgia. It was then that Farrow was given a two-week leave, reaching home on September 21, 1941, just two days before his twenty-third birthday. In celebration of that event, fifteen mem-bers of his family gathered for a birthday party in his mother's apartment at the McFall Hotel. His Aunt Margaret remembers that Bill, tired of wearing his army uniform after almost a year in service, rose that morning, went to the closet, and dug out an old pair of blue jeans and a sweatshirt. His mother looked at him aghast. She insisted that he don his officer's uniform that she had so carefully ironed that morning. After all, his Stem relatives were all coming to see him, she said, and they did not want to see him as he used to be. They wanted to see the new Bill Farrow. He had worked so hard for so long to amount to something, and now they all wanted to share in his success.

Bill flashed her his lop-sided grin and said, "Whatever you say, Mom."

In later years members of his family would recall with a mix-ture of joy and deep sadness Bill's twenty-third birthday party. Each of them entered his mother's apartment, yelled "Bill!" then rushed forward to give him a big hug. All congratulated him and presented him with gifts. Then everyone sat around enjoying cake and punch and questioning Bill about his life as an Air Corps pilot. His cousin, Peppy Stem, who perhaps knew Bill bet-ter than anyone else, regaled everyone with tales of their great misadventures while growing up. Following each of Peppy's anec-dotes, Jessie Farrow's hand would fly to her mouth, and she would say, "Why, Bill! I never knew about that."

Bill, tears of laughter rolling down his cheeks, finally rose and

*On leave in Darlington, Bill Farrow celebrated his twenty-third birthday at his mother's apartment at the McFall Hotel. Pictured (L-R): Granny Stem (she is about to cut the birthday cake), Marjorie Farrow, Fred Stem, Bill and Jessie Stem Farrow.* (Photo courtesy of the Darlington County Historical Society)

pretended to stuff a napkin into Peppy's mouth. Truly, the Farrows and Stems were in a festive mood.

Following the party Bill and Peppy walked downtown and saw many of Bill's old friends and classmates. Hugs and handshakes were exchanged, and then they all walked down to the corner drugstore to enjoy Cokes and catch up on all the latest news.

Bill's two-week leave passed in a flash, and he then reported back to Augusta, temporary headquarters for the Seventeenth Group. A week following his return to his squadron he invited his mother and fiancée, Lib Sims, down for the weekend. They went sightseeing all over the historic Augusta area, took in several movies, and had dinner in a fine restaurant. It was a wonderful weekend that both Lib and Jessie would long remember. Then, for Bill and the Seventeenth Group, it was back to Pendleton by way of March Field in California. To his mother Bill wrote:

> March Field is a swell place. The B.O.Q. [bachelor officers' quarters] is a mansion, the weather tops, the scenery leaves nothing to be desired. On my trip here, from March to Pendleton, I saw some of the most breathtaking rugged country—huge, stately snow-topped peaks rising majestically above us. It

*Bill Farrow, wearing his hat at a rakish angle, and his cousin and best pal, Peppy Stem, pose outside the McFall Hotel on September 24, 1941. Peppy would later have a ship shot out from under him in the North Atlantic, but he survived the war. Seven months after this photo was taken Bill Farrow would be a prisoner of the Imperial Japanese Army.* (Photo courtesy of the Darlington County Historical Society)

was a picture such as can't be put into words—the shadows and soft contours across the snow, the splendid fiery burst of California sunrise, tinting the mountains a delicate, shimmering pink. The whole so awesomely large and colorful as to put the puny words of man to shame.

Two months later the Japanese bombed the United States Pacific fleet at Pearl Harbor, in Hawaii, and the nation was suddenly at war.

Bill immediately wired his mother that he was fine and there was nothing to worry about. In turn, his mother wrote him the following letter:

So glad you wired and wrote me. I feel better about the great morale of the people over the country. That's one thing that will help defeat Hitler and the Japs—such a defiant, righteous and meaningful attitude. May the Lord let us carry on in just such a manner until victory shall be ours. We know our purposes are so right and just, we can't help being victorious. I hope you can patrol the West Coast and not have to go across, at least not real soon. We can hear from you oftener and more at length and you will have had proper training for combat after more flying time and experience here.

As Christmas 1941 approached, the news from throughout the Pacific Theater was totally grim. Not only had the United States lost most of its Pacific fleet at Pearl Harbor, but by that time two of America's most important island outposts, Guam and Wake Island, had fallen to Japanese military forces after hard and bitter fighting. Americans, who were only too aware of the cruelty of the Japanese military, could only shake their heads and wonder what terrible fate awaited the brave American servicemen on those islands who had fallen into the hands of the Japanese. Subsequent reports proved that their worst fears were justified: Some American POWs had been shipped to Japan to work and die in factories and coal mines, while many others had simply been marched down to the beaches of Guam and Wake Island and mowed down with machine guns.

As though those defeats were not bad enough, also in December a Japanese fleet unloaded tanks, artillery, and some 10,000 battle-hardened troops, cruel veterans of the Manchurian campaign, on the shores of Lingayan Gulf in the Philippines. Americans were later disappointed to learn that the Filipino soldiers, who were supposed to defend their island from attack, had fled in terror when those ferocious Japanese soldiers had stormed ashore. Completely overwhelmed, soon American and Filipino forces, nearly 100,000 men, were in full retreat down the Bataan Peninsula. As the weeks and months went by, American forces were flabbergasted to learn that their commander, Gen. Douglas MacArthur, had ordered that all ammunition dumps and food supply depots be blown up to keep them out of the hands of the Japanese. Unfortunately, that also kept them out of the hands of MacArthur's own starving army.

But of course MacArthur promised them that help was on the way. He assured them that President Franklin D. Roosevelt would immediately dispatch guns, planes, and thousands of American troops to save MacArthur's beleaguered army. Unfortunately, that was not true.

Unknown to MacArthur and the American and Filipino soldiers

now fighting for their very lives on Bataan, President Roosevelt had promised British prime minister Winston Churchill that all of America's resources would be sent to North Africa and the European Theater in support of Allied invasions there. Not a tank, not a gun, not a soldier would be sent to relieve America's starving and disease-ridden forces in the Philippines, and would not be for another two years. By then it was far too late since the embattled Americans and Filipinos had had no alternative but to surrender. Already some 10,000 American soldiers had died or been murdered in the infamous Bataan Death March, while more thousands had perished at the hands of the Japanese while held in that torture chamber known as Camp O'Donnell.

As for Filipino civilians under Japanese occupation, their fate was almost too horrid to recount. It has been said that for a period of two years, from April 1942 until April 1944, no Filipino woman or girl dared be seen on the streets of any town or village. They were only too aware of what their fate would be if caught out by Japanese soldiers.

Back in the States, on December 23, 1941, Bill Farrow was delighted when he was promoted to first lieutenant. Along with that promotion came an increase in salary, and young Bill tried to save every cent possible. He and Lib Sims planned to marry once she completed college in June of '42, so the additional money would certainly come in handy once that long-awaited event came to pass. His mother and the Stems were most happy for Bill. It seemed that he had life by the horns and knew just where to go with it.

He had vivid memories of being at home on leave during Christmas 1940, and the wonderful celebrations he and his family had enjoyed. Thus he was terribly disappointed when informed that this Christmas no member of the Seventeenth Group was being allowed time off for the holidays. They would all be out on patrol searching for Japanese submarines.

He later wrote his mother that he and his friend Ivan "Fergie" Ferguson tried to have their own party. They went out in the forest and, trudging through deep snow, found and cut down a small pine tree, which they took back to their barracks room and decorated as best they could. Still, they decided, after standing and looking at that little tree for several minutes, there was something missing. With a wrinkled brow, Farrow turned to Ferguson. Then he snapped his fingers—"Food!" So they drove to the Air Corps PX on base and purchased a small fruitcake, a can of peanuts, and some Cokes. Then they returned to their room and tried to have their own Christmas party.

After consuming half the cake and a Coke, Farrow stood staring out the window. The sun had gone down, and the outside world was now shaded in darkness. Fergie rose and turned on the radio. What they needed to make their party a real success, he said, was some good Christmas music. But it didn't work. Silently, they sat in chairs across the room from each other, each man lost in his own thoughts. Lonely and homesick, they stared glumly at the four walls. It was their first Christmas away from family and friends.

"White Christmas" began playing on the radio. They listened silently to the lyrics, both men choking back the tears. Suddenly, Farrow jumped to his feet. "Hey, what say, Fergie, let's go down to the gym and shoot some basketball?"

"Great idea, Lieutenant," Fergie grinned. And that was the end of their big Christmas party.

This was to be Bill Farrow's last Christmas ever. Fate's big wheel was turning—faster and faster.

# CHAPTER 4

# Training for Doolittle's Raid

By January of 1942 American morale was at an all-time low. The United States' Pacific fleet had been devastated at Pearl Harbor, and its defenses had crumbled everywhere west of Hawaii and north of Australia. The Japanese had overrun Hong Kong, Malaya, and the Dutch East Indies, Wake Island and Guam. As for the Philippines, the huge American and Filipino army there, more than 100,000 ill and starving soldiers, was in full retreat down the Bataan Peninsula, and their surrender was expected at any time. In a word, the Pacific Ocean was quickly becoming the private lake of the Japanese Empire.

Back in Washington, President Franklin Roosevelt spent sleepless nights hoping to devise a means of striking back at the Japanese, of performing a feat so sensational in nature and so daring in execution that it would both weaken the Japanese war effort and boost sagging American morale. But neither he nor his generals could come up with any great ideas. America's resources were all earmarked for the war in Europe. The Pacific Theater would just have to wait.

It was about that time that Capt. Francis S. Low, a submariner (of all people!), and a trusted member of Adm. Ernest King's staff in Washington, DC, experienced a sudden moment of inspiration. His great idea had actually begun to take shape a day earlier, on a cold, dreary afternoon in Norfolk, Virginia. There, Low had stood shivering on a reviewing stand with other high-ranking Army and Navy officials watching Air Corps bombers drop bags of sand on the outline of a carrier deck painted on the runway before them.

And, yes, at that moment a great idea did indeed began to blossom in Captain Low's mind.

Would it be possible, he asked himself, for a medium bomber, say the new Mitchell B-25, to take off from a carrier flight deck? If the planes were pushed to the very rear of the deck, they would have five hundred feet to make their takeoff. Would that be long enough? If so, he grinned to himself, then perhaps the Japanese heartland could kiss good-bye to its immunity to attack.

Low made it a point the next morning to head straight for Admiral King's office at the Pentagon. He explained his idea while King sat listening, his fingers folded in his lap, nodding his head, a smile playing about his lips.

When Low had finished speaking, King leaned forward across his desk. "Now, let me make sure I've got this straight," he said. "You believe that it might just be feasible for us to load up an aircraft carrier with our new B-25 bombers. Then the carrier would steam to within five hundred miles of the Japanese mainland. At that point, the bombers would take off, bomb various Japanese cities, then fly on across the Yellow Sea to friendly airfields in China. There they would refuel and fly on to India and safety. Is that essentially what you're suggesting?"

"That's it exactly, Ernest. Of course at this point I don't know that a B-25 can take off from a carrier. Certainly our B-25s can't *land* on a carrier deck, which is the reason I'm suggesting that they fly on to airfields in China."

"Well," said King, warming to the idea, "it won't take long to find out. I'll phone the commander of our B-25 base at Camp Pendleton, Oregon, and ask him to go out and mark off five hundred feet on his runway and see if his B-25s can take off within that distance."

Subsequently, the answer to this question was an unequivocal *maybe*. It was not easy, and it took some practice, but in the final analysis a B-25 medium bomber could indeed take off in less than five hundred feet, which meant it could take off from a carrier flight deck. Or perhaps it could. Still, no one was sure.

A week later, just after the first of the year, Captain Low and Admiral King paid a visit to Henry H. "Hap" Arnold, commanding general of the U.S. Army. Once settled in Arnold's office, King asked Low to explain his idea to the general.

Low gave King a wink. Then he turned back to Arnold. "Well, General, my plan is to bomb Japan. And I would suggest we do it as soon as possible."

Arnold glared at Low in disbelief. "Well, that is an excellent idea, Captain. And it's such a simple idea. I just wish I'd thought of it myself. Now do you fellows have any more great ideas, or can I take off for breakfast?"

"No, Hap," King grinned, "wait a second. You haven't heard the details yet. Believe it or not, Captain Low has worked out a feasible method of achieving just such a feat."

Arnold grew serious. "Well, let's hear it for goodness' sake."

Over the next five minutes Low and King laid out their plan.

King further explained that America's new air weapon, the B-25 medium bomber, would make an ideal plane for such an operation. "It can take off from a carrier deck, plus it carries a bomb load of 2,500 pounds, and can fly 2,200 miles non-stop. There's still a lot of details to be worked out, Hap, but on the whole I truly believe that this is an operation that can be pulled off. As far as furnishing a carrier, I can take care of that little detail myself."

Trying to hide his excitement, Arnold nodded agreement. "I believe you're right, Ernie. It's really a daring idea and most unorthodox, but I believe it's just a matter of working out the details. And it's just the sort of idea that would appeal to President Roosevelt. He, like the rest of us, could use some good news about now."

Arnold was quite correct. When he informed Roosevelt of Captain Low's great plan, the president was ecstatic and ordered that preparations for a raid on Japan be undertaken immediately. Also, Arnold was to keep him posted on developments on a daily basis.

At that point Arnold returned to his office and began racking his brain, trying to come up with a name, a super airman who could lead such a daring mission. It should be, he decided, someone who knew aircraft inside out, someone who was both an engineer and a pilot, and someone who could inspire those under him to undertake such a suicide mission. Plus, this special person

*Jimmy Doolittle in a photo taken just prior to the outbreak of World War II. At that time he was the world's foremost daredevil racing pilot. He also held a PhD in aeronautical engineering from MIT.* (Photo courtesy of the Air Force Museum)

must be one who could work out a thousand details and keep all of them straight in his head at the same time.

It took him only a moment to come up with the name of the very man he was looking for—Lt. Col. James Harold "Jimmy" Doolittle.

During the thirties Doolittle had been one of the world's most daring racing pilots. Then he had gone on to earn a PhD in aeronautical engineering from MIT. At the moment he was serving on Arnold's staff as director of special projects. Arnold's face broke into a grin. Doolittle was practically within arm's reach.

He turned to Captain Harrigan, seated at a small desk across the room. "Captain, go and ask Colonel Doolittle to report to my office at once."

Minutes later America's master airman entered Arnold's office. Arnold shook his hand, then said, "Here, sit down, Jimmy. Just make yourself comfortable."

"Well, what's going on, General?" Doolittle asked, seating himself across from Arnold. "You haven't been this nice to me since you asked to borrow my golf clubs last Saturday."

Over the next thirty minutes Arnold outlined Low's great plan for pulling off a raid on Tokyo and other Japanese cities. Doolittle leaned forward in his chair, and his jaw became slack as Arnold's incredible story began to unfold.

"My god, General, this is the darndest thing I've ever heard of. And you know what—"

"What?"

"The most wonderful part of all this is its audacity. I believe it might just work because it is so darned unbelievable."

"I'm glad to hear you say that, Jimmy. President Roosevelt, by the way, totally agrees with you."

"Have you decided which aircraft carrier will deliver the planes to Japan?"

"Yep. We've decided on the *Hornet*. It's brand new and has the longest flight deck in the Navy. It'll ferry the planes to within four hundred miles of the Japanese mainland. Then it'll turn around and hightail it out of there. We can't afford to lose a carrier at this point."

"I do have one question, something I don't believe you touched on."

"What's that?"

"The B-25 can take off from a carrier deck, which has been proven. But where will it land when all its gas is gone? We know it can't *land* on a carrier deck, and obviously it can't land in Japan. Neutral Russia sure won't let us land there, and China is occupied by the Japanese army. So just where in hell will it go? This is beginning to sound like a one-way trip, a real suicide mission."

Arnold nodded. "Believe it or not, Jimmy, that's a question we've already considered. It's a dangerous mission, but we do want the men to at least have a chance of survival. Therefore, we're now negotiating with Chiang Kai-Chek to arrange for our planes to land at Chuchow Air Field in an area southeast of Shanghai that the Japanese still have not taken."

Doolittle looked skeptical. "I'll take your word for it, General."

"You see, our B-25s will hit Japan about dusk, then fly on

southwest down the island of Honshu and then across the Yellow Sea and reach the coast of China about dawn. Thus they'll have plenty of daylight to fly another two hundred miles southeast of Shanghai to Chuchow Air Field where they'll land, a total distance of almost two thousand miles. The Chinese Air Force will be expecting them. They'll refuel at Chuchow and then fly on to Chunking. From there they'll fly on to India, and eventually back to America."

"That's a pretty daring plan, General."

"Yes, and it'll take daring airmen to pull it off."

"You got anybody in mind to head it up?"

"What if I asked you to do that, Jimmy?"

Doolittle nodded his head vigorously. "General, I'd give my right arm to lead this mission."

"Your insurance paid up?"

"Always."

"Good. That's what I thought you'd say."

"Oh, and how many B-25s will be involved?"

"Believe it or not, that's something else we've worked out. Sixteen planes is the most we can park on a carrier deck and still leave room for them to take off. And of course we'll have plenty of spare planes and crews in case they're needed."

"Will you put me down to fly plane number one?"

"You got it, pal."

Doolittle got to his feet and stuck out his hand. "When do we get started?"

"How about right now?"

"Let's go."

As for plans to land American warplanes at Chuchow Air Field in China, Generalissimo Chiang Kai-Chek agreed to the proposal with the utmost reluctance. He was only too aware of the horrible retributions the Japanese would exact from the Chinese population should they learn of any help given the American airmen by the Chinese. Subsequent atrocities would prove Chiang Kai-Chek totally correct in his estimation of the situation. Still, for political reasons, he had no choice but to cooperate with the Americans. Following the war Japanese records indicated that some 250,000 Chinese civilians were executed by the Japanese for assisting the Doolittle Raiders in their attempts to avoid capture.

In January 1942, nearly a hundred pilots, copilots, and navigators, plus another sixty crewmen, all from the Seventeenth Bombardment Group—consisting of the Thirty-fourth, Thirty-seventh, and Ninety-fifth Squadrons, plus the Eighty-ninth Reconnaissance Squadron—all stationed at Camp Pendleton under the commands of Col. William C. Mills and Maj. John A. Hilger, were ordered to an airfield in Minneapolis, Minnesota. Hilger, a tall, lean Texan, was named Doolittle's executive officer for this top-secret operation.

The airmen, still in the dark as to the purpose of this move, were awakened the morning following their arrival, fed breakfast, then taken by bus to a hotel in downtown Minneapolis. Snow was three feet deep all around them as they made their way to the hotel. Bill Farrow and Ivan Ferguson, relaxing as best they could on the front seat of the bus, speculated as to the reason for such a meeting.

"I think I've got it all figured out, Fergie," Farrow said, unfolding his long legs out into the aisle. "The war in the Pacific doesn't seem to be of any concern to the government. They're throwing everything they've got against the Germans."

"True," Ferguson nodded.

"So, I'll bet you they're going to move the Seventeenth Group to the East Coast. I hope it'll be the Myrtle Beach Air Corps Base in South Carolina. From there we'll go out on sub patrol over the Atlantic."

"I think you may be right on target, Bill. Those German subs have been raising hell all up and down the Eastern Seaboard. I've got an aunt in Jacksonville, and she says you can go out every day and see smoke on the horizon where those German subs have got another American ship. We've been patrolling the Pacific for six months now and haven't seen a single Japanese sub."

"I hope I'm right. I can get home on the weekends then. Plus you'll love Myrtle Beach, Fergie. It's the greatest resort town between New York and Miami—and has the best-looking girls. My uncle has a place down there."

At that moment the bus passed a group of heavily bundled coeds from the University of Minnesota. They were standing on the corner, trying to flag down a taxi. At the sight of the young females, the bus erupted in a virtual chorus: "Wooooeeeee" and "Hubba-hubba" and "Beat me, Daddy, eight to the bar" and "Well, all reet!" They were young Air Corps officers, yes, but they were also charter members of the "Swing" generation, and they wanted to identify themselves as such to the young coeds.

Laughing at his buddies' antics, Farrow nudged Ferguson. "So much for America's young heroes."

Minutes later the airmen were led into the banquet room at the hotel where they were treated to a fine lunch of roast beef and mashed potatoes. Then they watched eagerly as Maj. John A. Hilger strode up front to the podium. The pilots became hushed as he prepared to speak.

"Gentlemen," he said finally, "you are one of the most unique groups of airmen in America, flyers of our newest air weapon, the B-25 medium bomber. And that's why you were chosen to hear what I've got to say this evening. You see, the Air Corps is looking for volunteers, both pilots and crews, for a secret and highly hazardous mission. That's about all I know about it. Being a secret mission, they've told me almost nothing. I was told, however, to point out that this will be a highly hazardous mission, which is the reason that we're looking for volunteers." He paused and looked around at all the upturned faces. "I want you to think about that before you volunteer. I believe it must be a very important mission, and probably a very exciting mission. But again, it's also highly hazardous. Now, how many of you think you might be interested in volunteering for such a mission? As for questions, I probably won't know the answers, but I'll be glad to try to answer any questions you might have."

A pilot raised his hand and came to his feet. "Will this mission take us out of the country?"

Major Hilger shook his head. "That I don't know."

Another pilot raised his hand and stood. "What if we don't volunteer for this mission? Will it go against our record?"

"Absolutely not," Hilger answered. "This operation is strictly voluntary. But, let me caution you here, this operation is also top secret. So, once you've volunteered and begun your training, there can be no backing out. Once you're in, you're in. So think carefully before you commit yourself. If you try to back out once you're in," Hilger laughed, "we'll throw you out of a B-25."

Farrow raised his hand. The other airmen watched in awe as he unwound his six-foot four-inch frame and stood to address the major. "Sir, I understand about the secrecy, and I've already decided I'm going anyway, whatever it is and whatever it's for. But I do have one question. My fiancée is graduating from college on June first. Do you think this mission will have us tied up longer than that?"

Quiet laughter rippled through the assembled airmen. Major Hilger himself smiled. He studied the ceiling for a moment before answering.

"I sure wish I could tell you, son. I realize how important your fiancée's graduation from college must be to you. But again, I simply don't have an answer. That's something you'll have to take into consideration before volunteering."

"I've already volunteered," Farrow answered emphatically. "I wouldn't miss it for the world."

"Good man." Hilger turned to his executive officer standing nearby. "Captain, put Lieutenant Farrow's name on that list."

Farrow, though innocent of that action's impact, had just placed himself in the hands of that force directing his life, that strange chain of cause and effect that would ultimately lead to his death on October 15, 1942.

He sat back down and whispered to Ferguson. "What say, Fergie? Want to give it a shot? I'm telling you, they're going to send us to England to help bomb the Germans."

Ferguson shook his head. "This doesn't sound like my cup of tea, Bill. I'm not footloose and fancy-free like you guys. I've got a family to think about. But you go ahead. You're far more adventurous than I am. Believe me, my classification in this operation is 2-B."

"What's 2-B?" Farrow asked seriously.

Ferguson flashed him a big grin. "Simple, 2-B here when you guys get back."

Farrow chortled appreciatively at the joke. "Hubba-hubba."

"At this point," Hilger said, "take about fifteen minutes to think the situation over. At the end of that time, I'll ask those who want to volunteer to remain in their seats. Those who choose not to go will be taken back to base aboard the bus."

Farrow remained seated. Ferguson said, "Okay, Bill, I'll see you back at the base." He then rose and went out into the hallway.

Subsequently, although Jimmy Doolittle could use only forty-eight pilots, copilots, and navigators and some thirty-two crewmen, Hilger signed up all of those who remained in their seats, nearly a hundred and fifty men, including the excited Bill Farrow. After all, their training would last for the next six weeks, and it was highly hazardous training. A few substitute pilots and crews could hurt nothing.

Still, Doolittle could use only sixteen planes and sixteen pilots. Those would be selected from among the best once their training had ended. But even then they still would not know just what they had volunteered for. Nor would they be told until they were far out to sea aboard America's newest aircraft carrier, the *Hornet*.

Almost immediately, even as they were speaking with Major Hilger at the hotel in Minneapolis, airplane mechanics were installing extra gas tanks aboard the B-25s. If they were going to fly 2,200 miles, then every inch of space had to be utilized. Mechanics went through the planes, literally gutting them of any equipment or material that was not absolutely essential to the operation. Even their machine guns were removed. And in those empty spaces gas tanks were installed.

Those mechanics also removed the famous and highly secret Norden bombsights. Should any of these planes fall into the hands of the Japanese, they would not get their hands on the Norden. Thus the bombardiers aboard these planes would be forced to literally eyeball their targets once they reached Japan.

No time was wasted, and the plan to bomb Japan moved forward with incredible speed. On February 3, 1942, the Seventeenth Bombardment Group was sent to Owens Field in Columbia, South Carolina, for their initial training.

Bill Farrow was obviously delighted at this unforeseen twist in his fortunes. He would later write to his aunt that he had been able to spend time with his fiancée, Lib Sims, and that he had enjoyed a delicious steak dinner at her home. He remembered that at dinner that night Lib's father had asked the question that Farrow had been dreading. He asked him what in the world he was doing at Owens Field.

Farrow paused before answering, and Lib quickly spoke up and said, "Daddy, Bill's involved in something he's not allowed to talk about. So please don't ask him."

"That's right, Mister Sims," Bill said. "I'm sworn to secrecy. But to tell you the truth, I really can't talk about it because I still don't know what it is myself. They refuse to tell us anything. But when it's all over, I'll be glad to tell you all about it." Bill then changed the subject. He knew that Lib's father was a devoted fan of Carolina football, so he asked, "But what about the Gamecocks, Mr. Sims? Think they'll win the Southern Conference championship in '42?"

"Ah, Bill," Mr. Sims replied, growing serious, "this war's playing the dickens with college football all over the country. A lot of schools have discontinued the game totally. As for us, Coach Enright says he just hopes we'll have enough boys out to field a team. He's not making any promises. I guess we might win the conference if all the other schools drop football."

Farrow also visited with his old friends at the Pi Kappa Alpha house, and in fact spent several nights there, bunking with "Muddy" Mills, a young man from Mayesville, a small town near Darlington.

There was little he could tell Muddy, except that the volunteers slept in leaky two-man tents at Owens Field. The temperature in February in Columbia was below freezing, and Farrow and his mates were all required to stand nude beneath big metal drums each evening and shower in ice cold water. It was not exactly the heroic life they had expected, and Farrow took quite a ribbing from his shivering friends about the sunny South.

By that time Bill's mother Jessie Farrow had taken a Federal job with the Department of Defense in Washington, DC. Bill wrote her from Owens Field:

Hope you're liking your new job now—you're helping in National defense too, remember, so if things get tough, know that you are doing it for our country. And there's nothing too much to do for our country—remember that—nothing!

The last weekend in February Farrow was given a weekend pass, which allowed him to visit his family in Darlington. There, Saturday passed in a dizzying round of visitations with family and old high school friends. Then came Sunday morning, and his Aunt Margaret would later recall Bill accompanying her to the First Baptist Church of Darlington where he had a joyful reunion with his former pastor and Sunday school teachers, and told them that he truly missed attending church in Darlington. Then it was back to Aunt Margaret's house for a delicious home-cooked meal of fried chicken, rice and gravy, collard greens, corn bread, and ice tea. Bill ate voraciously. Yet he seemed strangely quiet.

"Bill, is anything bothering you?" Aunt Margaret asked.

"No, Aunt," he said, smiling for the first time. "I'm fine."

Following the meal, Bill went to visit with Peppy and all his Stem cousins. Later, he would ask his aunt if she had anything he could take to his Aunt Mary Stem's house for an afternoon party. He wanted to see the entire family one last time before taking off for Eglin Air Corps Base in Florida.

Later he would write his mother in Washington:

> Though it wasn't but a day, I got to see all the family; Peden [Peden Gardner of Darlington], who is based in Florence, and also Margie E. We had tea—everybody chipped in—Aunt Lil with a delicious cake, Pee Wee with sweet cakes and sandwiches, Aunt Mary with tea and sandwiches. Missed you very much.

Later, following news of his capture by the Japanese, his Aunt Margaret would recall that Bill had seemed uncharacteristically quiet during the tea, downright glum in fact, and at one point vanished for fully thirty minutes. His cousins looked around for him, but no one could find him. But then he walked in, excused his absence, and joined in the party as though nothing unusual had happened. Aunt Margaret could not help but wonder if perhaps Bill had experienced a premonition of sorts, if he somehow knew that this would be his last trip home. Indeed, when he told them good-bye that afternoon, it would be for the last time ever. He would see his mother once more, but he would never see other family members again.

Late that afternoon he caught a ride back to Columbia with an old friend, Jack McCullough, now a student at the university.

Jack, who was driving a 1936 Ford coupe, asked Bill, "Say, Bill, as much as you like to travel around, why don't you invest in an automobile? They don't cost that much, and I know you must be making good money as an Air Corps pilot."

But Bill shook his head. "They cost too much for me, Jack. I'm trying to save every penny for when I get married this summer. Lib graduates the first of June, and then we're going to make definite plans to get married. I guess I'll have to buy a car then."

Jack threw back his head and laughed. "Hey, haven't you heard, Bill? The Great Depression's over. President Roosevelt says so."

"Yeah, well, maybe he should tell that to all those poor guys standing in lines at soup kitchens in Darlington County this morning."

"Now, Bill," Jack needled, "don't be cynical. It doesn't become you."

"Facts are facts, regardless of what the president says."

On February 24, 1942, Bill Farrow and his fellow airmen from the Seventeenth Bombardment Group flew their B-25s on to Eglin Air Corps Base in Florida where their training became more intensive.

On March 3 Farrow wrote his Aunt Margaret:

> I'm setting up a joint account with you. If and when I'm sent over, you may draw on my account if any of you get in a pinch. And if I get knocked off, you take over the account.
>
> The weather down here is perfect—warm and clear. The Gulf is beautiful, sparkling in the sunlight, the white sands stretching serenely into the distance.
>
> Guess what! Colonel Jimmy Doolittle is here. Something's popping.

The airmen had perfected their carrier takeoffs at Owens Field. Under normal conditions the B-25 required a minimum of nine hundred feet for takeoff, but after hours of constant practice, the men of the Seventeenth Bombardment Group had reduced the distance to only five hundred feet, the length of the *Hornet*'s flight deck.

Now that they had mastered that little detail, they could practice

*A B-25 is shown practicing a takeoff on a 500-foot section of the landing field at Owens Field in Columbia, SC. The ability to take off from a short runway was essential to the success of the mission. If pilots could not do it on the ground, they could not do it once aboard the aircraft carrier* Hornet. (Photo courtesy of the U.S. Army Archives)

for the attack itself. With Eglin situated on the Gulf Coast of Florida, the pilots would take off and fly out over the Gulf westward to New Orleans. Then, from an altitude of only five hundred feet, they would "bomb" that city, then hit the gas and zoom back out over the Gulf and fly eastward all the way to the Naval Air Station in Jacksonville, then back to Eglin. It was excellent practice for the real operation that would begin in just a few short weeks.

Once they had touched down at Eglin, each pilot very carefully measured the amount of gas his plane had expended on the operation. Gas would be their lifeline during the raid on Japan, more precious than gold, and each pilot watched his gas consumption most carefully. They were unaware of it then, but once they had departed the *Hornet*, they would be required to fly a distance of some 2,200 miles to friendly Chuchow Air Field in China. If they ran out of gas before reaching it, they would undoubtedly fall into the hands of the Japanese. And if that happened, they would face terrible consequences, perhaps even death.

*Bill Farrow (far right) and his fellow pilots check their stopwatches during practice take-offs at Eglin Air Corps Base in March 1942. They became quite proficient at these take-offs, and all made it safely off the* Hornet *on April 18.* (Photo courtesy of the Air Force Museum)

On top of everything else he was expected to learn, Farrow was also required to master the job of every other man on his plane, the *Bat Out of Hell.* He had to become a marksman with the .50-caliber machine gun, become proficient as a navigator, and be able to drop a bomb on his target without destroying everything else in the neighborhood.

Still, the airmen were all totally puzzled as to what their assignment might be. But then one evening after their flight practice had ended for the day, a Navy officer from Pensacola came and gave them a lecture on Navy courtesy. Following his lecture, Farrow and his fellow pilots began talking excitedly, putting two and two together. Navy courtesy, then taking off in only five hundred feet. They looked at one another, light bulbs suddenly clicking on—why this must mean that they were going to be assigned to an aircraft carrier. They were going to take off from an aircraft carrier! But why? To that question they still had no answer.

By this time, the middle of March of 1942, the Imperial

Japanese Army had conquered the islands of the South Pacific, with the exception of the Philippine Islands. And there, the heroic soldiers of the United States Army, with dwindling supplies of food, medicine, and ammunition, and no means of resupply, somehow held out against overwhelming odds. They were retreating down the Bataan Peninsula and daily dying by the hundreds of disease, starvation, and Japanese bullets. It was just a matter of time, therefore, before they too would be overwhelmed. America held its breath, just waiting for the news to come that its brave men in the Philippines had finally been forced to surrender.

Before dawn on March 23, less than a month after they had arrived at Eglin, Bill Farrow was awakened from a deep sleep and told to pack his bags. Following instructions, Farrow walked out into the early morning darkness and climbed aboard his old trusty *Bat Out of Hell*. The airmen were now to fly across America all the way to March Field in Sacramento, California, then up to McLelland Field.

Well, this was certainly like the Army, they decided. Fly them from the West Coast to the East Coast, then back to the West Coast. So apparently they were not going to Europe aboard an aircraft carrier after all. It seemed now that the Pacific Theater would be the site of their big adventure.

Two days following his arrival at McLelland Field, Farrow wrote his Aunt Margaret:

> Guess what! Colonel Doolittle got here before we did! How? He flew across the Rockies on instruments. Sure am glad we have a leader who knows the answers.
>
> I understand we're to go on a dangerous mission. I have sent all my personal effects home so that you and Mom and the family will know that I won't be home anytime soon.

Jimmy Doolittle immediately met with the pilot and crew of each plane, asking them a series of questions: What did they think of their plane? Was it in good shape, or was it in need of repair?

Since only sixteen B-25s would fit onto the flight deck of the *Hornet,* Doolittle very carefully selected the planes, pilots, and crews he wanted for the real operation against Japan. With these he ordered that all radio equipment be removed, since such equipment was additional weight that would waste precious gasoline. Besides, they wouldn't need radios where they were going—not unless they spoke Japanese.

As for the pilots and crews of these planes, they still had not the least idea where they were going or what they would do once they got there.

# CHAPTER 5

# The Long Trip to Japan

It was April 1, 1942, the day Bill Farrow and his fellow airmen had awaited for so long, and now he stood aboard the USS *Hornet*, awed by the grandness of this megalith of the seas. Its flight deck was the length of three football fields strung together, and its superstructure stood some nine stories tall, truly a giant among giants. This morning it was floating peacefully in the bay at Alameda Naval Air Station near San Francisco. Tall cranes on its flight deck were lifting those sleek B-25s aboard.

Farrow, feeling about as significant as a gnat, stood off to the side of the flight deck, out of the way of all those seamen who had jobs to perform. He turned up the collar of his leather flight jacket against the cold wind blowing in off San Francisco Bay and watched apprehensively as his B-25, the *Bat Out of Hell*, became the first plane lifted aboard. Once the plane was set down, deck hands immediately rolled it to the very rear of the flight deck so that its tail section was actually sticking out over the Pacific Ocean. Crewmen then placed chocks behind its wheels and lashed it down. Thereafter it would be known as plane #16. Thus it would be the last plane to take off from the *Hornet* the day the operation began.

So this is the explanation, Farrow thought to himself, the reason behind a thousand practice runs down a five-hundred-foot runway. He still didn't have the whole picture, but what he could see so far—B-25 medium bombers taking off from a carrier on a secret mission—caused him to laugh silently to himself. How

*The Pacific Theater as it appeared in January 1942. By April these islands had all been conquered by the Imperial Japanese Army.* (Photo courtesy of the U.S. Army Archives)

audacious! How darned ingenious! And best of all, he himself would be right in the middle of whatever it turned out to be! Just wait till Peppy and Mr. Sims heard about this.

He thought with pride of his mother, Jessie Stem Farrow, and his younger sister, Marjorie, and all his aunts, uncles, and cousins back home in Darlington and how proud they would be when they learned that he had been chosen for such a hazardous mission. As always, their approval was paramount in his mind.

Some day, he thought, years after he and Lib Sims had married, he would have something to tell their grandchildren about, much as the old guys who hung around the courthouse in Darlington boasted about their World War I exploits. He tried to picture himself as he might look thirty years later.

He stuck a stick of Spearmint chewing gum in his mouth and began walking with long strides to the small room below deck that would be his home for who knew how long. Everyone he passed, it seemed, was humming the most popular song in America at the moment, "Deep in the Heart of Texas."

Just two days earlier, while waiting at Alameda Naval Air Station, almost every unfortunate pilot and crewman who had not been chosen to participate in the raid could be seen running around armed with hundred-dollar bills. They were searching out those lucky stiffs who had been chosen. "Hey, pal," they would say, "here's a hundred bucks if you'll let me take your place on this mission." Farrow had been approached by numerous other pilots holding out hundred-dollar bills, but he wouldn't miss out on this venture for a million dollars. It would make his family proud. Plus it would be something to tell his grandchildren about some day.

Like most other young men of World War II, Bill Farrow was truly a modern-day crusader. He was extremely patriotic and totally convinced that America was engaged in a holy war to stamp out the forces of evil throughout the world. This was a highly hazardous mission, true, and he might very well be killed, but that possibility was of little concern to this heroic young man. He sincerely wanted to do his bit, regardless of the cost. He was fighting to keep America free, and he knew it.

Now, on April 1, 1942, pilots, copilots, navigators, and crewmen, enough to man twenty-four planes, a total of a hundred and twenty airmen, were brought aboard the *Hornet*. They waited apprehensively to see what the next step might be.

The following day at 10:18 A.M., April 2, 1942, they found out as the *Hornet* very quietly weighed anchor and slipped away from

*The USS* Hornet, *a 20,000-ton behemoth, in the summer of 1941. In October of '42, the* Hornet *was sunk at the Battle of Santa Cruz, and most of the men serving aboard were lost.* (Photo courtesy of the U.S. Navy Archives)

berth 9. Now it was making its way beneath the Golden Gate Bridge and out into the calm waters of the gleaming blue Pacific, destination unknown, but they were following the fortieth parallel in a northwesterly direction.

Farrow and his fellow airmen wondered why the *Hornet* would depart the bay on a secret mission in broad daylight and in full view of thousands of San Francisco citizens. But the Navy later explained that the *Hornet* was sailing with a new and inexperienced crew, and the Navy was afraid of a nighttime departure in a busy harbor with tricky tides. A collision now, even a small one, could result in the scrapping of the entire operation.

Later that afternoon all airmen were ordered to assemble in front of their particular planes. Thus at three o'clock Farrow met for the first time with the four other airmen who would fly with him on this most secret mission. They knelt beneath a big gray wing of the *Bat Out of Hell* parked at the very rear of the flight deck. Such meetings were in progress at that moment all over the flight deck as the pilots and crews of fifteen other planes became acquainted for the first time. The sun, now sinking in the west, was warm and pleasant, and the sea was a peaceful lake. Certainly from their vantage point aboard the *Hornet* it was difficult to believe that American soldiers were fighting and dying terrible deaths in the jungles of the Pacific.

The identity of Farrow's first copilot is now lost to history, for he had earlier declared himself unable to continue in this venture. But it hardly mattered, for there were seventy-two officers—pilots, copilots, and navigators—and forty-eight gunners and bombardiers—positions generally held by enlisted men but on this trip occasionally filled by officers—from the Seventeenth Bombardment Group aboard, so making substitutions was no problem.

As a substitute for Farrow's missing copilot came the irrepressible Lt. Bob Hite, a tall Texan known for his hot temper. There was also Lt. George Barr, navigator; Sgt. Harold A. Spatz, gunner-engineer; and Cpl. Jacob DeShazer, bombardier.

In later years Bob Hite would remember that when Farrow chose him to replace his missing copilot, he thought he was the luckiest man on the face of the earth. He responded by grabbing his tall new friend in a jubilant bear hug and dancing him around the squad room.

Farrow broke away from his grasp, and with a big grin asked, "Does that mean yes?"

"YES," Hite responded. "I do. Till death do us part." Hite of course had no way of knowing at the moment how prophetic his words really were.

In later years, looking back at Farrow's acceptance of his proposal, Hite would comment, "Believe me, over the next three years I'd remember that morning, and I'd have some second thoughts about how lucky I really was. How I came out of it alive is still beyond me. As for poor Bill Farrow, I still don't like to think about what they did to him."

Farrow and the other members of his crew introduced themselves and shook hands all around. Farrow then told them that on this mission informality was the order of the day. There would be no Lieutenant This and Sergeant That. With their permission, they would all be on a first-name basis. The men all heartily agreed to this pronouncement.

Farrow's next move was to run down a checklist of possible problems with each crewman. Only Jake DeShazer, the bombardier, foresaw any problems.

"Bill, I don't know what our target's going to be. But I hope it's a big one. When you don't have a bombsight, those darned bombs can go anywhere."

"Oh, just use your opera glasses," George Barr kidded, and everyone laughed.

"Or just pretend it's one of those good-looking girls in your father's congregation back in Oregon," Bob Hite chimed in, alluding to the fact that DeShazer's father was a Christian minister. "You'll see it okay then."

"Oh, ye of little faith," DeShazer joked.

"But seriously, Jake," Farrow said, "you really don't have to worry. Colonel Doolittle has thought of everything, including dropping bombs."

"Yeah, but I just wish they'd go ahead and tell us where we're going and what we're to do when we get there. Then we could all relax a little."

"It's my understanding" Farrow said, "that we're to have a big meeting tomorrow, and Colonel Doolittle's going to break the news to us then."

Again the men shook hands all around, then went back to their normal activity, which was checking every inch of their plane for potential problems.

The *Hornet,* under the command of Capt. Marc Mitscher, did not sail alone, but was escorted by two cruisers, an oiler, and four destroyers. In addition, on April 12, just north of Hawaii, they were joined by Task Force 16.1, consisting of another giant carrier, the *Enterprise,* with its contingent of fighter planes and dive bombers which would provide air cover for the *Hornet* and the other ships. Accompanying the *Enterprise* were two cruisers, an oiler, and four destroyers. In all, there were a total of sixteen ships of varying sizes and purposes in this fleet, and all were under the command of Adm. William F. "Bull" Halsey. Together, they were known as Task Force 16. Their mission was to ferry the B-25s to within four hundred miles of the Japanese coastline. They were very much aware that to be sighted by Japanese ships, planes, or submarines would prove disastrous. Indeed, even the most optimistic among military authorities had to admit that they were taking quite a chance. America could not afford to lose more ships at that point.

But in April of 1942 the news from all fronts had been so bleak and the military so eager for a victory that they were willing to take almost any gamble. Colonel Jimmy Doolittle knew that his planes would do little actual physical damage to the cities of Japan, but such a raid would certainly prove that the Japanese High Command had been terribly mistaken when they assured the Japanese people that their country was immune from foreign attack. Once American bombers zoomed in, bombing targets in various cities, the Japanese High Command would be forced to admit publicly that they had made a terrible mistake, that they had blundered. Such an admission would cause them to lose face with the people (as well as with the emperor) and to a Japanese officer, losing face was a fate worse than death.

More important, news of such a daring operation would boost sagging morale among the American people, and they could certainly use a boost in April of '42.

On the morning of April 2, Doolittle's airmen were again ordered to assemble in front of their respective B-25s for picture taking.

"These photos are for posterity, so give us some big smiles," Doolittle joked to his men before sending them out. He didn't know just how prophetic his words really were. For in years to come Doolittle's raid on Tokyo would become one of the most memorable events of World War II, and those who participated in it recognized as immortal heroes around the world.

As of this writing—August 2006—eighteen of the original eighty airmen who participated in Colonel Doolittle's raid on Tokyo on April 18, 1942, are still living. Their names appear in bold print beneath their photographs.

Two of the sixteen planes that participated in that audacious operation on the afternoon of April 18 were lost over Japanese-occupied territory in China, and their crews became prisoners of the Imperial Japanese Army. Of the ten men who served aboard those two aircraft, only four would ever come home again. Bill Farrow was not among them.

*Crew #16 (Plane 4-2268). (L-R): Lt. George Barr, navigator; Lt. Bill Farrow, pilot; Cpl. Harold Spatz, engineer-gunner;* **Lt. Robert L. Hite, copilot;** *Cpl. Jacob DeShazer, bombardier. This crew was captured by the Japanese on the morning of April 19, and Farrow and Spatz were brutally executed in October of that year.* (Photo courtesy of the U.S. Air Force Archives)

*Crew #6 (Plane 4-2298) (L-R):* **Lt. Chase Nielsen, navigator;** *Lt. Dean Hallmark, pilot; Sgt. Donald Fitzmaurice, engineer-gunner; Lt. Robert Meder, copilot; Sgt. William Dieter, bombardier. Lt. Dean Hallmark and the crew of the* Green Hornet *would also be captured on April 19 after their plane crashed in the surf off the coast of China. Fitzmaurice and Dieter drowned in the surf. Hallmark, like Farrow, was executed in October of '42.* (Photo courtesy of the U.S. Air Force Archives)

*Crew #1 (Plane 4-2344) (L-R): Lt. Henry A. Potter, navigator; Col. James H. Doolittle, pilot; Sgt. Fred A. Braemer, bombardier;* **Lt. Richard E. Cole, copilot;** *Sgt. Paul J. Leonard, gunner.* (Photo courtesy of the U.S. Air Force Archives)

*Crew #2 (Plane 4-2292) (L-R): Lt. Carl R. Wildner, navigator; Lt. Travis Hoover, pilot; Lt. Richard E. Miller, bombardier; Lt. William N. Fitzhugh, copilot; Sgt. Douglas V. Radney, engineer-gunner.* (Photo courtesy of the U.S. Air Force Archives)

*Crew #3 (Plane 4-2270) (L-R):* **Lt. Charles J. Ozuk, navigator;** *Lt. Robert M. Gray, pilot;* **Sgt. Aden E. Jones, bombardier;** *Lt. Jacob E. Manch, copilot; Cpl. Leland D. Faktor, engineer-gunner.* (Photo courtesy of the U.S. Air Force Archives)

*Crew #4 (Plane 4-2282) (L-R): Lt. Harry C. McCool, navigator; Cpl. Bert M. Jordan, gunner; Lt. Everett W. H Jolstrom, pilot; Sgt. Robert J. Stephens, bombardier; Lt. Lucian N. Youngblood, copilot.* (Photo courtesy of the U.S. Air Force Archives)

*Crew #5 (Plane 4-2283) (L-R): Lt. Eugene F. McGurl, navigator;* **Capt. David M. Jones,** **pilot;** *Lt. Denver V. Truelove, bombardier; Lt. Rodney R. Wilder, copilot; Sgt. Joseph W. Manske, engineer-gunner.* (Photo courtesy of the U.S. Air Force Archives)

*Crew #7 (Plane 4-2261) (L-R): Lt. Charles L. McClure, navigator; Lt. Ted W. Lawson, pilot; Lt. Robert S. Clever, bombardier; Lt. Dean Davenport, copilot;* **Sgt. David J.** **Thatcher, gunner.** (Photo courtesy of the U.S. Air Force Archives)

*Crew #8 (Plane 4-2242) (L-R):* **Lt. Nolan A. Herndon, navigator-bombardier;** *Capt. Edward J. York, pilot; Sgt. Theodore H. Laban, engineer; Lt. Robert G. Emmens, copilot; Sgt. David Pohl, gunner. (Note: York's plane landed in Vladivostok, Russia, where he and his crew were interned as prisoners of war.)* (Photo courtesy of the U.S. Air Force Archives)

*Crew #9 (Plane 4-2423) (L-R):* **Lt. Thomas C. Griffin, navigator;** *Lt. Harold F. Watson, pilot; Sgt. Eldred V. Scott, engineer-gunner; Lt. James N. Parker, copilot; Sgt. Wayne M. Bissell, bombardier.* (Photo courtesy of the U.S. Air Force Archives)

*Crew #10 (Plane 4-2250) (L-R):* **Lt. Horace E. Crouch, navigator;** *Lt. Richard O. Joyce, pilot; unidentified crew member replaced by Sergeant Horton for the flight; Lt. J. Royden Stork, copilot; Sgt. George F. Larkin, engineer;* **Sgt. Edwin W. Horton, gunner,** *is pictured in the insert.* (Photo courtesy of the U.S. Air Force Archives)

*Crew #11 (Plane 4-2249) (L-R):* **Lt. Frank A. Kappeler, navigator;** *Capt. Ross Greening, pilot; Sgt Melvin Gardner, engineer-gunner; Lt. Kenneth Reddy, copilot;* **Sgt. William Birch, bombardier.** (Photo courtesy of the U.S. Air Force Archives)

*Crew #12 (Plane 4-2278) (L-R): Lt. William Pound, navigator;* **Lt. William M. Bower,** **pilot;** *Sgt. Omer Duquette, engineer-gunner; Lt. Thadd Blanton, copilot; Sgt. Waldo Bither, bombardier.* (Photo courtesy of the U.S. Air Force Archives)

*Crew #13 (Plane 4-2247) (L-R): Lt. Clayton Campbell, navigator; Lt. Edgar McElroy, pilot; Sgt. Adam Williams, engineer-gunner; Lt. Richard A. Knobloch, copilot; Sgt Robert Bourgeois, bombardier.* (Photo courtesy of the U.S. Air Force Archives)

*Crew #14 (Plane 4-2297) (L-R):* **Lt. James Macia, navigator-bombardier;** *Maj. John Hilger, pilot; Sgt Jacob Eierman, engineer; Lt. Jack Sims, copilot; Sgt. Edwin Bain, gunner.* (Photo courtesy of the U.S. Air Force Archives)

*Crew #15 (Plane 4-2267) (L-R): Lt. Howard Sessler, navigator-bombardier; Lt. Donald G. Smith, pilot; Lt. (Dr.) Thomas R. White, gunner; Lt. Griffith Williams, copilot;* **Sgt. Ed Saylor, engineer.** (Photo courtesy of the U.S. Air Force Archives)

As Farrow and his crew lined up in front of the *Bat Out of Hell* on the morning of April 2, they had no way of knowing that just to their front, posing in front of plane #6, Lt. Dean Hallmark, pilot of the *Green Hornet*, would also be executed by the Japanese, along with Farrow and Harold Spatz.

Indeed, at that moment all was right with the world. Out of all the pilots in the Seventeenth Bombardment Group, they alone had been selected to participate in this most special operation. They didn't know yet just what the operation entailed, but it would definitely be something memorable, something that would further America's war effort against a cruel enemy. Else why would the Air Corps select Lt. Col. Jimmy Doolittle, arguably the world's greatest pilot, to lead them? And why else would they be serving aboard the *Hornet*, America's newest unsinkable aircraft carrier, the leviathan of the seas?

Daily these young Americans listened angrily to the latest news reports concerning the "Battlin' Bastards of Bataan," as they had come to be called, and how they were still holding out against everything the Imperial Japanese Army could throw at them. They had little ammunition, food, or medicine, but by God they were apparently fighting to the last man, much as Texans had done at the Alamo. As for Generals Jonathon M. Wainwright and Edward P King, the commanders of the American and Filipino forces on Bataan, they had won the airmen's undying respect. As for General Douglas MacArthur, whom the soldiers on Bataan referred to derisively as "Dugout Doug" and who, by order of Pres. Franklin Roosevelt, had fled to Australia aboard a B-17, leaving his men to suffer and die, the airmen had deep reservations.

*The* Hornet *with B-25s lashed to its deck en route to Japan. The protective Navy F4F fighter overhead was based aboard the* Enterprise. (Photo courtesy of the U.S. Navy Archives)

Privately, the airmen speculated as to the nature of their mission. Most expressed hope that they might do something to save the beleaguered American army in the Philippines, if such a thing was possible at that late date.

That evening, April 2, 1942, Colonel Doolittle called the men into a large meeting room. Before he could speak, however, he was forced to give the podium three sharp raps to silence the excited chatter going on among his airmen. They suspected that finally the nature and purpose of their mission would be revealed to them, and they were all abuzz with speculation. Finally, with a big grin, Doolittle began to speak:

"Gentlemen, for almost two months now we have led you around, pushed you around, had you sleeping in leaky pup tents, freezing in the cold morning air, eating C-rations three times a day, practicing takeoffs on little bitty strips of runway that a pickup

*Aboard the* Hornet *on the morning of April 3, 1942. Bill Farrow's plane, the* Bat Out of Hell, *was the first B-25 lifted aboard, and was immediately rolled to the very rear of the flight deck, thus becoming plane #16. That meant that his plane would be the last off on the morning of April 18.* (Photo courtesy of the U.S. Navy Archives)

truck could hardly take off on. And you performed magnificently, regardless of what we asked you to do. And for what? Well, we couldn't tell you. So you were good enough to simply take our word for it that all that suffering and practicing was for a good cause. Let me now express the Air Corps' gratitude to you, and my own personal gratitude to you. You have proven an example to young men serving in the U.S. military everywhere."

The airmen wildly applauded at that point. Doolittle raised his hand for silence.

"But now, gentlemen, let me tell you what you have all been waiting to hear. We are now three hundred miles out in the Pacific Ocean, and unless the Japanese have their sneaky little spies aboard this aircraft carrier, which I don't believe they do, then my words will go no further."

He paused for a moment, looking around the totally silent meeting room.

"Gentlemen, we are headed for Japan."

His pronouncement was followed by another moment of stunned silence while his words sunk in. Then pandemonium exploded in the room, with the men turning to one another and loudly exclaiming their surprise and excitement. No one was listening, everyone was talking. Some of the men began yelling "Yahoo, yahoo!" and laughing wildly.

Doolittle gave them a minute to vent their emotions. Then again he rapped the podium for order. The room grew quiet.

"There are still many details to be worked out. But as for the big picture, just let me tell you that our launch date is April 18. The *Hornet* will ferry us to within four hundred miles of the Japanese coastline, then we will take off late that afternoon. Some of our planes will bomb *military targets* in Tokyo, others will bomb *military targets* in Osaka, Yokohoma, and Nagoya. You'll note that I underlined the words 'military targets.' Under no circumstances will you even look toward the emperor's Imperial Palace. You will not even look in that general direction. And that's orders from President Roosevelt himself. Nor will you, under any circumstances, bomb schools, churches, or hospitals, nor any other civilian centers that the Japanese always target when bombing our folks. We don't want to do anything to feed the Japanese propaganda mill. You will bomb only those military targets assigned to you in whatever city you might choose."

Several hands went up around the room. But for the moment Doolittle brushed them aside.

"Let me finish first, gentlemen, then I'll entertain whatever questions you might have. Now, I told you that we will hit Tokyo and the other cities late in the afternoon of April 18. Then, once we've finished our runs, darkness will be setting in. And that's good. That means that we'll have the cover of darkness as protection as we fly on a southwesterly course down the island of Honshu till we reach the Yellow Sea. We'll fly across the Yellow Sea into China. By then dawn should be breaking. Thus we'll have daylight hours to search for friendly Chuchow Air Field. Our government has already received assurance from Chiang Kai-Chek that Chuchow Air Field will receive us. That's a distance of some two thousand miles. We'll refuel there and fly on due west to Chungking. Once we arrive in Chungking, we'll be home free. From there we'll fly south to India. And from there we'll be brought back to the United States. Now that's just a broad outline of our plan. There are still many details to be worked out. Do you have questions? I'm sure you must."

A young captain on the front row of seats raised his hand. "Sir, are we to understand that you'll be making the flight with us?"

"Absolutely. I wouldn't have accepted this assignment otherwise."

Another hand went up. "Sir, what's all this about flying into China? Is that the best plan we could come up with? That's a long way off."

Doolittle nodded vigorously. "It is definitely the best plan we could come up with. I wish we could all just turn around and fly back to the *Hornet*. But you know as well as I do that a B-25 can take off from a flight deck, but it cannot land on one. So the *Hornet*'s out. Besides, once we hit those Japanese cities, the Japanese will have everything in their arsenal—planes, subs, ships—out looking for our takeoff point. So the *Hornet* plans to wheel around and hightail it back for Pearl Harbor the minute we take off. We can't afford to lose a carrier at this point. I just pray that she makes it."

Another hand went up. "Sir, it's my understanding that China is occupied by the Japanese Army. So how are we supposed to land there?"

"Certain regions of China are occupied by the Japanese Army. But Chuchow is not. Chuchow is about two hundred miles southeast of Shanghai and about one hundred miles inland. It won't be difficult to find, especially in daylight hours. Besides, we'll be there for only an hour at most, just long enough to gas up and continue on to Chungking."

"Sir, is Chuchow expecting us?"

"They will be expecting us, but they aren't aware of that at this point. A matter of secrecy. But don't worry, the moment we take off for Japan a Navy fighter plane from the *Enterprise* will be dispatched to Chuchow Air Field to alert them that we're on our way."

Doolittle looked around the silent meeting room. "Now, if you fellows will remain seated, I want you pilots to come up as your name is called, and you will be asked which Japanese city you might like to attack."

Subsequently, Bill Farrow, the last pilot called, chose the city of Nagoya, some two hundred miles south of Tokyo. His target would be the Mitsubishi aircraft factory, the largest aircraft factory in Japan.

Following the meeting the pilots went their separate ways. Farrow, always of an introspective nature, very possibly made his way up to the darkened flight deck, and looked eastward across hundreds of miles of black ocean that separated him from his home in Darlington, some four thousand miles away. The wind was chill, and the night was silent as he stood there in the moonlight pondering the strange twists of fate that had brought him to this particular spot at this particular moment. Just a few years ago he had been pumping gas for ten cents an hour with few prospects of ever doing anything better. Now he was an Air Corps officer, a bomber pilot, about to embark on one of the most daring military missions in his country's history.

He was also of a deeply spiritual nature, and he had read the works of the world's greatest philosophers. Now he wondered how one accounts for such bizarre twists of fortune. Should he call it fate, or chance, or God, or a combination of all three?

Some day, perhaps, when he was older and wiser, he could sit down and try to separate the different strands of events that had become so intricately interwoven to form his destiny. For long moments he pondered his strange life. Had he not been chosen to receive his pilot's license back at the university, he would not be here now. Had he chosen to remain at the university instead of joining the Air Corps, he would not be here now. But once those events were set in motion, whether for good or for evil, it seemed impossible to stop or even change them. Life was like a roller coaster. And now he saw himself as a helpless passenger on that roller coaster. He could neither jump out nor stop it. At this point he had no choice but to hang on and see where it would take him. He prayed it would be a place called home. But his intuition told him that home might not be in the cards again.

Later, after much soul searching, Farrow collected his crew, and they all sat down in the galley for a briefing. Bob Hite remembers that he and Farrow sat on one side of the table, while George Barr, Jake DeShazer, and Harold Spatz sat on the other. Each man had helped himself to a steaming cup of Navy coffee. Each man was filled with questions concerning the raid.

An exuberant Jake DeShazer opened the discussion. "Excuse me, sir, I mean Bill, but can you tell us now just where we're going, and what we're supposed to do when we get there?"

Farrow reached over and patted the smaller man's shoulder. "I sure can, Jake. We're going to Nagoya, just south of Tokyo, and we're gonna raise Cain when we get there."

DeShazer could not hide his disappointment. "Well, I guess Nagoya's okay, as far as Japanese cities go, but what's wrong with Tokyo? My folks back in Oregon never heard of Nagoya. Nobody has. And I certainly don't want to go down in history for bombing a place nobody ever heard of. I sure don't wanna bomb some little Japanese cafe."

"Yeah, well, I'm a little disappointed myself," Farrow agreed. "But Tokyo had already been taken care of by the time I was called up. Nagoya's really a very famous Japanese city. It's about two hundred miles south of Tokyo, and one of the largest aircraft factories in Japan is located there—the Mitsubishi plant. And that's our target."

Somewhat mollified, DeShazer smiled. "Oh, okay, Lieutenant. That's a little better. So we're going to knock out that factory that makes those darned Japanese fighter planes, the Zeroes."

"That's it, Jake. In fact, I can't think of a factory anywhere that's more important to the Japanese war effort than that Mitsubishi aircraft factory."

"And it covers a city block," Hite joked, "so you don't have to worry about not having a bombsight. You can't miss. In fact, you can do it with your eyes closed. Or I'll do it for you."

"Yeah, yeah, okay, but I sort of had my heart set on the Imperial Palace in Tokyo," DeShazer said. "You know?"

"So did I and fifteen other pilots in that meeting room tonight," Farrow laughed, "but Colonel Doolittle said nothing doing. We can't hit anything that's not of military importance. Believe me, Jake, if we'd had our way, there'd be sixteen B-25s zeroed in on that Imperial Palace."

George Barr took a sip of coffee and asked, "And just when is all this scheduled to come off, Bill? Or can you tell us?"

"Yeah, George." Farrow stirred his coffee. "The way things are set, we're to take off late in the afternoon of April 18. That's a Saturday, just a little over two weeks from now. By then we'll be within four hundred miles of the Japanese coastline. We'll hit Nagoya about dusk, then fly on southwest down the main island of Honshu and across the Yellow Sea. About daylight we should be over the east coast of China. Then we'll fly on to Chuchow Air Field where we'll land and refuel. Chuchow is still unoccupied by the Japanese, by the way—"

"That's nice to know," Harold Spatz interjected. "I'd hate to holler 'Fill 'em up, Mack' to some Japanese captain carrying one of them big swords." The others laughed.

"Then on to Chungking," Farrow said. "From there we'll fly to India, next stop the good old U.S. of A."

"That's a pretty good ride," Barr observed.

"About twenty-two hundred miles," Farrow agreed.

Barr, the navigator, did a quick mental calculation. "Like flying from Eglin to Sacramento."

"Yeah," Hite added, "that's the reason we can't sit down for all those darned gas tanks they added to our plane."

"Sounds like a pretty complicated process," Barr said. "I mean, twenty-two hundred miles is a long way to fly even if we didn't have Japanese Zeroes hung around our neck. What if something goes wrong along the way?"

Farrow put down his cup, looked Barr directly in the eye, and then, in a melodramatic tone, he said, "Then we're already dead, George my boy. We just don't know it yet."

"Oh, come on, Bill," DeShazer laughed. "Don't beat around the bush. Give it to us straight. Tell us the facts."

"No, in fact, George," Farrow said seriously, "I'm glad you raised that issue. It is a complicated process, but there's no reason for anything to go wrong. We're flying the greatest plane in the world, and so if we do our jobs the way we're supposed to, nothing will go wrong. And before we know it, we'll be sitting in our big easy chairs back in the good old U.S.A. polishing our medals."

"And you'll be home in time to see Lib Sims graduate," Hite kidded.

"Absolutely," Farrow grinned. "Colonel Doolittle planned the entire operation around just that one point."

"Just think," Harold Spatz moaned. "At this very moment I could be sitting at Molly's Grill back at Pendleton, having a cold beer, talking to a couple of good-looking chicks, and trying to decide how to waste the rest of my youth. Instead, here I am out in the middle of the damned ocean with a boatload of loonies. My, my! If my friends could see me now."

Initially, the Raiders were assigned to rooms already occupied by the *Hornet*'s naval officers. These Navy men simply shrugged off their new friends as mere interlopers, like poor relations who had arrived uninvited, and thus made it a point to see that these airmen were issued tiny cots with ultra-thin lumpy mattresses to sleep on, and in general treated them as non-persons.

But then, following the announcement that these brave heroes were on their way to bomb Japan, a near suicidal mission, the Navy did an abrupt about-face.

Bob Hite would later recall a conversation he had with Bill Farrow as they stood in the chow line that evening concerning the Navy's change in attitude.

"Have you ever seen such a thing, Bill? Those two Navy officers in my room actually insisted that I take one of their beds last night—a real bed."

Farrow nodded. "Yeah, I know. I'm beginning to feel like a special character of some sort myself. The Navy guys in my room very politely moved their nightly poker game to another room. I actually got some sleep for a change."

A young ensign approached the two men at that point. "Excuse me, sirs," he said quietly, "but why don't you gentlemen go to the head of the line? No sense in you having to wait. We know you're still in training."

Farrow and Hite winked at one another. "See what I mean?" Hite chuckled as the two forged ahead of a hundred hungry sailors, an action that could have resulted in severe bodily harm only the day before.

April 5 was Easter Sunday, and religious services were held aboard the *Hornet*. A solemn Bill Farrow, Bible in hand, made it a point to be in attendance along with the rest of his crew. He awakened early, dressed, then went by to arouse Jake DeShazer, son of a Christian minister. DeShazer remembers that he awakened and sleepily told Farrow that he was going to grab another quick nap, and that he would be there before services began. Farrow smiled and quietly exited the cabin. DeShazer then spent the rest of the morning sleeping blissfully away. (During his three years of captivity in various Japanese prisons, DeShazer would recall with deep regret having slept through Easter services. In 1948 he became an ordained minister, then returned to Japan as a missionary. Among those he converted was the Japanese pilot who led the attack on Pearl Harbor.)

From that moment on most of the airmen's time was occupied by additional training for their upcoming flight to Japan. Lieutenant Stephen Jurika, who had spent much time in Japan prior to the war, lectured the men on what to do if shot down. Lieutenant T. H. White, the flight surgeon who would take part in the mission, lectured the men on first aid, sanitation, and how to purify contaminated water. Commander Frank Akers, the *Hornet*'s navigator, gave the airmen classes designed to sharpen their navigational skills.

Colonel Jimmy Doolittle himself conducted gunnery practice, and the airmen practiced hour after hour, firing at target kites flown from the carrier.

While the airmen were preoccupied with lectures and practice, flight mechanics were going over every inch of every plane to make sure that they were in top shape. Soon every plane was pronounced ready for action.

On the whole, despite the great risks involved in this operation, Farrow and his fellow airmen assumed a carefree attitude. Still, very much aware of the atrocities committed by the Japanese upon prisoners of war, the most asked question concerned what they should do if captured. Colonel Doolittle told them they would have to decide that for themselves, that every situation was different. But as for himself, he said, if his plane was hit and going down, he would pick out the closest target and dive straight into it. He would not allow the Japanese to take him alive.

During their free time in the evenings, recalled Bob Hite years later, the airmen passed the time by playing poker. "It was just one long poker game. You could go from room to room, table after table, and all you'd see were men playing poker. I wasn't an habitual player, but I'd play occasionally. Farrow himself never played, but he enjoyed watching. I still remember, Bill would sit down between me and the fellow next to me. He'd have a cup of coffee in his hand, and he'd just squeeze in between us. He wouldn't take a hand, but he'd sit there and whisper advice to me. Whenever I won a hand, Bill was a happy fellow. You'd think he and I had just broken the bank at Monte Carlo. He was the friendliest guy in the world. I guess gambling went against his religion. But he could tell everybody else how to play."

Finally, on April 12, the USS *Enterprise* and its supporting vessels, all under the command of Adm. Bull Halsey, rendezvoused with the *Hornet* several hundred miles west of Hawaii. Now Task Force 16 would have air support should it be attacked. At last, Capt. Marc Mitscher and Col. Jimmy Doolittle could breathe a sigh of relief. Now all they had to do was to drive right up to the Japan's front door and let loose sixteen B-25 bombers whose mission was to destroy public morale in the Land of the Rising Sun. The Japanese High Command would not be amused.

As though they didn't already have enough to contend with, on the morning of April 14, still sailing westward at a speed of twenty knots, the task force encountered rain, fog, and heavy seas. Nor did conditions improve. To the contrary, as the days progressed, the weather worsened, and the waves grew even higher.

*On the morning of April 14, only about 1500 miles east of the Japanese coastline, the* Hornet *encountered rain, wind, and heavy seas. The men wondered what else could go wrong. They didn't have long to wonder.* (Photo courtesy of the U.S. Navy Archives)

Two days later, on April 16, preparations for the raid increased in tempo. Deck crews made sure the planes were battened down against the terrible wind now blowing in from the west. And they began to prepare for the impending takeoff. At each plane fuel tanks were filled, five five-hundred-pound bombs were hoisted aboard, and its single machine gun was loaded. Only a few hundred more miles to go, then both the *Hornet* and the *Enterprise* could do an about-face and sail at full steam back to Pearl Harbor—barring any unforeseen disasters.

Farrow's plane, the *Bat Out of Hell,* was plane #16, the last plane lined up on the flight deck. In fact, its tail section stuck so far out over the fantail, over the dark waves raging below, that tail gunner Harold Spatz could not enter the rear hatch.

At this point, on the morning of April 17, the Task Force was located about twelve hundred miles off the east coast of Japan, and speed was increased to twenty-eight knots. By that time, with giant waves actually crashing across the flight deck, it appeared that Task Force16 had sailed into a virtual spring monsoon. The men wondered if anything else could go wrong.

They didn't have long to wonder.

On the evening of April 17, Bill Farrow and his fellow Raiders hit the sack early in hopes of catching up on some much-needed rest. They knew that takeoff was imminent, scheduled for the next afternoon, and they hoped to be in top physical condition when that time came. And it was fortunate that they did. For at 5:58 the next morning the *Hornet* received a frantic message from an SBD Dauntless dive bomber observation plane from the *Enterprise* that a Japanese patrol vessel had been sighted just six miles ahead. Immediately, the big guns of the Task Force opened up, and that unfortunate patrol vessel was blown out of the water. Still, Admiral Halsey feared that the alarm had already been sounded. It was very possible that dozens of Japanese bombers were already on the way. If so, Task Force 16 was in big trouble.

Halsey pondered the odds, then reached the decision that all those sleek B-25s had to get off the *Hornet*'s flight deck immediately. America could not take a chance on losing more big ships at that point.

*Bill Farrow (second from right) and his crew stand by their plane looking out to sea on April 17, the day before they took off on their now immortal raid on Japan. Two days later, Farrow and his crew would begin to undergo unspeakable tortures at the hands of cruel Japanese interrogators.* (Photo Courtesy of the U.S. Navy Archives)

Thus at eight o'clock, on the morning of April 18, some eight hours ahead of schedule and still some seven hundred miles southeast of Japan, Halsey flashed a message to Mitscher: LAUNCH PLANES X TO COL DOOLITTLE AND GALLANT COMMAND GOOD LUCK AND GOD BLESS YOU.

Then aboard the *Hornet* the Klaxon horns sounded, and Mitscher's voice boomed out: "Army pilots—man your planes. Army pilots— man your planes."

Startled and alarmed, Farrow jumped straight up in bed. What in the world was this all about, he wondered. Takeoff was not due for at least another eight hours. Yet they were being ordered on deck—and it wasn't even daylight yet. Likely it was just another drill.

He yawned, stepped into his clothes, slipped on his flight jacket, and wished that he had a hot cup of coffee. But he supposed the coffee would have to wait until breakfast. At the moment he could visualize a dozen strips of bacon, several pieces of toast, and a big bowl of scrambled eggs.

All the other airmen were doing the same. They crawled out of their bunks, dressed, piled their belongings into their B-4 bags and rushed up on deck. In their panic, no one was given breakfast, though there was emergency food and water already aboard each of the planes, supplies that would prove invaluable over the next sixteen hours. As for Bill Farrow and Bob Hite, they had thought to visit the galley the night before where they picked up even more emergency rations. They had also thought to visit the ship's commissary where they loaded up on Baby Ruth candy bars. At least they wouldn't starve to death during this operation. Later, Bob Hite would remember that long after their emergency rations had been consumed, those Baby Ruths would become lifesavers for the hungry men of the *Bat Out of Hell*.

They were also loaded down with equipment—Browning .44 automatics in shoulder holsters, clips of ammunition, knives, flashlights, canteens, morphine, sterilized bandages, life jackets, and, finally, parachutes. But who would need a parachute? Just extra baggage.

Colonel Doolittle himself was dismayed at this change in schedule. He had to launch the planes eight hours early, meaning that they would hit the target areas at about noon instead of dusk. Thus there would be no searching for Chuchow Air Field during daylight hours. To the contrary, they would be flying blind over the coast of China about midnight. How in the world would anyone ever find Chuchow Air Field in the darkness? Even more daunting to his spirits was the knowledge that they would have to fly an extra three hundred miles, so he was faced with the overwhelming question: Where would his airmen get the gas to fly all those extra miles? He certainly sympathized with Admiral Halsey and his fear of losing more American ships, but still . . .

Once arrived on the flight deck, Doolittle called a quick meeting of his Raiders. Then he told them of his concerns. His final words were: "Men, once you leave this flight deck, you're on your own. Be careful, God bless you, and I'll see you in Chungking."

His Raiders, hail and hearty heroes every one, dismissed Doolittle's fears as probably groundless, then all gave a rousing cheer. At that point, pounded by heavy seas and gale-force winds, they began struggling down the flight deck to their respective planes, giving high signs and shouting to each other as they slipped and slid down the deck.

"Best of luck!"

"Tallyho!"

This was going to be their grandest day ever, the day they finally avenged Pearl Harbor. As far as their gas was concerned, they hoped that problem would take care of itself, as most problems do. At any rate, it was a little late to be worrying about it.

Lieutenant Chase Nielsen, the navigator aboard plane #6, the *Green Hornet,* piloted by Dean Hallmark, would later write an account of their experiences on the morning of April 18: "With the *Hornet* going full speed ahead into a 25-knot wind, it was almost impossible for us to stay on our feet. I slid down the deck on my hands and knees pushing my gear ahead of me in the general direction of the B-25s." He describes how several sailors, seeing his predicament and that of other members of the crew, rushed to help the men to their plane. Reaching the B-25, the crew stowed their equipment, checked the guns and bombs, finished refueling the aircraft, waved goodbye to the sailors, and took their positions.

Monsoon-like winds and a torrential rain were now sweeping the flight deck. Farrow and his crewmen, scrambling to reach the

*Bat Out of Hell,* found it difficult to keep their footing as the big carrier pitched in waves thirty feet high. They ran, slipped, and crawled to where their plane was tethered at the rear of the flight deck and wildly clambered inside.

Farrow, now dripping wet, strapped himself into his pilot's seat, then spoke over the interphone to his excited crewmen. "Okay, fellows, I know we're hours ahead of schedule. But there's one bright spot in all this. We'll be the last plane taking off this morning. That means we'll have an extra hour of fuel."

"Gosh, how lucky can we get!" Bob Hite exclaimed, and the crew burst into nervous laughter.

"That extra hour of fuel could mean the difference in life or death," Farrow said, "when we reach China tonight."

Hite grinned at Farrow seated beside him. "I was only joking, SIR!" Farrow leaned over and gave Hite a playful elbow in the ribs.

Seated in the well behind Farrow was navigator George "Red" Barr, while bombardier Jake DeShazer was seated in the nose cone, and gunner Harold Spatz was hunched over in the tail section.

In fact, had Farrow taken off ten minutes earlier or ten minutes later, he might well have avoided going down in Japanese-occupied territory and thus lived to a ripe old age. But, then, whether one lives or dies is often a matter of only seconds. With Farrow it was ten minutes.

Doolittle's plane, the first in line, cleared the flight deck at 8:20 A.M. Then it was another plane approximately every five minutes. At 9:15, with tall waves breaking over the bow, Farrow gripped the wheel as the Navy flagman used both hands to motion him forward into the takeoff position. It was then that disaster struck. As the plane in front of him, piloted by Lt. Don Smith, gunned its engines for takeoff, its strong prop blast propelled a Navy deckhand, Seaman Robert W. Wall, back toward the *Bat Out of Hell.* Farrow and Hite watched in helpless horror as the terrified seaman was devoured by the big blades of their left propeller. They looked away as blood splattered the deck. Luckily, as it turned out, Seaman Wall lost an arm but not his life.

Planes #1 through #10 were scheduled to bomb Tokyo; planes #11 and #12 Yokohoma; and planes #14, #15, and #16 Nagoya and Osaka.

Farrow received the signal from the Navy flagman to move into a takeoff position. He pushed the throttle forward, listening to the smooth whine of the two big engines, then he lifted the flaps, and the *Bat Out of Hell* began to move forward. Bob Hite would later remember that the men were filled with a mixture of anxiety and anticipation at that point, as proven by their frivolous conversations.

Just before revving up his engines for takeoff, Farrow called over the interphone: "Okay, anybody wanna resign? Last chance!" His comments were met with laughter.

"Oh, sir," it was gunner Harold Spatz. "I've got a big problem."

*Approximately an hour and fifteen minutes following Jimmy Doolittle's takeoff, in gale-force winds and high seas, the* Bat Out of Hell *began rolling down the flight deck. Just prior to this event, a Navy seaman lost his arm when it was caught in the plane's propeller, a most unsettling experience for Farrow and his crewmen.* (Photo courtesy of the U.S. Air Force Archives)

Farrow frowned. "Make it quick, Harold. What's your problem?"

"I forgot my toothbrush. Can I run back and get my toothbrush?"

Farrow grinned and shook his head. "How about we toss you out thirty minutes from now? And you can swim back for your toothbrush."

"Aw, Lieutenant, come on!"

"Yeah, okay, Harold. How about I pull over right down here?"

"Hey, Harold," Hite called, "bring me back a cup of java and a couple of doughnuts, okay?" The men all laughed.

"Sure, Bob," Spatz said with mock seriousness.

"Okay, everybody knock it off," Farrow ordered. "I'm about to get the GO signal from the flagman."

The flagman gave them the GO signal at 9:15 A.M., April 18, 1942, and Bill Farrow yelled to his crewmen, "Everybody hold on. Here we go." At that message, all the crewmen, though strapped to their seats, reached out and got a firm grip on the nearest immovable object.

Navy crewmen cheered and waved their caps as Farrow gunned his engines and the plane roared forward. His eyes were like silver dollars as he watched the flight deck quickly recede beneath them. Then, just as the *Hornet* crested a big wave and dipped downward, he eased back on the wheel and in a moment he could see nothing below but the huge dark waves of the

*A naval officer watches apprehensively as Bill Farrow and his crew take off from the flight deck of the* Hornet *at 9:15 on the morning of April 18. This time the next day they would be in the hands of the Imperial Japanese Army, a horrible fate for such heroic young men.* (Photo courtesy of the U.S. Navy Archives)

Pacific Ocean. Suddenly the *Hornet* was long gone, and the *Bat Out of Hell* was on its own. At last they were airborne. Next stop Nagoya, the third largest city in Japan.

The Raiders circled the Task Force below until finally joined by the *Bat Out of Hell,* the final plane off the flight deck. Now all the planes were in the air. Taking their cues from Colonel Doolittle, the Raiders began streaking toward Japan and immortality.

Flying at an altitude of only five hundred feet, beneath heavily overcast skies, the Raiders hoped they would not encounter enemy opposition from either the sea or the air, especially since each plane was armed only with a single .50-caliber machine gun. But so far, so good.

At approximately 2:00 P.M., after almost five hours in the air, the clouds finally broke, a brilliant sun burst forth, and Farrow

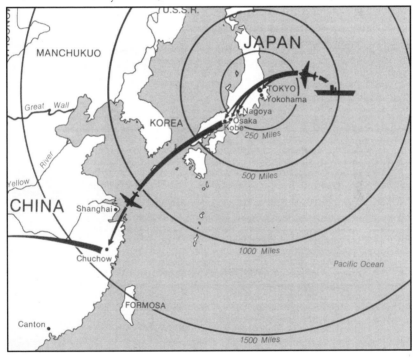

*Initially, the* Hornet *was to ferry the airmen to within 400 miles of the Japanese coastline. But due to the sighting of a Japanese patrol boat, the airmen were forced to take off some eight hours and 200 miles ahead of schedule. Already strapped for fuel, they wondered if they could possibly make it all the way to the Chuchow Air Field. (Photo courtesy of the U.S. Army Archives)*

could see the white beaches of Japan dead ahead. At that point
the Raiders formed five groups of three planes each. According
to previous orders, they spread out at this point, with ten miles
between each group, a ploy that Doolittle had devised in hopes
of giving the impression that there were far more than sixteen
planes involved in the operation. Spread out over a fifty-mile
front, the men of these various groups could barely see the
planes of the groups beside them. Farrow and his crew were in
the far-left group.

At this point, Hite remembers, in the midst of the Japanese,
the Raiders' comments grew more serious.

"Hey, George, how far to Nagoya now?" Farrow asked of
George Barr, the navigator.

"Just about three hundred miles."

"Okay, about ninety minutes of flying time. And how about
Chuchow Air Field?"

"Just a second." Barr studied his map. A minute later he called,
"Hey, Bill, according to my calculations Chuchow's about fifteen
hundred miles. About eight or nine hours of flying time."

"That's quite a hop," Farrow said.

"Wake me when we get there," Bob Hite said, sliding down in
his seat.

"Hey, no problem," Harold Spatz called from the rear turret,
"just go to the second light and take a left. We'll be there before
we know it."

The planes descended to an altitude of only two hundred feet.
Below them the white beaches of Japan glittered in the sun. The
men could clearly see small pleasure boats floating in the harbor,
and Japanese civilians romping on the beaches below. The civilians waved at them, and they waved back.

"Looks just like Myrtle Beach from up here," Farrow observed.

"Hey, did I ever tell you guys?" Harold Spatz called. "I'm from
Kansas, and I'd never even seen the ocean till I joined the Air
Corps."

"What'd you think of it?" Farrow asked.

"Well, it's not as big as I thought it would be," Spatz joked.

"Get outta here," George Barr laughed.

"Okay, guys," Farrow's voice was serious. "Believe it or not, we're now flying over the Land of the Rising Sun. That means Japanese, lots of Japanese. So I want every man to look out his nearest window and keep your eyes peeled for enemy aircraft. If you see anything, sound the alarm, and we'll try to take evasive action."

As luck, as well as the element of surprise, would have it, Farrow and his crew experienced little if any opposition from Japanese ground or air forces as they zoomed across the countryside at treetop level. Finally, Farrow spotted Nagoya dead ahead. Below them they could see Japanese civilians going about their business, walking the streets and waiting for city buses. It was now 3:30 P.M.

"Okay, Jake," Farrow called DeShazer, "heads up. We should be approaching the Mitsubishi works any minute now."

"Right, Bill," DeShazer replied nervously, "but remember, they took away my bombsight. I'll have to eyeball the target."

"Don't worry, Jake. You'll do a fine job, and we're all behind you all the way."

Minutes later, as his target came into view, DeShazer squinted hard at the Mitsubishi aircraft factory, took a deep breath, and released five five-hundred-pound bombs. Then he jumped to the nearest window and looked behind him to see just where his bombs might be headed. He was just in time to see great flames and billows of smoke shoot skyward as the Mitsubishi aircraft factory received direct hits. Farrow gripped the wheel tightly as the explosions rocked the *Bat Out of Hell.*

"YAHOO!" DeShazer yelled. "We got 'em, Lieutenant. We got 'em."

"Great going, Jake," Farrow and the other airmen responded. They were all looking back at the burning aircraft factory. They began cheering for Jake DeShazer.

"I'm just relieved that I didn't blast a hospital or playground by mistake," DeShazer said. "Thank goodness that's over!"

Farrow could feel the plane lift perceptively with the release of twenty-five hundred pounds of explosives.

"This should help our fuel consumption considerably," he said. "Maybe we'll make Chuchow after all."

Bob Hite joked, "I tell you what, Bill, if we need to jettison any

*Since all the planes involved in the raid were lost, this is the only photo taken over Japan that survived. It was taken by Lt. Richard Knoblock, plane #13. This is a shot of the naval base at Yokosuka. (Photo courtesy of the U.S. Air Force Archives)*

more weight, we'll just throw these three Yankees out. That oughtta lighten our load considerably."

"Watch it, Reb," Barr responded. "We got you outnumbered three to two."

"Those are odds we Southerners are used to," Farrow said.

"Excuse me for being a wet blanket," Spatz called from the rear turret, "but shouldn't we be getting the hell out of here?"

"Right you are, Harold my boy," Farrow said as he pushed forward on the throttle. "Next stop Chuchow Air Field."

The men all gave a hearty laugh. They had just bombed Japan, possibly the most daring venture in the history of American warfare, and now the world was their oyster. This time next week they would probably be starring in a big Hollywood movie.

It was probably just as well that they failed to realize at that point that it would be years before they would ever see America again. Indeed, several of those brash young heroes would never see America again.

# CHAPTER 6

# A Night Flight to China

In later years both Bob Hite and Dick DeShazer would recall that following the bombing the men were lighthearted and in a humorous mood, as they had been throughout the long flight.

"We were hardly more than kids," Hite said, "and we really didn't appreciate the gravity of what we'd just done, nor the danger we were still in."

With Nagoya now behind them, the men excitedly agreed that this operation had proven by far their easiest exercise to date.

"The toughest part," Bill Farrow said, "was taking off this morning. The way that crosswind was blowing across the flight deck, I was afraid we might wind up down in the galley somewhere."

"Yeah, but you know," George Barr said, "I thought the training we went through down at Eglin was a lot tougher than this. I don't know what I was expecting, but it really wasn't that tough."

"Oh, yeah," DeShazer agreed, "I just knew there'd be Zeroes all over us before we got out of there. But I didn't see a single enemy plane."

"Nor any antiaircraft fire," Farrow added. "We were really lucky."

"I think we just surprised hell out of them," Hite added. He checked his watch. Three-thirty, and dark storm clouds were beginning to gather again as they sped southwestward down the island of Honshu toward the Yellow Sea.

"Looks like we might be hitting more wind and rain before long," he observed.

"That's good," Farrow said. "Now if the Japanese come looking for us we can hide in those big clouds."

"Boy, do I feel like a hero," came Spatz's voice from the rear turret. Everybody laughed at that comment.

"Sure, we all do," Bob Hite said. Amid big chuckles, they began to refer to one another as heroes.

"Hey, Hero Jake," Hite called, "how'd you feel when you saw that big Mitsubishi plant go up?"

"Words can't describe it, Hero Bob," DeShazer replied.

All in all, the men were floating on cloud nine. After months of intensive training, the big operation was successfully behind them. They had braved everything the Japanese could possibly throw at them and completed the mission without a complaint or a whimper. Soon they would be going home to a hero's welcome.

Gone was the stress and worry that each had been carrying inside for weeks, and now they were all high on the adrenaline that had been pumping through their bodies since early morning. As soon as the mission was behind them everybody wanted to talk non-stop. And they did, recalls Bob Hite, with nobody listening to anybody else.

Later, by 7:00 P.M., the men could see black storm clouds roiling beneath them, and gale-force winds began rocking the plane from side to side. They had been in the air for the past thirteen hours, and the men began to express fatigue.

"Hey, George," Spatz called from the rear turret, "are we there yet?"

"No, not quite," Barr replied. "Chuchow Air Field's about two hundred miles southwest of Shanghai, so we've got a couple of more hours anyway."

Farrow and the other airmen were aware that Chuchow was a hundred miles east of Chungking, their ultimate destination this night, and dangerously close to Japanese-occupied territory. Alone now in the darkness, they could only hope and pray.

The Raiders had no way of knowing it at the time, and perhaps it was just as well, but the Navy fighter that had been dispatched from the *Enterprise* to warn Chuchow Air Field that the Raiders were on their way had been intercepted and shot down by Japanese fighters. Thus the Chinese were totally ignorant of the

Raiders' approach. That meant there would be no torches lighting the airfield that night. The Raiders were on their own.

Farrow reached behind him and tapped Barr on the shoulder. "How far till we reach the coast of China, George?"

"According to my calculations China should be just ahead."

At that point, as though on cue, Barr suddenly spotted a lighthouse on the Chinese coast and advised Farrow to climb, and climb fast, to avoid the mountains that reached up to the clouds behind the beach. Farrow nodded and climbed to 11,000 feet on instruments.

"Okay, George, which way now?" Farrow called, and Barr gave him an approximate heading to get them to Chuchow.

An hour dragged by, and, flying high above the dark clouds boiling below, there was still no sign of Chuchow.

"I hate to tell you fellows," Farrow called, "but we're in a tough spot. We can't find Chuchow from way up here, and I'm sure not planning to go down any lower. Those clouds out there are full of rocks, and we don't want to wind up plowing a tunnel through one of those mountains."

"How much gas we got left?" Hite asked.

"That's the problem," Farrow answered. "Free China and Chungking are situated southwest of Shanghai. We don't have enough gas to make it to Chungking, so I think we'll just keep on flying west and see if we can run out of this weather and make a forced landing somewhere near Chungking."

George Barr spoke up. "Look, Bill, you're the commander, and I'll stick with you all the way to New York if you say so. But in my opinion you'll be making a big mistake by flying west. Let me suggest that you fly west for fifty minutes and then due south—to make sure we're out of Japanese-occupied territory. Then when our gas is gone, we simply bail out. At least we'll come down in friendly Chinese territory."

But Farrow and Hite shook their heads. They wanted to bring the plane down in one piece if possible, refuel it, and then fly on to Chungking, their original destination.

Over the months and years to come, they would seriously regret this decision.

Still, at that point in the mission the Raiders were optimistic.

The way their luck had been running, they would find Chuchow, refuel the plane, and be happily on their way to Chungking before midnight. So despite their situation, their mood was still light.

Farrow called to Spatz back in the rear turret: "Hey, Harold, I don't think we're in any danger of being pursued at this point. Why don't you just come on up here and join the party with the rest of us."

"Great, Bill. Thought you'd never ask." There was relief in his voice.

"I guess it's getting a little lonely back there after thirteen hours."

"Yeah, it's awfully quiet and dark—scary as hell."

Moments later Spatz scrambled into the cockpit and squeezed into a seat behind Hite. "Hey, Bill, we there yet?"

"No," Farrow laughed, "but we soon will be."

"I hope so. I gotta use the bathroom."

"Hey, somebody hand Harold the pee jug," Hite called.

"Pee? You mean that's pee I been drinking? I thought it was orange juice."

The plane rocked with laughter.

"How many Zeroes you shoot down today, Harold?" Hite asked.

Spatz didn't miss a beat. "Eight. Damaged three others."

"Great! So you became an ace on your first flight out. That's not bad, Harold."

"I know. President Roosevelt wants me to come to Washington next week to pick up a big medal."

Hite grinned. "I just want you to know, my boy, that I'm awfully proud of you."

"Thank you, General. Merely doing my duty."

To kill time the men told little moron jokes and sang songs. Hite remembers that the number-one song in America at that time was "Deep in the Heart of Texas," and the men sang it until even he never wanted to hear of Texas again.

"We'd go, 'The stars at night, are big and bright,' then we'd take our fists and go bom-bom-bom-bom on the nearest object handy, then finish the line with 'deep in the heart of Texas.'"

And "Chattanooga Choo Choo" was another favorite. Dick DeShazer suggested "Tangerine," but the men all complained that that song was just too mushy and too tough to sing.

At that point, Bill Farrow suggested they do a few rousing choruses of "Dixie," and the men all began to sing, even the Yankees on board.

Hite remembers that they also sang "Praise the Lord and Pass the Ammunition," a little ditty that had hit the airwaves immediately following Pearl Harbor.

Then they sang everybody's favorite song, the Andrews sisters' version of "Don't Sit Under the Apple Tree."

After they had exhausted their repertoire of songs, the men decided to furnish brief biographies of themselves. George Barr said, "Okay, Bill, you're the commander of this ship. You go first."

Farrow smiled modestly. "Well, there's not much to tell. I'm just a poor old country boy from Darlington, South Carolina. I finished high school in 1935 and then served a couple of years with the CCC boys. Then in 1938 I entered the University of South Carolina. Met a wonderful girl there named Lib Sims, and as soon as I get back home we're getting married. But I got tired of never having any money, and in 1940 I joined the Air Corps. I received my wings in July of '41 and was assigned to fly a B-25 medium bomber at Camp Pendleton, and now here I am. Not much of a story, eh?"

"Okay, not bad," Barr said, "now you, Bob."

"Hey, George, who appointed you master of ceremonies?" Spatz joked.

"I did myself, young man."

Bob Hite cleared his throat dramatically, and then in his deep Texas drawl he said, "Ladies and gentlemen, it pleases me to announce that I was born and raised in Earth, Texas, on a small ranch where my daddy raised all sorts of animals, including cows and steers. Beef cattle, in other words. That's why they call us cowboys. But seriously, I did enjoy the outdoors, and I still do. I finished high school, then completed three more years of school at Texas State College before I joined the Air Corps. And, like Bill, I was assigned to fly a B-25, and here I am—for better or for worse. Oh, and by the way, I've been accused of being highly opinionated and overly aggressive, so don't ever disagree with anything I say. You don't want to annoy me."

"Oh, we would never do that, sir," Spatz said.

"And now," Barr intoned, "we shall hear from Jake DeShazer."

The quiet and reserved Jake DeShazer spoke up only after much prodding from his fellow crewmen. "Well, I was born and raised right there in Oregon. My father was a farmer and a lay minister. Had a little Christian church where most folks in the neighborhood went to church on Sundays. But Dad and I are a lot alike. We both enjoy hunting and fishing in the great outdoors. I was pretty easygoing growing up, and never took school very serious. So when I finished high school, I joined the Air Corps because I didn't have anything else to do. But I am very proud that I completed the mechanic and bombardier schools once I got in the Air Corps. I might just stay in service once this war's over. There's not much demand for bombardiers out there in civilian life."

"Thank you, Doctor," Barr said. "And now our next contestant is Mr. Harold Spatz, a sassy little kid from Kansas. Take it away, Harold."

Spatz grinned and began to speak. "Well, I was born and raised in Lebo, Kansas, not exactly the garden spot of the universe. My mother died when I was real little, and so it was always just me and Pa there on the farm. But like Jake says, I wasn't ever too serious about school, so when I graduated in 1939 I decided to join the Air Corps. I went in at Fort Riley and finished mechanics school. Then they sent me to Camp Pendleton. As for staying in, the Depression was pretty tough on us farmers, so I think I'll probably stay right where I am for the next twenty years. At least you get a place to sleep and plenty to eat. And like Bill, I'm engaged and plan to get married once we get back to America."

"Get married?" Bob Hite asked in disbelief. "Why you're just a kid."

"I'm twenty, Bob. And back in Lebo, people look at you kind of funny if you're twenty and not married."

"Aw, I was just kidding, Harold."

"My fiancée's named Julie, and she works at the dime store. We're both saving our money so we can get married soon."

"Yeah, well, we don't want anybody to think you're funny," Hite laughed. A moment later, his voice now serious, Hite added, "I'm only kidding, Harold. You send me an invitation, and I promise I'll be seated on the front row at that church at your wedding. And I suspect all these other mugs will be there too."

"Thanks, Bob."

"Okay, George," Bill Farrow said, "we've heard from everybody else. What about you now?"

George Barr spoke up: "Well, my mom died when I was an infant, and then when I was six my father was lost at sea when he was fishing off Long Island. I grew up in a home for boys until I started to college. I've never really had any foster parents, but Charles and Martha Towns were sort of my unofficial foster parents, and they stepped in when I finished high school and helped me attend college. The Towns are wonderful people, and I know my real parents couldn't have been any better to me than they were. So I attended Northland College in Ashland, Wisconsin. I played a little basketball for Northland, and after the war I want to finish college, become a high school teacher, and coach basketball."

After the biographies were finished, the men tried to think of something else to do—anything to kill time and take their minds off their current situation. Each silently faced the overwhelming question: "What if we can't find Chuchow Air Field in the darkness and in the midst of this darned monsoon! What'll we do then? We can't fly all the way back to the United States, and eventually we're going to run out of fuel. So just what will we do?" Most of the crew told themselves, "Well, the pilot and copilot voted to ride this baby in. And their votes are the ones that count, so that's what we'll do."

They had consumed their emergency rations hours earlier, and now the men were living on Baby Ruth candy bars and washing them down with water from their canteens.

"Hey, Lieutenant," Spatz called to Farrow, "did you guys see that big airplane place explode when DeShazer dropped his bombs? I had a bird's-eye view from back in my turret, and he dropped those bombs right down their chimney."

"Yeah, I know," Farrow agreed. "We saw it too."

The minutes passed, and soon both Spatz and DeShazer were snoring away.

Barr tapped Farrow on the shoulder. "Bill, I can't see a darned thing for that cloud cover down there, but according to my calculations we're about a hundred miles south of Shanghai."

"We sure don't want to wind up in Shanghai. Those Japanese soldiers would have us for breakfast."

"That's right. How's the fuel situation?"

"Fuel's no problem right now. We got maybe two hours left."

(The crew of the *Bat Out of Hell* had no way of knowing it, but at that very moment Capt. Edward York, flying plane #8, saw his fuel slipping away at an alarming rate and knew that he would never make it to China. Thus, hoping that the Russians would greet him as a friend, he flew straight across the Sea of Japan and into Siberia. But with the Germans now at the gates of Stalingrad, the Russians dared do nothing to endanger their neutrality pact with Japan. Certainly they would not allow American planes to bomb the Japanese and then take refuge at one of their airfields. Captain York finally spotted an airfield just north of Vladivostok and landed there. But the Russians did not welcome the Americans. Instead, they interned York and his crew, and they remained prisoners of the Russians for the next eighteen months, until they were finally able to escape and make their way to India via Iran.)

Another hour slipped away, and by that time only Farrow and Hite remained awake. Still, they could see nothing beneath them but huge dark clouds.

"Bill, whatta ya think about trying to drop below those clouds? We'll never see anything from this altitude."

"I know, Bob. But I don't want to fly into the side of a mountain either. And you know Doolittle warned us that the east coast of China is ringed with a high mountain range."

"Damned if we do, damned if we don't."

"Yep. In fact, I'm not sure what to do."

Hite pushed his cap back off his forehead. "Well, let's just give it a try briefly. Try to get under those clouds for just a minute, just long enough to see if we can spot any lights anywhere."

"We'll give it a try." At that Farrow pushed forward on the controls, and the plane began to descend. Finally, at five hundred feet, Farrow eased back on the controls. "See anything?"

Hite, whose eyes had been intensely searching the darkness for friendly lights, shook his head. "Not a darned thing. The Empire State Building could be dead ahead and I couldn't see it in this darkness."

"Well, we'll just stay at five hundred feet for a few more minutes and see if anything develops."

Another hour dragged by, and it was now almost midnight.

Farrow looked at Hite. "Whatta ya think?"

Hite shrugged. "I'm out of ideas, Bill. Just keep on flying."

"Hey, George," Farrow called, waking his navigator, "where in the dickens are we?"

Barr opened his eyes and shook his head. He checked his watch, then looked down at his map. "What's our speed?"

"About one-seventy."

A minute later Barr said, "According to my calculations we are now about two hundred miles to the west of Chuchow Air Field. In fact, we passed near Chuchow over an hour ago."

Farrow and Hite greeted this news with loud groans. "Okay, so Chuchow's out," Farrow said. "That really limits our options. All we can do now is continue flying west until our fuel runs out. At that point we'll just have to hit the silk. Any of you guys ever use a parachute before?"

His question was met with dismal silence. Bob Hite looked out his window. It was totally black outside. Even for experienced jumpers it would be a daunting exercise to bail out under the conditions they were now facing. Indeed, the thought of jumping out of the plane, from an altitude of five thousand feet, in the total darkness, with the wind howling and the rain coming down like bullets, was a discouraging prospect. But what other option did they have? If they jumped, they would at least have a chance of surviving. If they refused to jump, they would face sudden death when the plane crashed.

Finally, Bob Hite said, "Let's just hope that our fuel runs out when we're in territory occupied by the Chinese and not the Japanese."

"Oh, happy thought," Barr laughed. "From the frying pan into the fire."

For another hour Farrow and his crew flew westward, at an altitude of five thousand feet, their fuel almost depleted. Finally, at

*This map shows the sites where Doolittle's Raiders crashed in China following the bombing of Japan. Farrow and his crew (in plane #16) bailed out near Nanchang in Anhwei Province, an area occupied by the Japanese. Dean Hallmark and his crew (in plane #6) crash-landed in the surf off the coast in Chekiang Province, also occupied by the Japanese. (Photo courtesy of the U.S. Army Archives)*

about midnight through a break in the clouds they spotted the lights of a city in the distance.

"Hey, fellows, look!" Farrow said excitedly, pointing at the lighted city that lay dead ahead. "Lights! Maybe we're saved at the last minute after all."

Hite leaned forward, staring hard out the window. "By George, you're right, Bill. Now if we can just find a level spot to sit this baby down . . ."

Then came Barr's voice. "Sorry, fellows, but that's Nanchang." His chilling words came like the kiss of death to Farrow and Hite, for it was well known that Nanchang and the surrounding area was occupied by the Imperial Japanese Army.

In the weeks and months to come, Farrow would seriously regret his decision to fly westward when he could have flown south into Free China. But he made his decision based on the best information available at the time.

Minutes later, coming like a clap of doom, they heard the sound they most dreaded. Their engines began to sputter. Now, truly, it was decision time. Out of fuel, they could either bail out or take a chance on a crash landing. Considering the mountainous terrain, their decision was made for them. Farrow switched on the automatic pilot and yelled for everyone to wake up.

"Get ready, fellows, it's bail-out time. Line up there by the nose hatch."

"That's our only option?" DeShazer asked, shocked to learn that he would now have to use his parachute for the first time.

"It is," Farrow said. "Believe me, I don't want to do it either, but we have no choice at this point. It's either hit the silk or face sudden death. You can take your choice."

"And it's too late to resign," Spatz said.

"Forget the jokes, Harold, and line up there by the hatch. We're flying at five thousand feet, so you'll have plenty of time to pull your rip cord and see your chute open before you hit the ground."

"Bill," DeShazer called, "in case things don't work out for me, thanks for everything you've done. You're a great leader."

"Thanks, Jake, but don't worry, everything's gonna be fine."

"Oh, well, you win a few, lose a few," Bob Hite joked as he pulled open the hatch. Freezing wind suddenly filled the fuselage. "Okay, let's go, fellows, and God bless you." Bob Hite was the first in line, followed by DeShazer, Barr, and Spatz. Farrow gave Hite a tap on the back. "GO!" The four airmen slipped quickly, one after the other, from the plane into the inky blackness of night.

During the months to come, while sitting in their filthy prison cells, Farrow, Hite, and the others would pass the time by recounting their experiences between bailing out and being captured by the Japanese. Bill Farrow told the following story.

He remembered sitting in the escape hatch, his long legs dangling in the dark sky far above the earth. He glanced quickly at the gold Bulova his Aunt Margaret had given him for his twenty-first birthday. It might be important some day for him to know the exact time of their bailout. It was exactly 12:05, Saturday morning, April 19. It was a moment he knew he would never forget. If he lived to tell about it.

It was then that the blades of the twin propellers stopped turning, and the nose of the plane tilted alarmingly downward. Now Farrow could no longer postpone the inevitable. He looked down, eyeing with deep fear the black abyss that surrounded him. With his heart pounding, he took a deep breath, said a silent prayer, and slipped out of the hatch. Falling head over heels, he could feel himself hurtling toward the earth some five thousand feet below.

Recalling the instructions he had received in flight school, he searched desperately for the small metallic rip cord handle. Finally he found it and pulled. Then he counted to four and looked up, hoping to see that big silver canopy opened above him. But on such a dark moonless night he could see nothing, not even his hand in front of his face. So maybe that big canopy was spread out above him, maybe not. Should his chute not open, he reasoned, he obviously would not know it when he hit the ground. At least he would experience a painless death. At that moment the prospect of a painless death was about all he had to look forward to.

But as the seconds dragged by and he was still aware of the rain and soupy gray fog enveloping him, so thick that he could hardly breathe, he concluded that his chute had indeed opened. Then he wondered if his crewmen had made it, and if so where they were and if he could find them once he hit the ground.

Big raindrops were pelting his face and hands, and the wind was shrieking around him like a banshee.

Then another problem occurred to him—just what to do when his feet touched solid ground in Japanese-occupied China. That, unfortunately, was one question that no one had taken the time to explore. He had seen numerous photos of

*The lucky crews of four American aircraft who bailed out over China were rescued by Chinese guerillas and helped to safety in Chungking. Here they are being secreted in a mountain cave until they can make their getaway. The crews of two planes, the* Bat Out of Hell *and the* Green Hornet, *piloted by Bill Farrow and Dean Hallmark, were captured by the Japanese. They were not so lucky.* (Photo courtesy of the U.S. Army Archives)

those short, stocky Japanese soldiers armed with rifles and those long, wicked-looking bayonets, and he dreaded being taken alive by such fiendish savages.

As luck would have it, he finally plopped down in what felt like a soft muddy field of some sort, maybe a rice paddy out in the countryside. In the darkness, with the rain still coming down in sheets, it was really difficult to tell just where he was. But at least his landing had been an easy one, and he was at last standing on firm soil. In fact, it was the first time he had stood up since leaving the *Hornet* some sixteen hours earlier.

For long moments he stood motionless, breathing deeply, the blood pounding in his ears, listening for the least sound, expecting at any minute to be taken by a squad of Japanese soldiers. But the silence was broken only by the sound of falling rain and the croaking of a million frogs. His intuition told him that he was alone.

Mustering the energy to take action, he gathered up his collapsed parachute, wadded it into a big ball, and placed it aside. Then with his bare hands he dug a shallow hole in the muddy soil and buried the telltale white silk where the Japanese would not find it any time soon.

He was mildly amused to recall that this was a trick he had learned not in flight school but from watching a 1940 Errol Flynn movie about an OSS agent dropped behind enemy lines in occupied France. He hoped it would work in China as well.

It was then that he heard the unmistakable sound of a plane crash. It was the end of his beloved *Bat Out of Hell,* which had finally slammed into the side of a mountain several miles to the west. Thank God that George Barr had destroyed all the maps, charts, and other papers before bailing out.

Not knowing what to do at this point, but feeling that as an Air Corps officer he should do something, Farrow began sloshing slowly through the muddy field, making his way westward toward Chungking and safety. According to his best reckoning, Chungking was only some fifteen miles to the west. If only they could have stayed in the air another few minutes, they would be home free now. If only . . . If only . . .

In the total darkness he kept stumbling over knee-high mounds of soil, and soon he was as muddy as the field he landed in.

Except for several Baby Ruth candy bars, he had not eaten in almost two days. And now his stomach rumbled with hunger. And, too, the extraordinary events of the past sixteen hours and the unreality of his present situation left him feeling terribly disoriented. He wondered if he could be going into shock.

Very likely he was keenly aware that it was now early afternoon back in Darlington and Columbia, and he wondered what his family might be doing at that very moment. He wondered how Lib Sims might be spending her afternoon. He supposed she was probably preparing for her final exams and getting terribly excited about her pending graduation.

Perhaps they were even thinking of him just as he was thinking of them. Indeed, he would have given the world to be with them, instead of there, in that stinking field of mud. Despite himself, he thought of his Aunt Margaret's fried chicken and potato salad, and of Mrs. Sims's big thick steaks and french fries.

It was then that he heard a sound somewhere off to his right, and he knew that he was not alone. Quickly, he knelt behind a mound, then reached for the .45 automatic in his shoulder holster. He knew that his Browning .45 would do little good if he was surrounded by a Japanese patrol, but at least he could go down fighting. He wiped the water from his eyes and tried to peer through the darkness, but he could see nothing. Perhaps he was mistaken after all. Perhaps—but no, there it was again—the unmistakable sound of someone sloshing through the mud.

His heart racing now, his senses finely attuned to the least disturbance, he strained to pick up the sounds he had heard a moment earlier. Images of cruel Japanese soldiers armed with those long evil-looking bayonets flashed through his mind. He pulled back the hammer on his Browning.

Then from out of the darkness, not twenty feet away, came the sound of a familiar voice—"Hey, who's that? Is someone there?" That voice rang a bell. Farrow felt his lips spread in a big grin. It was the unmistakable voice of Jacob DeShazer.

(Note: DeShazer at the age of twenty-nine was the senior member of Farrow's crew. The author interviewed him on several occasions over the years, and his recollections of his interactions with Farrow have proven invaluable.)

This chance meeting struck Farrow as incredible. Despite their time lapse in bailing out in almost hurricane-force winds, then blowing around "all over hell and half of Georgia," they had landed within a stone's throw of one another there in that muddy field.

"Jake!" Farrow answered in a loud whisper. "It's me, Bill Farrow." A feeling of exhilaration swept over him at the sound of DeShazer's voice. "Just hold what you got, Jake. I'll be right there."

Farrow gave his smaller companion a big muddy embrace. Both men were mentally and physically exhausted at that point, and terrified that Japanese patrols might well be at hand. But still, to feel solid ground beneath their feet and to have friendly company gave them a feeling of well-being unjustified by their precarious situation. If they stuck together, maybe they would make it home after all.

"You okay, Jake?"

"Yeah, I'm fine, Bill. A little shaky maybe, and I could sure use some food. But everything considered, I'm fine. How about you?"

"Sure, I'm fine too, Jake. But what about the others? You haven't heard anything?"

"No more than you, Bill. But I guess they're in the same boat we're in—if their parachutes opened, that is."

With the rain streaming down their faces, both men shivered in the cold morning wind. Farrow stuck his Browning back into its holster, then both men sank down behind a low mound.

"Look, Jake, there's no sense in us stumbling around here in the dark. Let's try to get some sleep. When dawn comes and we can see, we'll try to decide what to do. Maybe we'll just start walking toward Chungking."

"What time is it now?"

Farrow looked at the luminous hands on his gold Bulova. "It's two o'clock, or right at it."

They sank to the muddy ground. DeShazer yawned. "So we've been on the road now for seventeen hours, blown Japan off the map, and flown halfway 'round the world. Not a bad day's work, eh, Lieutenant?"

Farrow totally agreed. "You said it, Jake. Everything considered, it's been a swell day."

DeShazer scratched his chin, then pulled his cap lower on his head to keep it from blowing away. "Say, you think maybe we should take turns staying awake? To watch for the Japanese?"

Farrow shook his head. "Naw, I don't think so. As dark and nasty as it is, it's not likely they could spot us even if they were standing right on top of us. And I know we couldn't see them. So let's just try to get some sleep. We'll worry about what to do when daylight comes."

The two flyers then stretched out in the soft mud, using the mound as a pillow. It was April 19, well into spring, and the wind though cold was not frigid, so they were in no danger of freezing to death. And at that point they sought blessings wherever they could find them.

Minutes later, however, they found to their disappointment that despite their exhaustion they could not sleep. Instead, they spent the remaining hours of darkness in whispered conversation, excitedly rehashing the events of the past twenty-four hours.

At one point Farrow lamented in a regretful voice his decision to fly on toward Chungking instead of heading south into safe territory. "Listen, Jake, I'm sorry I got you all into this mess. I should have listened when you all tried to get me to change course back there."

"Ah, don't worry about it, Lieutenant. Besides, you were almost right. If we could've stayed in the air another ten minutes we'd have been out of this province and over friendly territory again."

"Just ten minutes," lamented the philosophical Farrow. "That's a mighty short time if you're having fun. But in a life-or-death situation it's forever." He shook his head at the irony of it all. "Just another ten minutes and we'd be on our way home now instead of stuck here in this darned mess."

"Yep," DeShazer agreed. "Ten more minutes and we'd be in Chungking right now instead of lying here starving to death."

Once again it seemed that the dark hand of fate could almost be seen as it worked tirelessly to bring Bill Farrow's young life to its conclusion. Just ten more minutes and he would have been home free. Perhaps he might have lived to a ripe old age and been able to boast some day to his grandchildren about his exploits in Japan and China way back during World War II. But now, thanks to the path that Farrow had been directed along, nothing more rewarding than a Japanese prison and a brutal early death awaited him.

"You know," Farrow said wistfully, "back in March, just before we left Eglin, I told my fiancée that I'd be out of the country for maybe two months. You think we'll make it back by then, by the middle of May? I told her I'd be back in time for her graduation, and then we'd get married."

DeShazer silently calculated. "Well, that's almost a whole month from now. With any luck at all, I'd say that by the middle of May I'll be sitting right there in the front-row pew of that church watching you swear your life away. Say, what's that girl's name anyway?"

"Lib Sims, and she's really a swell girl, Jake. I'd sure be disappointed if you didn't make it to our wedding."

"She got any good-looking friends?"

"Dozens. And they won't leave you alone once they've seen you."

"Oh, sure," DeShazer laughed.

"You know, life's funny, Jake. If I hadn't joined the Air Corps I'd be up there myself walking across that stage on June first to receive my own diploma."

"Yeah, life's funny all right. You never know."

"It does make you wonder sometimes. A year ago my greatest concern in life was making it through calculus. And now, thanks to several moves on my part that probably weren't too smart, here I am sitting in this godforsaken muddy field in the middle of China somewhere. Just sitting here waiting for my head to be shot off by a bunch of stupid Japanese soldiers. Who'd believe it? What am I doing here? What are you doing here?"

"My father's a Christian minister, Bill, and I'm sure he's got the answers to questions like that. As for me, I don't know. I guess I'd just say it's a matter of what God ordained."

"You do see the hand of God at work here?"

"Maybe, but it's hard for me to believe that God would punish us this way. God is a good God, and what's happening here ain't real good."

DeShazer wiped the rain from his eyes with his muddy sleeve and pushed himself to a sitting position. "Gee, I wonder what happened to the other guys. They could've been captured for all we know, or even dead."

Farrow nodded forlornly. "Well, we'll find out eventually, if we live long enough. And I wonder what happened to all the other Raiders. Wonder if they found Chuchow. Or maybe they're in the same boat we're in."

"Who knows, Lieutenant? I'm just wondering what the heck we're gonna do. If I remember the map correctly, Anhwei Province is one big province. And it's swarming with the Imperial Japanese Army. So we've got a lot of walking ahead of us if we're ever gonna get out of here. And we're gonna need a lotta prayer and a lotta luck."

Farrow was thinking the same thing. But as the officer in charge, he felt he should show some confidence, pretend that he had a plan even if he didn't.

"Look, Jake, as soon as it gets daylight, we'll scout around and try to find some friendly Chinese. I've got five hundred dollars that Colonel Doolittle gave us for just such an emergency, bribe money you might say, and we'll pay the Chinese to lead us out of here. All the way to Chungking."

Farrow and DeShazer had no way of knowing it at the time, but there was one other crew in about the same predicament. At dusk the previous evening the *Green Hornet,* piloted by Lt. Dean Hallmark, had crashed a mile off the Chinese coast as Hallmark attempted a desperate landing in the surf. Two of his crewmen, Sgt. Don Fitzmaurice and Sgt. William Dieter, had died of injuries almost immediately. But Hallmark and the others—Lt. Chase Nielsen and Lt. Charles Meder—though painfully injured, managed to swim ashore. They too would soon be captured by the Japanese.

Following the war Capt. Chase Nielsen (he had been promoted during his internment) would write a series of articles for the Associated Press that were carried in newspapers across America. Nielsen's articles were so articulate and written in such a readable style that many critics suggested that he had missed his calling: he should have been an author instead of a navigator. Nielsen, by the way, as of this writing, is alive and as feisty as ever. The following account of his plane's crash on April 19, 1942, is based on his recollections immediately following the war.

It was just past 9 P.M. and the outside world was cloaked in darkness as the *Green Hornet* came in low over the waves off the coast of China. Pilot Dean Hallmark eased back on the throttle and put down his flaps. At that point there was such complete darkness that he could not see his hand in front of his face, but according to Nielsen's calculations, the coast lay only a mile or so ahead and

Hallmark wanted to set the *Green Hornet* down as gently as possible, hopefully right there on the beach.

Too late he realized that the huge waves raging below were much higher than he had anticipated. The result was disastrous, as his nose section slammed into a wall of black water and the *Green Hornet* plummeted into the sea.

From his position just behind the pilot's seat, Chase Nielsen heard an agonized scream from Sgt. William Dieter, the bombardier stationed in the nose cone. Suddenly Nielsen was surrounded by black water pouring in from everywhere. Apparently he had hit his head against the rear of the pilot's seat, for at that moment he briefly lost consciousness. Then he came to and was surprised to find himself standing in water up to his waist, blood streaming from gashes to his head and arms. He raised his hand and touched his nose. It was broken and beginning to ache terribly.

Then Nielsen became aware that both Hallmark and his copilot, Lt. Bob Meder, were nowhere to be seen. Both had apparently been catapulted through the windshield. Gone too was Bill Dieter from his place in the nose cone.

The plane was quickly filling with water, so Nielsen climbed up through a hole in the top of the plane where the turret had been. Then he inflated his Mae West, his life preserver, and climbed to the top of the slowly sinking plane. He was delighted to find that Bob Meder was already there, though hanging on for dear life. Moments later both men were joined by Dean Hallmark, who had bad cuts on both knees. Then came Bill Dieter swimming up out of the darkness. A moment later the crew was joined by the engineer, Sgt. Don Fitzmaurice, who had somehow managed to climb out of the rear turret despite his severe head wound. Nielsen gave him a hand and pulled him atop the slowly sinking plane.

Now Nielsen appraised their dangerous situation. The plane's left wing had been torn away and was nowhere to be seen. Waves fifteen feet high towered above them and hit them with terrific force. The night was still totally black, and the plane was beginning to sink more rapidly.

All the men were injured, but Bill Dieter and Don Fitzmaurice were in particularly bad shape. Fitzmaurice had a deep hole in his forehead where he had been struck by some protrusion in the rear compartment and now he was bleeding profusely. As for Dieter, he was babbling incoherently. Nielsen suspected he had been crushed on impact when the nose cone slammed into the ocean. How they had made it out of the plane was a mystery.

Hallmark and Bob Meder, after several agonizing minutes, somehow managed to open the compartment atop the fuselage and lift out the life raft. Deliverance was at hand. But then, just as Meder pulled the lanyard on the $CO_2$ cylinder that would inflate the raft, the cord broke off flush with the cartridge. Now they must use the hand pump. Nielsen felt his heart sink. Only that hand pump stood between the airmen and a watery death. He immediately jumped to the side of Hallmark and Meder and began frantically rummaging around inside the raft compartment for that golden hand pump, but in the darkness and under the circumstances it was impossible to find. As though things were not already bad enough, a huge wave chose that moment to sweep Bill Dieter off the fuselage. Dean Hallmark noted his situation and make a desperate dive for him. But he was too late. Dieter was gone.

Then came another huge wave and suddenly the *Green Hornet*, their last connection with the United States and home, slipped quietly beneath the waves. Now all were in the water, each man totally alone in the darkness, each swallowing sea water, each gasping for air. Nielsen was keenly aware that his chances of survival were growing increasingly slim.

Don Fitzmaurice, now unconscious, washed against Bob Meder, who made a grab for him. But Meder could not hold on. He could only watch helplessly as Fitzmaurice floated away.

At that point the men, in hopes of locating one another in the darkness, began to shout at the top of their lungs. But within a few minutes the voices of both Hallmark and Meder were out of range and Nielsen was aware that he was all alone.

They had been in the air for a little more than twelve hours when the crash occurred and Nielsen was exhausted—and extremely hungry. Still, as ever, Chase Nielsen was determined to survive. He knew that the beach would have to be to the west, to his left. And so he began to propel himself in that direction. For what seemed like hours he would alternately swim then float for a while. Thoughts sped through his mind. He thought about his family back in Utah and wondered what they were doing. He wondered about the crews of the other fifteen planes and where they might be at this moment. He wondered if Jimmy Doolittle had survived his first combat mission. And where could Hallmark and Meder be? As for Fitzmaurice and Dieter, they were so badly injured and unable to care for themselves, their chances of survival were extremely slim.

Then Nielsen began to worry about his navigation and he wondered if it had been accurate. Were they only a mile off the coast of China? Or maybe a hundred? He prayed that he had been right, but there was that lingering doubt. A huge wave broke over his head and shoulders and he found himself coughing and struggling to breathe.

By that time Nielsen's broken nose was burning terribly from the saltwater, and his strength was quickly ebbing away. Still, he couldn't give up. To give up was to die, and he wasn't ready for that. A dedicated Mormon, Nielsen began to pray. He prayed as he had never prayed before in his life. The hours passed; then, after floating aimlessly in the dark, he heard the unmistakable sound of waves breaking against the rocky shore. His feet touched bottom, and he somehow managed to crawl up onto solid ground.

Fearing discovery by the Japanese, he found a place to hide in a wooded area about a hundred yards up from the beach. Gasping for breath, he lay down in the tall weeds. Then he quickly fell into an exhausted sleep. Hours later he awakened to find the sun up and the skies clear.

He raised himself and looked down at the beach. Just below him some thirty Chinese fishermen were readying their boats for the day. Several hundred yards down the beach he noticed more Chinese congregated around what appeared to be the bodies of two men.

Nielsen quickly crawled to a better vantage point. Were these the bodies of his fellow airmen? Just as he raised up to get a better look, he was suddenly startled to find he had been discovered. Standing just above him in the tall weeds was a man wearing a shabby uniform. Nielsen could tell from the six-pointed star on his

A Japanese newspaper, the Japan Times and Advertiser, *written for English-speaking citizens of Japan, announced the bombing of Tokyo and other Japanese cities on April 19, 1942. In fact, no American planes were brought down, though the crews of two did fall into Japanese hands.* (Photo courtesy of the U.S. Air Force Archives)

cap that he was a Chinese guerilla fighter. He was holding a big rifle pointed straight at Nielsen's head. "You stand," he was told.

Nielsen obeyed the command and raised his hands. He could see now that the bodies down the beach were indeed those of Fitzmaurice and Dieter. The guerilla fighter said, "They dead.

Bury them after hour. You go with me. We fight Japs. You no worry now. We go see my chief. Talk all about you then. Go fast, follow me."

Nielsen writes that he was puzzled by the strange relationship between the Chinese and Japanese military forces. Both were well established in the area, but they apparently took a hands-off attitude toward one another—sort of "you don't bother us, and we won't bother you."

He was led to a small garrison manned by about a dozen Chinese guerillas. There the commander of this force, a Captain Ling, a young, well-dressed officer, informed him that his friends' bodies had been removed from the beach area, and that the Chinese were busy making coffins to hold their bodies.

At that point a guerilla entered the room and informed Ling that another American flyer had been found and was being hidden until he could be brought to the garrison. Ling promised Nielsen that his men would begin searching for the fifth member of his crew immediately.

That afternoon, after being fed a meal of rice and odious fish, Nielsen was led to a small nearby village. There, he entered a dark cottage occupied by an ancient Chinese man. He was about to speak when a sudden noise to his rear caught his attention. Alarmed, he whirled around, and there stood the imposing figure of his pilot, Dean "Jungle Jim" Hallmark. Fearing that their new visitors might be Japanese, Hallmark was standing behind the door holding a big club over his head.

Following a joyous reunion, Nielsen and Hallmark were led back to the garrison where they were delighted to meet the other member of their crew, Bob Meder. He had been found, and had been awaiting their arrival. Meder told them that he had helped both Dieter and Fitzmaurice to shore, but both had died soon afterward. It was he who had pulled their bodies high up on the beach away from the raging surf.

That afternoon the three survivors were led to the bodies of Dieter and Fitzmaurice. Their bodies were placed in crude wooden coffins and buried while their comrades stood silently praying nearby.

The next morning Captain Ling placed the three Americans

aboard a big sampan crowded with Chinese soldiers and civilians. They sailed upstream in a muddy river throughout the day. Then with the arrival of darkness Ling ordered the boat to anchor near a small village. Here the airmen spent a dreamless night in a small thatched hut. The next day they again boarded the sampan and sailed for several hours until they reached the walled city of Wenchow. Here they spent another night. But with morning Captain Ling informed them that the Japanese were searching everywhere for the Americans who had bombed Japan three days earlier, and that he could take them no farther. Ling then left them in the care of an elderly man named Wong who spoke perfect English.

Sage Wong illustrated in some detail the hardships the Japanese had imposed and the sadistic way they treated the Chinese people. He described how the Japanese soldiers loved to drag a young girl from her home, gang rape her, then slit her stomach open with a Samurai sword and how Japanese soldiers would behead hundreds of Chinese boys and men with their heavy swords. All this was done, said Wong, with no restraint from the Japanese officers—because they were no better than the Japanese soldiers.

Curious, Nielsen asked him why many of the Chinese guerrillas avoided fighting the Japanese and was surprised when Wong answered that many of their guerrillas were no better than the soldiers. Both preyed on the Chinese people, taking what little they had then murdering them. Everything considered, said Wong, life really was not worth living any more and he hoped that his Buddha master would soon send for him.

After only a few minutes of conversation, a young Chinese boy rushed into the room and began to speak very rapidly to Wong. His eyes were large and he was gasping for breath. Looking at him, Nielsen became fearful. It was then that the interpreter reached for his rifle. His eyes had all but closed, and as he stepped toward the doorway, he was met by two of his comrades. They spoke quickly, then Wong explained to the American that Japanese soldiers had entered the gates and were searching that area of the city. They must try and hide from them the best they could.

Despite Wong's efforts to spirit the Raiders out of the city, all their avenues of escape were cut off by Japanese soldiers carrying submachine guns. Thus Wong took them to a small warehouse and told them to go inside and hide as best they could. Hallmark dove into a corner, and his two comrades covered him with several ragged blankets. Then they themselves climbed rough columns to the ceiling where they hid in the rafters. Mr. Wong, meanwhile, as though he had not a care in the world, sat down on the bare cement floor and attempted to light a charcoal fire in a small metal container.

At that point, their old friend, Captain Ling, entered the room accompanied by a Japanese officer and two soldiers. Captain Ling spoke harshly to Mr. Wong. But Mr. Wong simply shrugged his shoulders. Ling then gave him a sharp slap across the face. Wong still did not reply. At an order from the Japanese captain, a soldier began kicking at the blankets in the corner where Dean Hallmark was hidden. Three kicks and there lay Hallmark for all to see.

The Japanese captain, speaking very good English, said, "You, you in the corner, stand up and walk out only two steps. If you don't, I'll have you shot immediately."

Hallmark had no choice but to comply.

The Japanese captain then asked him, "Where are the other two men?"

Hallmark, a man famous for his courage and cool approach to danger, gave him a blank look and asked, "What other two men?"

The Japanese captain then drew his pistol. He began yelling at Mr. Wong and beating the old man about the head. But still Mr. Wong made no reply.

It was then that a Japanese soldier looked straight up at Nielsen hiding atop a rafter. He shouted something to his captain in Japanese.

The captain looked up, grinned, and ordered the other two Americans to climb down. Sick with apprehension, Meder and Nielsen obeyed the order. The three Americans were handcuffed, tied with rope, and marched to a Japanese garrison only a mile outside the city. There they were locked in a barred cell. They knew the war was over for them.

Nielsen heard the big door clang closed behind them and was overwhelmed with a feeling of complete depression. For the first time in his life, he was at the mercy of a cruel enemy. Based on the stories he'd heard of the Imperial Japanese Army, he had a sick feeling that his future might be much shorter than he'd planned.

But of course none of this was known to Bill Farrow and Jake DeShazer as they wrestled with their own problems on the morning following their famous raid on Tokyo.

As dawn finally lit the eastern sky Farrow gently nudged DeShazer who had dropped into a troubled sleep. In later years DeShazer would remember that the rain had stopped, and now both men sat up and tried to peer through the ghostly white mist that shrouded everything as far as they could see. Somewhere off to their front they could hear roosters crowing.

They looked at their immediate surroundings and were not amused to find that what they had taken for a rice paddy was in fact a Chinese cemetery. They had spent the past six hours reclining on a fresh Chinese grave.

Farrow's limbs had grown stiff during the cold damp night. He stood, stretching his long legs, and rubbed the sleep from his eyes. Then he gazed about him. He was surprised to see through the early morning fog what appeared to be a dozen small huts. Gray, shabby structures, they stood less than a hundred yards away in a clearing at the edge of the cemetery. He could see no signs of life anywhere.

"Hey, Jake, stand up. See what I see?"

DeShazer rubbed his eyes, then stood and gazed in the direction Farrow was pointing. "Yeah, houses. What do you think, Lieutenant?"

Farrow patted the .45 Browning in his holster. "We gotta start somewhere, Jake. Let's scout 'em out."

"Yeah, that's what I was thinking."

Bending low, moving quickly from one mound to the next, ready to make a run for it should any Japanese patrols suddenly materialize, the two men warily made their way toward the little village. Then, just as they reached the edge of the cemetery, two men and several small boys emerged from the nearest hut.

Suddenly they stopped in their tracks, mouths agape, and stared in amazement at the six-foot four-inch creature crouching just a few yards to their front. Never had they seen such a tall man, a veritable giant

Farrow flashed them a disarming smile and waved in greeting. DeShazer held up a pack of Chesterfield cigarettes.

"American, American," Farrow called excitedly, hoping the name would elicit a positive response from the Chinese who had suffered so terribly at the hands of the Japanese.

Other villagers began to emerge from their huts at that point. Then, from around the side of a hut came an aged man with white hair and a deeply lined face. He looked to be in his seventies at least. He was tall for a Chinese man, with strong Asian features. The other villagers bowed and made way for him as he took tentative steps toward the American flyers. Obviously he was the village headman.

Farrow and DeShazer smiled and bowed, then Farrow reached out and grasped the astounded headman's hand in a firm grip. He began pumping it up and down, repeating, "American, American."

"Melican, Melican," the headman repeated in a puzzled tone.

Farrow then held out his right hand, thumb extended, and began flying it from side to side, making the sound of a motor with his mouth: "Whoom, whoom." A grinning DeShazer stood by, nodding encouragement.

"Airplane," Farrow said.

"Melican," the old headman replied.

"AIRPLANE," DeShazer corrected him. "WHOOM, WHOOM!"

At last the headman apparently got the idea. With a big grin he held out his right hand and began imitating Farrow's motions. By now all the villagers were grinning and flying their hands around.

"You got it," Farrow laughed. He then took out his wallet and withdrew two one-hundred dollar bills, bribe money for just such a contingency.

"Chungking," he said, pointing west. "Chungking. Melican, Melican."

The headman took the money and nodded his understanding.

Then he motioned for the two flyers to follow him. Farrow grinned and gave DeShazer a pat on the back. Things were beginning to look up already. They still had a long way to go before reaching Chungking and safety, but they were a heck of a lot better off now than they had been since running out of gas early that morning. Now they just had to take things a step at a time. They had no other choice.

The crowd of villagers, approximately fifty in number, now chattering excitedly, parted as Farrow and DeShazer followed the headman across a small courtyard to a two-room hut. They then entered the dark interior where they found two women and a small child sitting on stools eating a breakfast of rice and fish. One of the women was elderly and toothless, while the other was fairly young and apparently the wife of the headman. There followed a flurry of conversation in Chinese, and the two women rose and without expression dipped two small bowls of rice and fish from a blackened pot hung above an open fire. The headman motioned for the two airmen to be seated on the stools just vacated by the women. But the two airmen shook their heads and insisted on squatting on the hard earthen floor.

The small child, his mouth agape, could not take his eyes off the two giant Americans.

The two men ate voraciously, though the rice was somewhat tough and chewy, and the fish hardly cooked at all. Still, it was the first real food they had had since the evening of April 17, and now it was the morning of the nineteenth, and they were ravenously hungry. Besides, they didn't want to offend their host.

Once they had finished their repast, Farrow again waved his money in the headman's face. "Chungking, Chungking," he repeated. The headman, who still had not changed expression, then motioned for Farrow and DeShazer to enter the small room that was connected to the kitchen.

"Chungking," he said reassuringly. Then he closed the door of the small room and placed a solid beam across it. For better or for worse, the two Americans were now firmly locked in.

There was a small window in the room across which boards had been nailed to keep out the chill winds of winter. There were cracks between the boards just big enough to allow the airmen to peek outside. They looked at each other and shrugged. Their fate was now in the hands of the headman, and there was nothing they could do about it.

The fetid odor of human waste from the village's big open toilet assaulted their nostrils as they sat quietly on the earthen floor, waiting, hoping against hope that Chinese guerillas would soon arrive and lead them out of their latest dilemma. Still, their intuition told them that things were not going well.

"You're a religious man, Jake," Farrow said. "Do you believe in the power of prayer?"

"I do. My father's a Christian minister back in Oregon, and so I was raised in a Christian home. In fact, my ambition once this is all over is to become a minister myself. But in answer to your question, I firmly believe in the power of prayer. I've seen it work a thousand times."

"That's wonderful, Jake, and I've seen it work too. Maybe it wouldn't hurt if we started a little prayer service right now."

"Well, yeah, I agree." Suddenly DeShazer frowned and shook his head. "Do you remember Easter morning? You awakened me for religious services aboard the *Hornet,* but I lay back down and slept through the services?"

"Sure, I remember."

"Well, that's really bothered me ever since. And I can't help but wonder if it's my fault we're in this mess—because I was so disrespectful of Jesus on Easter Sunday."

Farrow gave DeShazer a reassuring pat on the back. "Hey, Jake, don't take it that way. Look, we had been up half the night training for this operation, and I almost slept through services myself. Now take my word for it, Jesus knows you didn't mean to sleep through services or show any disrespect in any way. No, Jake, Jesus is not punishing us for any sins right now. Jesus loves us. He loves everybody."

"Then what is it?"

"Why we're here?" Farrow hung his head. "Because of my own stupid decision to fly on westward when I should have listened to you guys and flown south, out of Japanese-occupied territory. I'm the reason we're here, Jake."

A sudden commotion outside the hut roused Farrow from his

reverie. He jumped to his feet and peered through the cracks in the boards covering the window. First, he saw a dozen or so emaciated dogs trotting up the path that led into the woods. They were whining peevishly, their tails tucked between their legs. Behind them hurried the villagers, their faces expressing no emotion. And then came what Farrow feared most, the sounds of marching feet followed by a company of Japanese soldiers, hardened veterans of the Manchurian campaigns. They were led by a Japanese officer, armed with a handgun and the ubiquitous Samurai sword.

At that point the headman came forward and bowed low to the Japanese officer. The officer shouted something to him in Chinese. The headman shrugged and shook his head. He no doubt knew from harsh experience that the Japanese would be merciless if they learned that the villagers were harboring enemy soldiers.

"How'd they find us so fast?" DeShazer asked, the hope gone out of his voice.

"I guess they investigated when our plane crashed. They didn't find any bodies among the wreckage, so they probably assumed that we had bailed out. So they sent patrols out all over the province to find us. Obviously they've succeeded."

The officer gave the headman a sharp slap across the face and began shouting at him. Again, the terrified headman shook his head. At that, the officer yelled orders to two of his soldiers. They saluted, then ran to one of the villagers who was carrying a large blanket. This they tore from the villager's grasp and returned with it to the officer.

The officer shouted more orders, and the two soldiers knocked the headman to the ground. Then they rolled him up in the big blanket. Another soldier ran forward at that point with a small can of gasoline, which he used to soak the blanket.

Farrow, seeing what the officer had in mind, began to knock violently at the window with his fists. "Come on, Jake, we can't let those poor people die on our account. Try to get their attention."

But with all the commotion in the yard, no one heard their frantic knocks.

The grinning Japanese officer took a match from his pocket

and lit a small stick. This he handed to the headman's terrified young wife. He shouted for her to ignite the blanket, but she began to weep hysterically, shaking her head no.

The officer, laughing heartily now at the wife's dilemma, knelt down by her small son and gleefully grabbed him by the throat. Slowly he began to squeeze. The child began to struggle for breath. The poor woman, in agony at having to make a choice between her husband and her son, closed her eyes and tossed down the burning stick.

Farrow and DeShazer watched in horror as the blanket—and the headman—burst into flames. The officer and his contingent of soldiers began to cheer as the headman's screams of pain reverberated throughout the village.

Minutes later, once the flames had died down and the head-man lay dying, two Japanese soldiers finished him off by smash-ing in his skull with the butts of their rifles.

Farrow and DeShazer wanted to turn their gaze away from the hellish scene going on before them, but they stood as though transfixed. This was their introduction to the Imperial Japanese Army, and it would prove a memorable one.

The headman's young wife was now lying on the ground. She was sobbing uncontrollably and clutching her son to her bosom. The other villagers, witnesses to what had just transpired, remained silent. They knew their time would soon come.

The Japanese officer began issuing orders in a quick excited voice and motioning toward the hut. Japanese soldiers then ran inside followed by the officer. Moments later Farrow heard the heavy beam being moved away from the door. He and DeShazer backed into a corner, their hands raised high. His Browning was useless now. They had no hope but to surrender.

The door burst open, and six burly Japanese soldiers rushed into the room, surrounding the American flyers. Grinning wickedly, the soldiers began to prick the airmen with the points of their long bayonets, drawing blood on several occasions. Then the stocky Japanese officer roughly shoved aside one of his sol-diers and pointed his pistol at the two airmen.

He stood silent for a moment, eyeing the six-foot four-inch Farrow from head to toe as one might examine an oddity never seen before. Then he shouted a question in Japanese.

Farrow replied, "My name is Bill Farrow. I'm an American air-man."

"Yeah, me too," DeShazer said.

"Melican," the Japanese officer repeated knowingly. He turned his head to look back at his soldiers. "Melican," he said, and they all nodded. It was just what they had all expected.

Then stepping aside, the officer barked an order, and two soldiers rushed forward and began frisking the two flyers. They confiscated their knives and handguns. With each discovery the excited soldiers would emit a delighted "aaaahhh!"

The airmen were then rudely shoved from the room back into the headman's yard. Now they could see that the villagers had already been divided into two groups—some twenty men and boys in one group, and a similar number of women and girls in the other. All had their hands upraised.

They had violated the rules by trying to help these American airmen escape, and now they likely knew from harsh experience what their terrible fate would be. The men and boys would be slaughtered immediately, while the women and girls would furnish the grinning soldiers with sexual gratification before they were murdered. The men remained amazingly stoic as they awaited their fate, giving no sign of the fear and revulsion they must have felt. But the females, now on their knees weeping and pleading, sought mercy.

But they would receive no mercy. Already their Japanese captors were greedily eyeing the younger girls. The freedom to rape would be their reward for tracking down these American criminals.

Farrow and DeShazer were handcuffed and shoved into the back of a covered truck parked some twenty yards from the scene of horror now in progress. They eyed the opening in the cover, but escape at this point was totally impossible. Farrow looked at DeShazer and shook his head. Outside, they could hear the moaning and wailing of the women and girls.

"My God, Jake, I didn't know such evil existed in the world."

"Me neither, Bill. Wonder what makes 'em this way?"

"Power, Jake. They have the power to do it, and they know they won't be punished for it. I saw a very similar thing at my fraternity back at the university when some members would mistreat pledges. It was against the rules, but those members had the power and freedom to do it, and they took advantage of it. It gave them a tremendous sense of power to mistreat those guys and know they would get away with it. The other members were scared to interfere because they were afraid they would be accused of being killjoys."

"You run into bastards wherever you go."

"Yep. And people who're afraid of stopping 'em from being bastards. They're almost as bad. But what we're seeing here, Jake, is evil on a grand scale."

They then heard the Japanese officer shout a command, and gunfire immediately erupted. The screams of the females intensified. Moments later, after a brief period of silence, there came the sounds of individual gunshots as the soldiers walked around happily delivering the *coup de grâce* to the wounded. There must be no survivors.

Then came more commands from the officer. His words now sounded cheerful and jocular. The two airmen knew what was coming.

"I think we'd better cover our ears, Jake."

The screams of the women and girls again intensified, and the airmen could visualize what was going on outside. They knew they would not forget.

"May they roast in hell," DeShazer said.

Farrow agreed. "But you know, Jake, there is still an out for them. They can become Christian and ask God for forgiveness. But that will be their only salvation."

"I hope they do. In fact, I might come back here some day and help 'em do it."

Some ten minutes elapsed, and the loud screams subsided to low murmuring moans. Apparently the soldiers had satisfied their lust.

Then came another harsh command from the Japanese officer, and more gunfire erupted. Now the females were being slaughtered.

"What a heck of a way to start the day," DeShazer said. "The folks back home would never believe this."

"We've got to hang in there, Jake. We'll just take it a day at a time, a minute at a time. But in the end, we will survive. Keep telling yourself that. And trust in God."

At that point twenty soldiers piled into the rear of the truck, pushing the two airmen tightly against the cab. The Japanese officer rode up front with the driver.

Where they were to be taken, what their fate would be, the airmen did not know. Perhaps it was just as well.

# CHAPTER 7

# A Prisoner of the Kempei Tai

After a seemingly endless trip over a bumpy, deeply rutted dirt road, the Japanese soldiers and their prisoners finally arrived at their destination, a small town some ten miles to the west of the village where Farrow and DeShazer had been captured. The trip had lasted for more than an hour, and during that time their Japanese guards had totally ignored them. Instead, they had laughed and joked and rubbed their loins suggestively as they recounted to one another their cruel experiences with the females of the village. And all were excitedly speaking at the same time.

It reminded Farrow of his experiences riding home on the school bus after a big win in basketball for St. John's High School back in Darlington. All the guys had been excited, and all were speaking at the same time. No one was listening to anyone else. It had been just a Babel of excited teenage voices. I did this, and I did that, and I did this, and then I did so and so. By the time they reached home, no one had the least idea what anyone else had done. But no one cared.

By now the very spiritual Bill Farrow didn't care whether these Japanese bastards ever accepted Jesus as their Lord and Savior or not. They certainly deserved whatever they got for their terrible sins.

They drove through muddy congested streets, filled with people and animals, until they approached what was obviously a jail of some sort with barred doors and windows. By now the noon hour was approaching, and a bright warm sun beamed down from directly overhead. A medley of street odors made Farrow and

165

DeShazer nauseous. Then the truck halted, and the two Americans were roughly yanked to the ground and led inside.

They were then shoved into a small bare cell with whitewashed cement walls. There was not even a stool in the cell, and so they sat down on the cold cement floor. Their guard clanged shut the heavy metal door, a heartrending sound to two men who had known nothing but freedom all their lives. What horrors lay ahead they could only imagine.

Farrow noted the time. It was 12:10 P.M., exactly twenty-seven hours since they had departed the *Hornet* the previous morning—already a lifetime ago.

Totally exhausted, the two Americans leaned their heads against a wall.

"Wonder what happened to the other guys," DeShazer said.

Farrow rubbed his chin thoughtfully. "I don't know, but I sure hope they're better off than we are."

"Yeah, me too."

(Farrow and DeShazer were unaware of it at the time, but George Barr, Bob Hite, and Harold Spatz had also been rounded up and were now on their way to a Japanese military prison in Nanchang where Farrow and DeShazer would soon be taken.)

"By the way, Jake, I don't know what these fellows have up their sleeve for us. But whatever you do, don't tell them anything about Colonel Doolittle or the *Hornet,* or about bombing Japan. We could be endangering the lives of a lot of other airmen walking around out there if we tell 'em who we are, where we came from, or what we did."

DeShazer nodded agreeably. "That's true, Bill, but I've kept up with this war pretty closely, and these Japanese are pretty smart cookies—smarter'n anyone gives 'em credit for. In fact, I'll bet they already know more about all that bombing and stuff than we do."

"You're probably right, but let's not take any chances. Besides, we're American airmen, and according to the Geneva Convention we're required to give them our name, rank, and serial number, and that's all."

"Yeah, that's true. But I don't think these bastards can read. They've probably never heard of the Geneva Convention."

"Yeah, the same thing occurs to me."

*Jacob DeShazer became a proud member of the Army Air Corps in 1939. He underwent terrible tortures at the hands of his Japanese captors, but instead of hating the Japanese he felt sorry for them. Following the war he returned to Japan as a Methodist missionary and converted thousands of his former enemies to Christianity. As of this writing, Jake is ninety-three years old, the oldest of all the surviving Raiders. May he live forever!* (Photo courtesy of Jacob DeShazer)

"Nobody thought about the Geneva Convention when they were murdering two hundred thousand Chinese civilians in Nanking. You read about that?"

"Yep."

An hour later the two airmen stiffened as the heavy iron door swung slowly open. But it was only a lowly private bringing them a plate of strange food, consisting of two hunks of meat, a helping of rice, and two slices of bread. He silently placed it down on the floor before them. Then he bowed low and backed out of the cell. Farrow and DeShazer looked at each other and shrugged.

"See, I told you these Japanese are really very nice people," DeShazer joked.

They then devoured the food, though they hadn't the least idea what it was—and were afraid to ask.

Following their repast, they sat silently, each pondering the strange series of events that had led them from the security of home and family to this godforsaken hole in the ground.

At this point the introspective Farrow must have wondered why God, the good merciful God that he had worshipped since infancy, would allow him to work and struggle for so long, to overcome so many hardships, and to accomplish so much, only to have it all end this way. It just didn't make sense. It seemed that he was being punished for his good work instead of being rewarded. Had he offended God in some way?

But then his life was really a long way from over. Maybe God had something in mind for him that he was simply unaware of at this point. Maybe this suffering would make him a better, stronger, and more compassionate man. Only time would tell.

Still, if only he hadn't resigned from the university. If only . . . if only . . . He knew he could drive himself mad by replaying the past, by playing *what if*. He and DeShazer removed their flight jackets, folded them up, and made pillows for themselves. Then they fell into an exhausted sleep, the screams of those poor Chinese women still ringing in their ears.

Later that afternoon, Farrow could not tell how much later, he and DeShazer were startled awake when the big door swung slowly open on its iron hinges. Two Japanese soldiers armed with rifles with long bayonets quickly entered the cell. They were immediately followed by two Japanese officers. One was tall and slim with a severely pockmarked face, the other short and stocky wearing big thick glasses. Both bore grim expressions. Both spoke broken English.

The airmen started to rise to a standing position, but the short officer motioned for them to remain seated.

"Don't be stupid," he said. "Tell us who you be and where you coming from."

Farrow shot DeShazer a meaningful glance, then gave the two officers his name, rank, and serial number.

"You are being stupid," the short officer hissed. "You think you protected by Geneva Convention. But Geneva Convention not here to coddle you now. You up against real men here. We ask no surrender, we take no surrender."

"Besides," the tall officer added, "no one even know you here. We kill you, and no one even know you been here. Your poor family wonder forever what happened to you."

"No one even know you been here," the short officer repeated.

Such a terrible fate had already occurred to Farrow. He found it most unsettling to know that he could die, and his family would never know what had happened to him or where they might find his body. To die anonymously was a cruel way to die.

Again, Farrow repeated his name, rank, and serial number.

The tall officer gave him a quick kick in the ribs with the sharp toe of his boot. Then he shouted, "You officer. You answer questions now."

Farrow grabbed his side and doubled over in pain.

"Hey, look," DeShazer said, hoping to defuse the situation, "we're just American soldiers. Nothing else. There's nothing special about us. We got lost, and here we are. You're just wasting your time."

"Just soldiers, eh?" the short officer said. He bent over and fingered the emblem on Farrow's collar. "Look, see? That is Air Corps pin. And you wear flying jackets. And you only soldiers? Ha! You lie!"

"We think you very special," the tall officer said. "You answer questions now, or you be beheaded now. Then your bodies be thrown into deep holes in ground, and no one ever know where you are."

The short officer adjusted his thick glasses, then drew his

Samurai sword and began waving it around menacingly.

"Where you come from?"

Farrow took a deep painful breath. "We can only give you our name, rank, and serial number." He then pointed to the insignia on the officer's collar. "You're an officer. You know that."

For some reason, a reason that would somehow register with the Asian mind, Farrow's mentioning the word "officer" seemed to establish a strange link, a bond of sorts, between the two men.

The short officer paused and replaced his sword in its scabbard. He seemed to be reflecting on Farrow's words. "Very well, Lieutenant, but I regret you cannot be more cooperation."

As the two officers turned to exit the cell, one of them uttered a statement these American airmen would hear many times over the coming months—"Americans' heart not right."

"Quick thinking, Lieutenant," DeShazer said, wiping the perspiration from his forehead. "That could have become a very ugly deal for both of us."

Farrow nodded and massaged his bruised ribs.

For hours the two men sat pondering their fate and wondering what might happen to them next. That night, having heard nothing further from their captors, they closed their eyes and dropped into a troubled sleep.

The next morning, April 20, they were again startled by the appearance of two burly guards who came storming into their cell. They were handcuffed and blindfolded, then led outside where they were shoved into the rear of a truck. Twenty minutes later they arrived at a small airfield where they boarded a transport plane and were flown to a military prison in Nanchang, the city of lights they had seen from the air the previous night just before bailing out. Though blindfolded, Farrow could sense that this was not some small village jail but a real military prison. Once inside, he and DeShazer walked down several long hallways and past dozens of cells before they were halted. Their guard then removed their handcuffs and blindfolds and pushed them into a bare cell, containing only two wooden benches and a large bucket for body wastes.

(That same day Chinese guerillas, with intentions of rescuing the American flyers, stormed the small jail where Farrow and

DeShazer had initially been taken. But they were hours too late. Had they arrived sooner, Bill Farrow might be alive today.)

Farrow and DeShazer rubbed their eyes as they entered the dark cell. Then they were startled and delighted to see the other three members of their crew. The five of them were thrown together into one cell where they had quite a reunion, with warm embraces and pats on the back. They all seem to have experienced the same emotional reaction—sadness on the one hand that their fellow Raiders had not made it back to safety, but joy on the other that their comrades were at least still alive.

They began taking turns rattling off their experiences since coming down in China. Corporal Harold Spatz, at twenty the youngest member of the crew, had been immediately captured

*A native of Lebo, Kansas, and the youngest of all the Raiders, Harold Spatz had just turned twenty when captured by the Japanese. This photo was taken by his captors following one of their infamous question and answer sessions. His face appears swollen and both his eyes blackened from the beatings he received. Still, he would tell the Japanese nothing. Despite his youth, he was executed along with Bill Farrow and Dean Hallmark. Today, along with each of them, he is remembered as a great American hero.* (Photo courtesy of the U.S. Air Force Archives)

when his parachute had brought him down in the center of the village where Farrow and DeShazer had been jailed. He said it was like the whole Japanese Army was standing there just waiting for him. He had been slapped around a little, but had gotten nothing he couldn't handle. He had been questioned and then brought to this jail in Nanchang.

As for Bob Hite, Farrow's copilot, he had been picked up by a squad of Japanese soldiers the previous afternoon. He later recalled that these soldiers, for reasons known only to themselves, had tried to make him believe that he had been rescued by a squad of Chinese guerillas. Among much laughing and good fellowship, they had put

*Two Japanese officers of the Kempei Tai lead Lt. Bob Hite from a transport plane to a waiting 1938 Ford sedan. Like the other airmen, Hite was then driven to Kempei Tai headquarters in Tokyo where he underwent weeks of starvation and torture in an effort to force him to admit to war crimes against the Japanese people.* (Photo courtesy of the U.S. Air Force Archives)

him in the back of a truck with promises to drive him to Chungking and safety. But only a half-hour later they arrived at a small village a few miles away. And there, right in the middle of the village square, Hite jumped down from the truck and saw what appeared to be a jail. From a tall pole atop the jail flew the flag of the Japanese Empire, the Rising Sun. His heart turned to ice at that point. He had obviously been deceived. Later he was trucked to Nanchang.

Oddly enough, George Barr said he had received the same reception as Bob Hite. He had been picked up by Japanese soldiers who assured him they were friendly Chinese and taken to a small village jail where he was shocked to learn that he was a prisoner of the Imperial Japanese Army. This morning, like the others, he had been brought to this military prison in Nanchang.

Farrow and DeShazer then related in broad detail the terrible atrocity they had witnessed the previous morning, when all the denizens of that small village had been murdered in cold blood. This story had a sobering effect on the others. Still, despite their unenviable situation, the men were at least together once again.

*Lieutenant George Barr, Farrow's navigator, was initially captured by Japanese soldiers who, for reasons known only to themselves, assured him that they were Chinese guerillas and that they would lead him to safety. Extremely lucky, Barr survived three and a half years of confinement in various Japanese prisons. Here, accompanied by "Chinese guerillas," he has his photo taken only minutes following his capture.* (Photo courtesy of the U.S. Air Force Archives)

As the days passed they would derive courage and solace from one another.

Time went by, and Farrow tried to smile as his fellow crewmen related their adventures of the past twenty-four hours. But his heart wasn't in it. They were all in the same boat now, totally at the mercy of a cruel band of veritable thugs. In the end it was very likely that those thugs would murder them all, throw their bodies into a deep hole, and cover them up. And that would be the end. There would be no survivors to tell the outside world what had happened to the crew of plane #16, the *Bat Out of Hell.*

Very likely his thoughts wandered to his family and his fiancée, Lib Sims. They might well spend the rest of their lives wondering whatever had happened to him; what had been his fate; and if he were dead, where his body could be found. Such thoughts tortured his soul. He thought of Amelia Earhart and realized that he and his fellow Raiders could suffer the same fate she did when she simply disappeared over the Pacific Ocean in her failed attempt to fly around the world. A hundred years later people might well be saying about them what they said about her, "Gee, I wonder whatever happened to all those Doolittle Raiders. Probably they ran out of gas and crashed in the Pacific."

If only there was some way to let his folks know where he was. But there wasn't. As of now he and his crew had only the Japanese to trust with their future. And that was not a reassuring prospect.

Some two hours later Japanese guards entered the cell and took the men out, one at a time. In order to prevent their communicating with one another, they were placed in solitary cells.

Farrow had just enough time to familiarize himself with his new surroundings when his cell door suddenly swung open Two guards took him by the arms and led him to a large interrogation room. He was to be questioned by a Japanese interpreter, a dapper little man wearing the uniform of an army lieutenant. He was standing to the left of a stocky captain who was seated behind a scarred desk. They watched impassively as the two guards forced Farrow to his knees before the desk.

Like most of the interpreters the Raiders would encounter, this one spoke excellent English. He smiled and explained in a friendly conversational voice that he had attended San Francisco State College and had worked for many years as an attorney in that city before returning to Japan. He had the utmost regard for America and Americans, he said, and deeply regretted that America had pushed Japan into a war.

Returning his civility, Farrow asked him what he thought of President Roosevelt.

The interpreter pondered the question as though the fate of the Japanese Empire depended on his answer. Then he said, "I'd like to hit him in the face with a rotten tomato."

Farrow chuckled agreeably. "Believe it or not, I know quite a few Americans who share your opinion."

The interpreter laughed at his response, prompting the Japanese captain to give him a harsh glare. The interpreter straightened and gave the captain a deep bow. Words in Japanese passed between them.

The interpreter then said, "Tell me, Lieutenant, what do the letters H-O-R-N-E-T spell?"

Farrow was shaken by the question. Apparently the Japanese knew far more than he had anticipated.

He shrugged innocently. "Hornet?"

"And what is a hornet, Lieutenant?"

"It's a bug. With a stinger. You know, like a bee or a wasp."

The interpreter smiled maliciously. "And what, Lieutenant, about the letters D-O-L-I-T-T-L-E?"

"Do little? Like the opposite of do a lot?"

The captain's fist came down with a bang on the desk. Then, without a word, he rose and left the room. Moments later another Japanese officer and six hefty Japanese guards entered. The interpreter whispered to Farrow that he would be painfully tortured  unless he cooperated in answering their questions. As though to punctuate the interpreter's warning, a short, stocky soldier walked up behind Farrow and struck him hard in the small of his back with his rifle butt.

Farrow fell forward, wondering if his spine had been broken. He was immediately jerked to his feet.

Still, he refused to answer any questions. His arms were then pinned to his sides, and he was slapped and beaten in the face. Blood poured from his nose and lips. Yet he insisted on answering each question with only his name, rank, and serial number.

At last the captain shrugged, gave an order in Japanese, and

Farrow was led back to his cell. There he could await . . . what? He didn't know. And the not knowing made it all seem that much more terrible.

That evening he was fed his first meal of the day, a cheese sandwich and a cup of tea.

The following morning, April 21, Japanese guards again handcuffed and blindfolded the five airmen, and they were then driven to the airport and loaded aboard a big transport plane. Each man was separated from the other by a Japanese guard, so it was impossible for them to communicate or compare notes. They flew for about an hour, finally landing in Shanghai.

Bob Hite would later write an account of their experiences there. "We were put in solitary cells and forced to sit cross-legged on the floor. I still had my heavy flight jacket on but I shivered uncontrollably—probably from the cold but also because I was hungry and, I guess, scared." By 9 P.M. that night, the guards had brought him a cheese sandwich and tea, a meal the hungry man found delicious. Exhausted he promptly fell asleep after eating his small dinner.

He was awoken only hours later by two guards who abruptly forced him to his feet. He was roughly led to a room where a Japanese major, an interpreter, and four guards waited. Asked to sit down, Hite was offered a cigarette. But when he reached for the cigarette with his shackled hands, the interpreter withdrew the extended offering. He explained that he could have a cigarette "afterward." "After what?" Hite naively asked.

The Japanese wanted information from him, but as a prisoner of war, Hite knew he was required only to supply his name, rank, and serial number, information he had already offered his captors. Angry at his response, the interpreter shouted that he would have Hite shot if he did not give them the wanted information.

With that threat hanging in the air, the officer, a man of stern military bearing, leaned forward with a smile on his face. He shoved some papers toward his prisoner and in faultless Oxford English, he told Hite to study the stack before him. The American leaned forward and saw that the major had a complete roster of the eighty men who had been part of Doolittle's raid.

Even at this early date the Japanese already knew who their captives were and what they had done. But still the Japanese were puzzled as to the site of their takeoff. Hite and the others lied, telling their interrogators they had taken off from the Aleutian Islands.

Initially, the Japanese were satisfied with this explanation. But even at that there remained one major bone of contention. Now

*Lieutenant Bob Hite, a native Texan, was a handsome young man of twenty-three when this photo was taken in 1941. The Army Air Corps had just awarded him his silver pilot's wings and his commission, and he could see nothing but sunshine ahead. Then in January of '42 he volunteered for Doolittle's raid on Japan. Following his capture by the Japanese, the next three years and four months would be a struggle just to survive. But with the help of God, he made it.* (Photo courtesy of Bob Hite)

the Japanese wanted them to confess to having committed war crimes during their raid on Japanese cities. They had bombed and strafed hospitals, schools, and other civilian centers, said the Japanese, and they wanted the airmen to sign documents confessing to such crimes. They failed to mention that the penalty for such crimes was death.

Farrow and his comrades refused to sign anything.

Such being the case, Japanese officers in Shanghai threw up their hands and decided that the Raiders needed prodding from professional interrogators. Thus the following morning the five Raiders were loaded aboard a big transport plane, destination Tokyo.

Following a four-hour flight they finally touched down in Japan's capital city, and there they were turned over to the Kempei Tai, the equivalent of the German Gestapo, or secret state police. Already the Kempei Tai were infamous throughout the Far East as a sadistic bunch who excelled in breaking men both physically and mentally. They had perfected their craft by torturing thousands of Chinese civilians and soldiers in Manchuria over the past ten years.

First the Japanese confiscated the airmen's ties and belts. Then they were placed in solitary cells where there was no furniture whatsoever, not even a mat to lie on at night. For a bed there was only cold cement. For a toilet, there was a hole cut in the floor. Farrow found the stench overwhelming.

For nourishment, the men were given two small cups of rice per day along with two cups of unsweetened tea. Worst of all, perhaps, the men were required to sit upright in the middle of that cold floor at all times. If they did otherwise, they ran the risk of a terrible beating from the guards.

It was here that the interrogations began in earnest, and Farrow immediately noticed the cold professional atmosphere. The Kempei Tai devoted most of their time to interrogating enemies of the state and other such "undesirables," and they knew their business. They knew how to make a man talk.

Each airman was taken to a bare interrogation room where stood another dapper interpreter and four impassive guards. It was their business to carry out the orders of a grim-looking captain seated behind a polished desk.

Farrow was forced to sit in a chair across the desk from a captain smoking a Lucky Strike cigarette. The interrogation began slowly enough with the interpreter asking fairly innocuous questions, which Farrow could answer without fear of endangering the lives of any other airmen who might also have fallen into the hands of the enemy.

But in time the interpreter began to pepper him with questions concerning the raid on Tokyo. These Farrow refused to answer, shrugging and pleading ignorance, or giving misleading answers.

At one point the interpreter shocked Farrow by pointing out that on his flight jacket he was wearing the patch of the Thirty-fourth Squadron of the Seventeenth Bombardment Group. It was an observation that he could not deny.

"And how did you like Camp Pendleton, Lieutenant? I believe it gets very cold there in winter."

"Very cold," Farrow agreed. Apparently these people had quite an intelligence apparatus in place. By now he was beginning to understand that the Japanese already knew more about Doolittle's raid on Tokyo than he did. He wondered why they were bothering to ask him questions.

Still, when asked directly about the raid, he refused to answer, or he gave misleading answers.

"We know that you bombed Tokyo and other Japanese cities," the interpreter stated at one point. "But we are puzzled as to your embarkation point. Where did you take off from, Lieutenant?"

Thinking quickly, Farrow answered, "Okay, I think you already know this, so it won't hurt if I tell you that we took off from the Aleutian Islands."

The interpreter roared with laughter. "Not a bad try, Lieutenant. But it won't work."

Farrow shrugged.

"But the most important question, Lieutenant, is why did you intentionally bomb our hospitals and strafe our schoolyards? You killed many innocent women and children. Why did you do that?"

"No, that's not true," Farrow protested. "We bombed only military targets."

"You had better tell the truth, Lieutenant."

"That is the truth."

"You are all guilty of terrible war crimes, Lieutenant."

"No, we are not."

After an hour of such give and take, the captain threw up his hands in frustration and issued orders in Japanese.

First, came the water treatment. Two of the guards grabbed Farrow and threw him to the bare floor. They held his arms outstretched over his head while two more guards sat on his legs. Then a folded towel was placed around his mouth and nose like a funnel. A Japanese guard poured water from a gallon container into the funnel, so that Farrow could not breathe. He could only gulp down the water as quickly as possible. This procedure was repeated until he lost consciousness. He was allowed to revive, then the procedure was repeated.

Thirty minutes later, when the captain tired of this game, Farrow was allowed a few minutes to catch his breath. But the torture was not over. At that point a rubber hose was painfully forced down his throat. Then water was poured down the hose and into his stomach. When he was so filled with water that it began to gurgle out his mouth, a husky guard jumped up and down on his stomach. Water and vomit poured from his lips.

After two hours of such treatment, Farrow was too weak to answer questions even if he had wanted to. He was then dragged back to his cell to recuperate. Several hours later the questions and torture would begin all over again.

Late that night, his body racked with pain, his mind spinning in confusion, still in shock from the last torture session, Farrow thought he had seen it all, at least for one day. It was then that two Japanese guards entered his cell and kicked him to his feet. Without comment, they handcuffed him and dragged him over against the far wall. They looked at the six-four Farrow, then at each other. Apparently, for some reason, his great height presented them with a dilemma. One of the guards walked to the door and shouted an order. Minutes later another guard appeared carrying two short stepladders.

The two guards then mounted the ladders, while the other guard grabbed Farrow around the knees. Together the three of them hoisted him off his feet. He looked up to see what they were

# U. S. AWARDS MEDALS TO 80 HEROES OF THE ARMY'S BOMBING RAID ON JAPAN

Here are the faces of Americans who bombed Japan. Opposite you see their leader, Brigadier General James H. Doolittle, who on the morning of April 18 swooped astonishingly down out of the Far Eastern skies at the head of his volunteer squadron and spread destruction along a 40-mile swathe in the very heart of the remote island empire. Where these fliers came from and how they returned from their perilous mission are secrets known to few in the U. S. High Command. But

on May 19, at an unexpected ceremony in the White House, President Roosevelt personally bestowed the Congressional Medal of Honor on General Doolittle and let it be known that Distinguished Service Crosses would be awarded to the 79 airmen who soared with him on his brilliant flight.

With Air Chieftain Arnold and Mrs. Doolittle looking on, the President pinned the emblem of the nation's highest honor on General Doolittle's blouse. An accom-

panying citation emphasized that he had undertaken his task "with the apparent certainty of being forced to land in enemy territory or to perish at sea." Before one of his fast B-25 bombers was shot down or prevented from reaching its destination. "We flew low enough the flier told newspapermen, "so that we could see the expressions on the faces of the people." "And what was that expression?" he was asked. Replied Herr Doolittle: "It was one, I should say, of intense surprise."

*On June 2, 1942,* Life *magazine carried photos of some of Doolittle's Raiders. Bill Farrow is pictured bottom row, second from left.* (Photo courtesy of the Darlington County Historical Society)

about. Above him, high up in the wall, was a thick wooden peg. The two guards on the ladders reached up and hooked his handcuffs over that peg. Now he hung suspended, his toes inches above the floor. The guards then stood back and looked up at him. Initially they had been stymied by his great height, but thanks to their sadistic ingenuity they had accomplished their mission after all. Now he could hang like his crewmen in the other cells. Laughing cheerfully, the guards made their exit.

After a few minutes Farrow's hands and arms became numb. The metal handcuffs were supporting all his weight, and the handcuffs were biting deeply into his wrists, causing him the most excruciating pain he had ever experienced. He felt as though his limbs were on fire. It was, he supposed, the closest thing to being crucified he had ever experienced. Surely, he thought, no man could endure such pain for very long. Certainly the guards would return and free him.

But he was left hanging there throughout the night. Besides, there was no one—only the guards and the other prisoners—to hear his screams. It was supposed to teach him a lesson.

When he was taken down the next morning, he managed to stumble about the cell on shaky legs, but his arms and hands hung useless at his sides.

"Oh, yeah, I remember that day," recalled Jake DeShazer in later years. "That was the day the Japs introduced us to another amusement. We were each taken into a different interrogation room. But Farrow and the others were all suffering the same tortures I was. The Japs would place large bamboo joints behind our knees, and then we'd be forced to kneel. The pain was terrible. Felt like my kneecaps were coming off. Then to make matters worse, they'd kick us on our kneecaps. I really thought mine would just pop right off.

"After about five minutes of that, we'd be ordered to stand upright. But of course we couldn't. I remember how the Japs would laugh at me crawling around on the floor like a bug trying to regain my feet."

Chase Nielsen, the navigator aboard Dean Hallmark's *Green Hornet,* would later recall guards stretching him out on a long table. "They tied one rope around my ankles and another under my chin. Then two burly guards would start pulling in opposite directions. It felt as though my spine was being pulled apart."

After hours of such treatment Farrow could hardly stand. Walking about in his cell was out of the question. Never was he or the other airmen shown any mercy. Indeed, immediately following a torture session, two guards would take him by his feet and drag him back to his cell, his head bouncing on the hard cement floor. There he would be left in isolation and forced to sit at attention. Then he had nothing more to look forward to than his next interrogation session. If he was careless enough to fall over, his Japanese guards would rush into his cell and force him to stand on his feet.

It is well known that Farrow was of a deep spiritual nature, a man whose trust in God knew no bounds. But there must have been times when even his faith was tested. There must have been times when even Bill Farrow would recall Jesus' words on the cross when he said, "My God, my God, why hast thou forsaken me?"

But through it all, Farrow and the other Raiders remained true to their vow of silence. There were many times during their torture sessions when they were tempted to tell all and thus spare themselves the terrible ordeal they knew they were in for. But it must be remembered that Farrow and his crewmen had been kept in solitary confinement since their capture and thus knew nothing of the fate of the other Raiders. Such being the case, they were afraid that if they yielded to temptation and talked, they could very well cost some other flyer his life.

Still, Farrow and the others were puzzled. The Japanese obviously knew everything there was to know about Colonel Doolittle and his raid on Tokyo. By now they even knew that the planes had taken off from the *Hornet*. So why were they so intent in hearing the flyers verify what they already knew to be true?

About a week after beginning their sessions with the Kempei Tai, Farrow and the others learned for the first time the enemy's real purpose in all these interrogations. They, of course, were unaware of the great controversy raging among high-ranking generals in the Japanese High Command concerning their status and just what should be done with them. General Sugiyama, chief of the General Staff, was particularly enraged by the raid, since it was he who would be required to offer explanations to both the Emperor and the Japanese people. It was a task he did not relish. Thus it was Sugiyama who insisted that these luckless airmen should be treated as war criminals. They should be forced to sign confessions stating that they were guilty of war crimes; then General Sugiyama could have them condemned in a court of law and subsequently executed.

But now, standing in Sugiyama's way, stood a very reasonable Gen. Hideki Tojo, premier of the Empire, who argued that these men were indeed prisoners of war, and that they should be treated as such according to the Geneva Convention. In other words, argued Tojo, these men should be interned in a prisoner of war camp for the duration.

And that's where the Kempei Tai came in. General Sugiyama knew that if he could persuade Farrow and the others to sign confessions that they had intentionally committed war crimes, he would have the advantage when debating with Premier Tojo. Now, thanks to orders from General Sugiyama, the Kempei Tai was determined to get those confessions.

The surviving Raiders recently recalled that in early May of 1942, they were taken in one at a time for another session, and this time they were introduced to a new torture.

After being dragged by the feet from his filthy cell to the interrogation room, Farrow was slammed down in a chair. He was asked some innocuous preliminary questions, then the interpreter suddenly asked: "Tell me, Lieutenant, why would you go out of your way to murder Japanese civilians during the raid?"

Farrow replied weakly, "We didn't."

"Lieutenant, it is well known that you both bombed and machine-gunned women and children in Nagoya."

Farrow managed to shake his head. "No."

"Why do you lie, Lieutenant? We have dozens of witnesses who saw your plane strafe our poor children in a schoolyard. Many of them died. And you dropped your bombs on a hospital. Many people there died."

Farrow had to struggle not to laugh. How infuriating to hear these Japanese officers, who were guilty of every sordid atrocity imaginable against every civilian population in southeastern Asia and the Pacific islands, now just oozing with piety when it came to accusing someone else of murdering their own people.

As for the interrogator's accusations, they were totally baseless. Farrow himself had seen DeShazer's bombs land squarely on the Mitsubishi aircraft factory. And Harold Spatz had not fired his machine guns a single time once they departed the *Hornet*.

"I'm sorry, but you're mistaken."

At that point the Japanese captain gave a brief order, and Farrow held his breath. He had been through this routine enough to know that the order was a signal for the tortures to begin. Sure enough, two Japanese guards came up from behind him, grabbed his arms and held them straight out so that he could not move his hands. Then two other guards took sharpened bamboo rods, about the size of pencils, and jabbed them through the skin where his fingers met his hands, between the knuckles. The rods were then shoved back and forth, up and down, tearing the tender membranes and bruising the bones.

Farrow clenched his teeth to keep from screaming. Perspiration streamed down his face. The smiling interpreter lit a cigarette and blew smoke toward the ceiling.

"Now, Lieutenant, are you ready to admit your role in the war crimes committed against the Japanese people?"

Farrow made no reply.

The interpreter nodded his head, and the two guards reached out and gripped Farrow's hands as though giving him firm handshakes and squeezed. Mercifully, he fainted from the intense pain.

Undaunted at this show of weakness, the guards simply threw a bucket of water in his face. Still, he would say nothing.

At this point Farrow was treated to the same terrible emotional torture experienced by all the other Raiders in captivity. The interpreter spoke again, saying, "American officer, your heart is not right. We regret it must come to this. But you see, since you refuse to cooperate, we have no choice but to take you out for immediate execution." The interpreter then pretended to wipe away a tear. "And to think, Lieutenant, your poor family will never even know what happened to you or where your body lies."

Dazed, Farrow could not believe what he was hearing.

Execution? Did the Geneva Convention mean nothing to these animals? His heart pounding with fear, he realized that the Geneva Convention worked only in normal situations. As the interpreter had pointed out, the world did not even realize that he was there. Thus the Japanese were free to do with him, and with all his friends, exactly as they liked. And no one would ever know.

He was then forced to his feet, blindfolded, and led down a long hallway and out the back door to a large courtyard at the rear of the Kempei Tai headquarters building. He was aware that several soldiers were marching down the gravel path behind him. The firing squad, he thought. His throat felt dry, and his heart pounded with fear.

Several minutes later he heard an order in Japanese, and the soldiers halted. He was marched a few feet farther down the path, then forced to his knees, his back to the squad. The sergeant in charge gave a command in Japanese, and he could hear the soldiers working the bolts of their rifles.

"Too bad, Lieutenant," said the interpreter. "You refuse to confess to your crimes, and now you must die. My sympathy goes to your family."

Convinced that he was about to die, Farrow's life flashed before his eyes. He remembered life at home back when he was a boy, his family, and his schoolmates. He remembered working the tobacco markets with his cousins, and his life as a CCC boy. Then there was the university and his fiancée Lib Sims. Now, in moments, his life would vanish as though it had all been a mere dream. His life would end, and none of them would ever know what had happened to him.

His blood pounding in his temples, he began to silently pray as he had never prayed before.

Then he heard another command. But now, instead of the dark oblivion he had expected, he was roughly pulled to his feet. Then he heard the voice of the interpreter. He was laughing.

"We are the Knights of the Bushido, of the Order of the Rising Sun. We do not execute men at sunset, but only at sunrise. It is now sunset, so your execution will take place in the morning. We will execute you then, Lieutenant Farrow, unless you decide to confess in the meantime."

Dragged back to his cell, dreading what sunrise would bring, Farrow just lay there on that cold cement floor, thinking what if . . . what if . . . what if . . .

Likely he tried to mentally calculate the days of his captivity. How many now? Three days? Four? Five? Was that all? It seemed that he had spent his entire life here. Everything else was a mere dream. Only weeks ago he had been a free man. He had never even spoken to a Japanese before. How long ago all that seemed now. Had he really lived a life somewhere before? Or was all that just a figment of his imagination? How his life had changed, and in only a few days. Now his only reality was hunger and pain.

Yes, he decided, he had been here always. That previous life that floated through his mind from time to time had been nothing more than a hallucination, a beautiful dream.

By May first, all the crews of Doolittle's Raiders had arrived in Chungking. All except for the crews of the *Bat Out of Hell* and the *Green Hornet*. It was obvious, by now, that they would not return.

On the morning of May 5, 1942, while on his way to the interrogation room, Bill Farrow was led through a small waiting room containing rows of brown benches. There, to his amazement, sat the three surviving members of the *Green Hornet*—Lt. Dean Hallmark, Lt. Chase Nielsen, and Lt. Bob Meder. They looked back at him in similar disbelief. They were not allowed to speak, of course, but they nodded enthusiastic greetings and gave the thumbs-up sign.

Farrow could see from their swollen faces and dark bruises that they had been exposed to the same harsh mistreatment he had endured. He grinned at them and returned their thumbs-up sign. Feeling a bayonet prod him in the back, Farrow kept walking. He wondered what had happened to Sgt. Bill Dieter and Sgt. Don Fitzmaurice.

Back home in Darlington, it was late April, and the flowers and dogwoods were in bloom everywhere; after a cold dismal winter, light had returned to the world. And life was wonderful!

At her home on St. John's Avenue, Bill's Aunt Margaret Stem, like everyone else in America, heard the news of the bombing of Tokyo on the radio on the evening of April 18. There was jubilation across the country. Margaret would later remember a visit from her sister that very evening.

"Margaret," she said, "tell me I'm crazy, but my sixth sense tells me that—what's Jessie's little boy's name? Bill? Well, I know as good as I'm standing here that Bill Farrow was in on that raid. You remember him telling us that he was going on a secret mission? And you remember how funny he acted, like there was something bothering him, which was not like Bill at all?"

"Well," said Margaret, "I started thinking over her words. Before I went to bed that night I was as convinced as my sister that Bill had helped bomb Tokyo."

Then the next day America's newspapers headlined the news. But still there were no details. No names were mentioned. Nor was the *Hornet* listed as the takeoff point.

Nor were there any comments emanating from Washington. President Roosevelt was silent on the matter, as were both the Army and the War Department. Indeed, the first word that the raid had been conducted by B-25 medium bombers came from newspapers in London, which reported that one such bomber had been forced to land on the coast of Siberia.

Then on May 10 the War Department confirmed the report that American planes had indeed made the raid on Japan. When asked their takeoff point, President Roosevelt joked that they had taken off from Shangri-La.

Ten days later, on May 20, newspapers across the country carried photos of President Roosevelt pinning the Congressional Medal of Honor on newly promoted Gen. James Doolittle. The accompanying article stated that it was Doolittle who had led the raid on Japan.

Also for the first time, it was then that newspapers carried the names of the eighty airmen who participated in the raid. Among them was Lt. Bill Farrow of Darlington, South Carolina.

His mother, Jessie Stem Farrow, now employed by the Federal Board of Economic Warfare in Washington, DC, read his name and nearly fainted. To think that her son had participated in such action, and at the risk of his own life! But now, thank God, it was all over, and Bill would soon be coming home. Indeed, now that it was all over and Bill was safe, she was overjoyed to think that her son had just gained immortality for himself by helping to pull off one of the most heroic military operations in the history of this great nation. Well, wasn't that just like Bill? To be involved in something that big and never even mention a word of it to his family, not even to his own mother.

Jessie immediately picked up the phone and called her sister, Margaret Stem, back home in Darlington.

"Have you read the news?" she asked, her voice shrill with excitement.

"Oh, Jessie, have I!" Margaret said. "In fact, I believe everybody's read it. My phone has been jumping off the hook all day, people calling to express their congratulations—and not just people from Darlington. Folks from all over the state have been calling. This is the biggest thing to hit Darlington since Sherman came through in '65."

"I'm so proud," Jessie said. She was weeping now. "But let me get off this phone, Margaret. I know Bill will be calling soon from wherever he is, and I want to make sure he can get through when he does."

"You're right, Jessie. And I'll do the same in case he calls here. I'll hang up on these callers just as quickly as possible."

In later years Margaret Stem would remember May 20, 1942, as one of the happiest days ever for herself and Bill Farrow's mother and other relatives. She remembered joyfully sitting in her swing on the front porch that afternoon in the bright spring sunlight talking with visitors from all over town who dropped by to offer their congratulations. "For some reason," she said, "almost every fellow who dropped by said he was Bill's best friend growing up. I guess time plays tricks on our memory."

Then that evening came a phone call from Gen. Jimmy Doolittle to Jessie Farrow. Initially, she was thrilled to get a call from the illustrious Jimmy Doolittle, but then she heard his devastating message, and suddenly his words changed her life forever. She would remember them in detail for the rest of her days. Indeed, after some pleasant preliminary remarks, Doolittle broke the heartbreaking news to her that her son was a prisoner of the Imperial Japanese Army. He spoke as softly and tactfully as possible, but his words came like a clap of thunder. It was a kiss of death that she had never even considered. Now she sank to her knees and burst into tears.

Bill would not be calling after all. He would not be coming home after all. Now she could only pray that he might somehow survive the war. That was all she had left. She had read the atrocity stories concerning the Japanese and their treatment of prisoners of war, and now she dreaded to think of what poor Bill must be going through.

She then phoned Margaret and repeated General Doolittle's words. Margaret's reaction was just as hers had been. Then Jessie said, "Margaret, I'm taking a thirty-day leave from my job, and will catch the noon train out of here tomorrow. Can you meet me at the depot in Florence at seven tomorrow evening? I just don't think I can handle this without your support."

"Oh, yes, Jessie. Don't give it a second thought. I'll be at the depot in Florence to meet you. We want you here with us."

A week later Margaret invited her friends and neighbors to her home for a prayer service. "Not just for Bill," she said, "but for all the boys in service. We prayed that God would look after them and help them survive that terrible war."

And of course Farrow's fiancée, Lib Sims, was devastated by the terrible news of his capture. She would write to his mother:

> He told me of his great love for flying, and his Boy Scout days, the fish stews and high school dances. He made me love and appreciate life as I had never done before. He made the good and worthwhile things become real to me. The stars were always brighter when I walked with him. The saddest and most heartbreaking thing about his departure is that he who taught me to love life should have it so cruelly denied him.

Truly, Farrow's relatives, who had reveled in the bright sunshine of May 20, were suddenly plunged into the darkest gloom. Jessie and her relatives went into mourning, and all the area churches announced immediate plans to conduct special prayer services. All citizens of Darlington began wearing black armbands.

At this point they could only pray.

Back in Tokyo, the Japanese finally decided that the airmen

perhaps needed some rest. Thus, after four weeks of endless interrogations, Farrow and his companions were allowed to sleep at night, though they were constantly questioned during the daytime.

Then, during the first week in June the Japanese decided to break their rule of solitary confinement and to put two men to a cell. Farrow's morale lifted tremendously at that point. Into his cell, cell #2, came Lt. Chase Nielsen, the navigator aboard Dean Hallmark's *Green Hornet,* and perhaps the toughest of all the prisoners; in cell #3 Lt. Dean Hallmark and Lt. Robert. J. Meder were put together; in cell #4 were Cpl. Harold Spatz and Cpl. Jake DeShazer; while in cell #1 went Lt. George Barr and Lt. Bob Hite.

Farrow's cell door opened, and to his delight in stumbled Chase Nielsen wearing a big grin on his battered face. Ignoring the guards, the two men embraced warmly. Then, without speaking, they seated themselves upon the floor.

Nielsen would later remember that the guards left at that point, and the two men checked every inch of their cells for listening devices. They also soon learned that though their guards would scream "Don't talk" and bang on their cell doors, they would not enter the cells. The two airmen therefore ignored the guards, and began to converse openly. This represented their first freedom to communicate with one another since their capture almost seven weeks earlier, and they indulged in conversation almost constantly.

"What happened?" Farrow asked. "How'd they get you fellows? I've seen you and Dean Hallmark and Bob Meder. But what happened to Bill Dieter and Don Fitzmaurice?"

Nielsen shook his head sadly. "Dieter and Fitzmaurice are dead. Both dead. You see, we approached the coast of China just after dusk and decided to try a surf landing. We thought that would be better than trying to find Chuchow in the dark."

"Yeah, good thinking."

"Later we learned we were in Ningpo, an area occupied by the Japs. But of course we didn't know that at the time."

"No, of course not."

"At any rate, we were going to land just off the coast, and then make our way to Chuchow on foot."

"Yeah, that was a good idea," Farrow agreed.

"But as we came in low over the water, a high wave snagged our landing gear, and we crashed in the ocean, crashed hard, about three miles off shore."

"Wow, that was really tough luck."

Nielsen exhaled loudly. "Absolutely. Dieter and Fitzmaurice were terribly injured when we hit the water. I really don't know how Hallmark survived. He was thrown through the windshield and got a nasty cut on his forehead. But somehow he and Bob Meder and I battled those huge waves and swam our way to shore."

"Just to wind up here," Farrow said. This was a theme he had explored with increasing frequency over the past few weeks. Why would God, a good and merciful God, allow him to struggle so hard for so long just to wind up here, being tortured to death in a stinking Japanese jail? What did it all mean? It was something he would like to discuss with his pastor and his Aunt Margaret some day—if he lived through it.

Nielsen swore under his breath. "These Japs are real sweethearts, aren't they?"

"Real swell fellows," Farrow agreed.

Farrow and Nielsen were curious as to what the others had told the Japanese and what sort of tortures they had undergone. As for their ultimate fate, it seems that they had reached similar conclusions.

"So what do you think, Chase? Think we're gonna be shot?"

This was a question that Nielsen, like all the others, had pondered for the past seven weeks.

"Look at it this way, Bill. We caused the Jap High Command to lose face with Emperor Hirohito, and that's a fate worse than death to these people. They hate us for that, and if they can get away with shooting us, I'm sure they'll do it. I'm sure they're trumping up all sorts of war crimes to charge us with. Then they can shoot us and feel totally justified."

"Yeah, just what I've been thinking."

"And another big problem," Nielsen continued, "is that nobody knows we're here. They could take us all out and shoot us today, and nobody would ever know what happened to us."

"And of course there's no way to escape."

"Nope."

"I mean, if we could break out of here," Farrow said, "where would we go? We've got white skin, and the average Jap comes up to about my belt buckle. We'd stand out like sore thumbs wherever we went."

Nielsen nodded. "Yet I don't know how long we can survive the way we're going. Sometimes I think death would be a relief."

It was a gloomy conclusion, but one that Farrow totally agreed with.

"But I will tell you this," Nielsen continued, shaking his fist and speaking with total confidence, "come hell or high water, one way or another I will survive this war, and some day I will be back to tell the world just what bastards these Japs really are."

In addition to all their other discomforts, these American airmen had not been allowed to shower, shave, or change clothes since their capture back on April 19. In their enclosed airless cells, their body odor, added to the stench of the open hole in the floor that served as a toilet, just added to their miseries. And by now their hair and beards were long and matted. Indeed, they were beginning to look like the monsters their captors were trying to make them out to be.

Also by now all eight of the airmen were suffering from dysentery. Their diet had been reduced to six thin slices of bread and three cups of unsweetened tea per day. By now they didn't feel that they would have the energy to escape even if their captors threw open their cell doors and invited them to do so.

A week later Farrow and the other airmen were taken out for interrogation. But this time the situation was different. All eight were marched into a small meeting room. And now, instead of being stabbed with bamboo rods, they were seated at a long table and handed pens. The interpreter placed down on the table in front of each airman a document written in Japanese. They were then ordered to write their signatures on the lines provided.

"What is it?" Farrow asked, the question they were all thinking.

"It is a confession," the interpreter answered. "A confession that you bombed Tokyo and several other Japanese cities."

"Yes, we did that," Farrow replied, "and no one denies it, but we certainly haven't committed any war crimes."

The interpreter smiled broadly. "You have a choice, gentlemen, you can either sign the document lying before you or be taken out at sunrise and shot. The decision is yours. And this time we are not joking."

The interpreter snapped his fingers, and a dozen Japanese guards rushed forward and began slapping and kicking the prisoners. Then came another snap of the fingers and they backed off.

The airmen looked at the documents lying there on the table. They were written wholly in Japanese and therefore had no meaning whatsoever. But by now the airmen truly had stopped caring. Besides, if they refused to sign they would be taken out and shot at sunrise. On the other hand, perhaps by signing they might very well prolong their lives—at least until America could win this war and force their liberation. In the end, all eight signed those meaningless documents.

In fact, they had just unwittingly signed their death warrants.

In September 1945, in secret Japanese archives, American authorities discovered Noboro Unit Military Police Report No. 352. According to this document the eight Americans had fully confessed to their war crimes and admitted they had intentionally bombed and strafed schools and hospitals instead of military targets. The entire document is obviously a lie, and the falsification of the confessions is clear to any American who speaks English. Indeed, the responses recorded here are spoken in the sort of English a Japanese interpreter might speak, but certainly not American airmen. The following excerpts are from the Kempei Tai report:

Q. Did you do any strafing while getting away from Nagoya?

Bob Hite: Heretofore, I haven't revealed any information on this point, but the truth is that about five to six minutes after leaving the city we saw in the distance what looked like an elementary school with many children at play. The pilot steadily dropped altitude and ordered the gunmen to their stations. When the plane was at an oblique angle, the skipper gave firing orders, and bursts of machine gun fire sprayed the ground.

Q. Didn't you strafe children of an elementary school?

Bill Farrow: There is truly no excuse for this. I have made no mention of this before, but after leaving Nagoya, I do not quite remember the place—there was a place which looked like a school, with many people there. As a parting shot, with a feeling of "damn these Japs," I made a power dive and carried out some strafing. There was absolutely no defensive fire from below.

Q. What are you thinking of after killing and wounding so many innocent people?

Dean Hallmark: Since it was our intention to bomb Tokyo and escape to China quickly, we also dropped bombs over objectives other than those targets specified, and made a hasty escape. Therefore, we also bombed residential homes, killing and wounding many people.

Q. After the bombing of Nagoya, did you not actually carry out strafing?

Harold Spatz: It was an extremely inexcusable deed. Shortly after leaving Nagoya, while flying southward along the coast, the pilot immediately upon perceiving a school, steadily reduced altitude and ordered us to our stations. I aimed at the children in the schoolyard and fired only one burst before we headed out to sea. My feelings at that time were "damn these Japs" and I wanted to give them a burst of fire. Now I clearly see that this was truly unpardonable and in all decency should not have been committed.

Q. Even if you were instructed by the pilot to drop the bomb properly, didn't you as the bombardier think that in the name of humanity you shouldn't have bombed innocent civilians?

Jake DeShazer: With our technique and methods used in that air attack such things, even if we thought about them, would have been impossible.

Q. State the conditions at the time of the bombing.

Chase Nielsen: At that time I was mainly observing the situation

outside from the windows. At an altitude of 1,500 meters, as
soon as we crossed the Noka River in the northeast part of
Tokyo, the pilot frantically ordered the bombing. In general
the main objective was the factories but with such a bombing
method, I believe we missed it.

Q. You not only bombed the factories, but you also bombed
homes of innocent civilians and killed many people. What are
your reactions in that respect?

Robert Meder: It is natural that dropping bombs on a crowded
place like Tokyo will cause damage in the vicinity of the target.
All the more so with our technique of dropping bombs while
making a hit-and-run attack, so I believe it was strictly unavoidable. Moreover, Colonel Doolittle never did order us to avoid
such bombings and neither were we particularly worried about
the possible damage.

Q. Did you not strafe an elementary school while headed out to
sea after the Nagoya raid?

George Barr: I am quite sure that was done. Only when the
pilot steadily dropped altitude and the strafing was executed
was I aware of it.

Now, based upon these falsified "confessions," General
Sugiyama, chief of the Japanese High Command, had the excuse
he had been searching for to justify his trying these eight
American airmen as war criminals in a military court of law and
to sentence them to death. Now, even the emperor would have to
agree, let Hideki Tojo weep all he liked.

Again, the airmen had no idea that they had just signed their
own death warrants, but they did notice that their interrogations
and torture sessions immediately ceased once they had given the
Japanese what they wanted.

Then, one week later, on June 15, 1942, they were given back
their shoes and socks, and taken out to the courtyard where they
were photographed. These photos would appear in newspapers
throughout Japan within the coming week, along with an
announcement that these evil American airmen had laughingly

*It was June 15, 1942, and Bill Farrow and his crew had just had their heads shaved. More important, they had just signed "confessions" that would later convict them of war crimes against the Japanese people. Here they are posed on the front steps of Kempei Tai headquarters in Tokyo. (Top, L-R): Bill Farrow, George Barr, Bob Hite. (Bottom, L-R): Jake DeShazer and Harold Spatz. (Photo courtesy of the U.S. Air Force Archives)*

confessed to committing war crimes against the Japanese people.

Following the photo session, Farrow and the others were hand-cuffed and led to four waiting cars—1939 Ford sedans—and driven to a railroad station. There they were placed aboard a train crowded with hundreds of Japanese civilians who stared at these strange Americans, especially at the giant in their midst. At that point, to their amazement, they were given fruit and box lunches containing fish, rice, and cabbage. Nearly starved, the men ate with gusto.

They spent a miserable two days rumbling through the countryside before boarding a ferryboat to the island of Kyushu, and there they boarded another train for Nagasaki. In that city they spent the night in a stinking cell in a small jail.

The next morning they were led aboard a small leaky freighter for the two-day trip to Shanghai. During their two days at sea they were allowed to converse freely, and the two crews eagerly became acquainted with one another.

*This photo was made June 15, 1942, on the steps of the Kempei Tai headquarters in Tokyo. But this time the American airmen had been joined by their Japanese hosts who felt it might be good for their military careers if they were photographed along with these American war criminals.* (Photo courtesy of the U.S. Air Force Archives)

Farrow and his men learned that Dean Hallmark, who had piloted the *Green Hornet,* like Bob Hite, was a native Texan, born and raised in Dallas. He was a husky individual with ruddy features, and had attended a junior college in Paris, Texas, before enrolling at Auburn University. There, because of his muscular build and swaggering walk, he soon became known as Jungle Jim Hallmark. He liked the life of an Air Corps pilot and planned to remain in service after the war. "My only regret," he told them, "is that I didn't join sooner. If I had, I'd probably be a captain by now. Then I'd be getting more pay for being in this miserable hole than the rest of you guys." Hallmark, it was said, feared neither man nor devil, and during the ensuing months he became the unofficial spokesman for the flyers in their dealings with the Japanese.

They learned that Bob Meder, Hallmark's copilot, a quiet reserved man in his early twenties and a native of Cleveland,

*A smiling Chase Nielsen had just received both his officer's commission and the silver wings of an Air Corps pilot when this photo was taken in 1940. A man of indomitable courage, for three long years he refused to break under the most brutal treatment the Japanese could dream up for him, and lived to testify at the War Crimes Trial of 1946. He later returned to his beloved Utah, and is alive and well today.* (Photo courtesy of Chase Nielsen)

Ohio, was the intellectual among the prisoners. He was tall and well built, and had distinguished himself in track in both high school and college. In fact, Meder was the only college graduate in the group. His ambition, he said, was to become a high school teacher and coach. He would soon become popular among his fellow airmen for his keen wit and fine sense of humor. He enjoyed reminiscing about his childhood and high school days, and usually his anecdotes would remind the others of stories they wanted to tell.

Chase Nielsen, Hallmark's navigator, because of his black hair and dark features, was often mistaken for an American Indian. But in fact he was of Swedish descent. He had been born and raised in Hiram, Utah, and loved hunting and fishing in the great outdoors. He had studied engineering at Utah State University before dropping out to join the Air Corps in 1940. He planned to remain in service once the war was over, but, he later wrote, he eventually planned to return to Utah "and settle down forever where the sky is blue, the mountains are tall and a man's only limitation is his own imagination."

Nielsen was noted for his indomitable will to live, one born of a deep-seated hatred for his Japanese captors. Repeatedly, he swore to the others that somehow he would survive, and that one day he would return to Japan and make those "damnable thugs" pay for their crimes against him and the other Raiders.

And in fact Chase Nielsen did just that!

Of course these captive Raiders had no way of knowing it, but on June 3 and 4 the seemingly indomitable Japanese Army and Navy had just suffered a terrible defeat at the Battle of Midway, their first setback of the war. Earlier, they had captured Wake Island and Guam rather easily, but their attempted invasion of Midway became a disaster. Their carriers and troop transports were sent to the bottom by American B-17s, and the Japanese were at last turned back. This victory, the first for America, became a tremendous moral boost for the entire Free World. Now the outcome of World War II was no longer in doubt. Now it was just a matter of time until the Axis forces surrendered and the Allies were victorious.

But the Battle of Midway was of no help to the eight Raiders now in the hands of the Kempei Tai. Now only their executions would satisfy the blood lust of General Sugiyama.

# CHAPTER 8

# Death in a Foreign Land

In late June of 1942 Jessie Farrow, alone in her drab apartment in Washington, DC, received a phone call from an aide to Gen. Jimmy Doolittle. He told her that a neutral embassy in Tokyo had contacted American authorities and told them that several American aviators were being held at a prison in Shanghai. His source, said the aide, had further informed them that one of the prisoners was named Farrow, and that all the prisoners were in good health. The aide also informed her that the War Department was desperately trying to get additional information about the flyers through the International Red Cross.

At about this same time the Air Corps delivered Bill Farrow's personal effects to his mother in Washington. It was with trembling hands that she opened and examined the contents of his luggage. There, among a stack of papers, she found a journal containing a creed of sorts that Bill had written for himself back in the summer of 1940. After reading it, she released copies to Washington newspapers. Within weeks it was being reprinted in newspapers and magazines across America. Indeed, in October 1942 noted *Washington Post* news columnist David Lawrence devoted an entire article to it.

Farrow's creed, entitled "My Future," reads as follows:

> The time has come to decide what rules I am going to set myself for daily conduct. My aim is decided—I am going into some branch of aviation. I have only to apply myself daily toward this end to achieve it.

First, I must enumerate my weaknesses and seek to eliminate them. Then I must seek to develop the qualities I need for this type of work. It's going to be hard, but it's the only way. Work with a purpose is the only practical means of achieving an end.

First, what are my weaknesses?

1. Lack of thoroughness and application.
2. Lack of curiosity.
3. Softness in driving myself.
4. Lack of seriousness of purpose—sober thought.
5. Lack of constant vigilance.
6. Scatterbrained dashing here and there and not getting anything done. Spur of the moment stuff.
7. Letting situations confuse the truth in my mind.
8. Lack of self-confidence.
9. Letting people influence my decisions too much. I must weigh my decisions, then act.
10. Too much frivolity and not enough serious thought.
11. Lack of clear-cut, decisive thinking.

Second, what must I do to develop myself?

1. Stay in glowing health. Take a good fast one-hour workout each day.
2. Search out current, past and future topics on aviation.
3. Work hard on each day's lessons. Shoot for an "A".
4. Stay close to God. Do His will and commandments. He is my friend and protector. Believe in Him, trust in His ways and not my own confused understanding of the universe.
5. Do not waste energy or time in fruitless pursuits. Learn to act from honest fundamental motives: simplicity in life leads to the fullest living. Order my life: in order there is achievement, in aimlessness there is retrogression.
6. Fear nothing, be it insanity, sickness, failure. Always be upright. Look the world in the eye.
7. Keep my mind always clean. Allow no evil thoughts to destroy me. My mind is my very own, to think and use just as I do my arm. It was given me by the Creator to use as I see fit, but to think wrong is to do wrong!
8. Concentrate! Choose the task to be done, and do it to the best of my energy and ability.

9. Fear not for the future. Build on each day as though the future for me is a certainty. If I die tomorrow, that is too bad, but I will have done today's work.

10. Never be discouraged over anything. Turn failure into success.

To cap it all off, on January 23, 1943, Dr. J. Rion McKissick, president of the University of South Carolina, walked out on stage to deliver his farewell address to the senior graduating class. He fumbled around in his coat pockets for a moment, then took out several pages of a manuscript and laid them on the lectern. At that point, in a voice trembling with emotion, he read Farrow's "My Future." Following that reading, McKissick said, "All that I would add to this as the hour of parting strikes, is the prayer from the heart of your alma mater that wherever you go and whatever you do, God will bless you and guide you and take care of you every one." Then he wished the seniors godspeed and without further comment turned and walked away. His words were met with overwhelming applause.

Under a blistering sun Bill Farrow and his fellow airmen now stood on the bobbing deck of their small black steamer as it chugged into Shanghai Harbor. It was June 19, 1942, and before them stood Shanghai, one of the great cities of the world. But handcuffed and blindfolded as they were, they could see nothing. They could only listen to the medley of sounds and smell the sharp odors of a bustling seaport city. Silently, they tried to absorb as much as possible of their surroundings.

They were aware that Shanghai, despite the war, was still considered an international city, and was inhabited by thousands of neutral Europeans, Westerners like themselves. Indeed, they knew that the streets of Shanghai were filled with people from Sweden, Switzerland, Portugal, and other European nations. Which meant that should they be able to effect an escape, they could easily mingle with the other Caucasians until they could manage to find help in getting out of the city and back to America. Or at least they had a chance now, slim though that chance might be, and that bit of hope gave them a sliver of optimism they had not felt since their capture two months earlier.

Once their steamer had docked, the flyers were led ashore and shoved into the back of a truck. Then for the next thirty minutes they were driven across the city until they reached their destination, the infamous Bridge House. This seven-story building, located in downtown Shanghai near the International Settlement and the bridge over Soochow Creek, was formerly a British hotel, but the Japanese in typical fashion had converted parts of it—mainly the hotel parking garage—into a prison. Now it was called, with chilling realism, the Butcher Shop. From the outside there appeared nothing ominous about the Bridge House, but the interior, to those who had suffered the great misfortune of being incarcerated there, was more terrible than the Black Hole of Calcutta.

Here for the next seventy-two days, from June 19 until August 26, Bill Farrow's worst nightmare would become a living reality.

All eight airmen were forced into a small cell, cell #6, some ten feet wide and fifteen feet long. Worse, there were already other inmates in the cell—Chinese men and women, several Japanese thugs, and one Russian. All in all, thirty people were crammed into a cell of 150 square feet. One elderly Chinese man, nearly dead with dysentery, lay motionless on the floor. And there were two corpses lying in a corner. No one knew how long the bodies had been dead, and the Japanese didn't seem to care. Everyone, of course, was forced to stand. Periodically, they would take turns sitting down, their knees drawn up under their chin.

The heat in this unventilated cell was overpowering, but it was the stench that went beyond anything Farrow had ever experienced. The toilet hole cut in the floor constantly overflowed, and that smell combined with the body odors of the inmates caused the airmen to retch.

Of course the airmen themselves smelled no better. By now, after two months in captivity, their long matted hair was down past their shoulders, and their beards were down to their chests. Nor had they been allowed to shower or change clothes during those two months. Truly, they were not a pretty sight or scent, but their hygiene was the least of their worries at this point. They were struggling just to stay alive.

And of course everyone was suffering from dysentery.

They were fed two cups of wormy rice per day and two cups of unsweetened tea. At first, they very carefully picked the worms from their rice, but then one day Chase Nielsen said, "By God, I'm going to make it one way or another. I'm going to live, just to tell the world what these bastards have done to us. So if you fellows don't want your worms, give 'em to me. At least there's some fat on 'em."

Nielsen's words put a different light on things. From then on, the flyers ate the worms and whatever else they could find.

Bob Hite would later recall that the cell was crawling with roaches and houseflies. And the rats, he noted, were beyond description: "They were giant rats. They crawled around the cell like they owned the place. They'd crawl over our feet as though we weren't there. We were afraid to kill them, afraid they'd just lie there and rot, and then we'd have another stench to put up with."

The only bright spot in their present situation was the knowledge that the Japanese could do nothing to them that they had not already done. And so the flyers, in defiance of orders, talked openly to one another. When the guards screamed for silence through the tiny slot in the cell door, the flyers would laugh derisively, scream back at the guards, and go on talking.

On June 22 the other prisoners, both living and dead, were all removed from cell #6, and Farrow and his fellow Raiders were left to their own devices. They still had not been allowed to shave, shower, cut their long hair, or change clothes, so they presented a frightening appearance, even to each other. As for the Japanese, Bob Hite remembered that even high-ranking officers would stand for minutes at a time staring at these strange freaks through the opening in the cell door. They were especially fascinated by the giant six-four Bill Farrow.

Despite the unbearable heat, which sometimes reached over a hundred degrees, the men would stuff their pants cuffs into their socks, and button the necks and sleeves of their shirts to keep from being eaten alive by the crawling insects that infested the cell. At night they would take turns staying awake to fight off the giant rats that crawled into their cell through the toilet opening in the floor.

After a week in the Bridge House, Farrow and the others were beginning to congratulate themselves for having suffered no beatings or torture sessions since their arrival on June 19. And it was a good thing, for they were still nursing the terrible wounds they had received at the hands of the Kempei Tai in Tokyo. Their faces and bodies were still bruised black and blue from the beatings, and their hands were practically useless from having bamboo rods thrust back and forth between their knuckles. But through it all, they now had each other for comfort and support. To them the company of their fellow airmen was worth a mint.

It was then, on a terribly hot afternoon when tempers were running unusually high, that the feisty Bob Hite shook his fist and shouted an insult at a Japanese officer who was peeping in through the door slot. The enraged officer rushed into the cell and swung his scabbard at Hite's head, giving him a nasty gash on the forehead. Hite, undaunted, kicked at the officer, then reached forward and wrenched the scabbard from his hands. That reaction was poor judgment, for now the humiliated officer stood there, his naked Samurai sword gleaming in his hand, ready to plunge it into Hite's stomach.

The other airmen, terrified at this latest crisis, sat in stunned silence. All except Bill Farrow, the Darlington daredevil. An incredibly calm Farrow leaped forward from his sitting position against the wall, grabbed the officer from behind, pinning his arms to his sides. Then he roughly dragged him from the cell and slammed the door.

Time seemed to stand still as the dazed flyers stood in watchful silence for the officer to return. With that razor-sharp Samurai sword he could behead every flyer in that cell in less than a minute, and they had no doubt he would do it. Certainly he had enjoyed plenty of practice in Manchuria.

Minutes later, and still no Japanese soldiers, the Raiders relaxed their vigil and turned their attention to Bob Hite, his shirt now soaked in blood from his nasty head wound. Hite himself simply smiled and patted Bill Farrow on the shoulder. "Thanks," he said, "I think I owe you my life."

Years later, when this incident was related to Dr. John Wilson, a Darlington physician and a boyhood chum of Bill Farrow, he grinned and said, "That would have been typical of Bill. He was a very circumspect young man, yet a total daredevil. If anybody here ever had a problem, no matter how big that problem might be, he had only to tell Bill Farrow, and Farrow would stand by him till the end."

Following the incident with the Japanese officer, the men noticed that their guards seemed to become friendlier. Now, instead of screaming through the cell door opening, the guards would look in and smile. Perhaps they applauded the airmen's attack on a not very popular officer.

Now a lack of food was their biggest problem. Chase Nielsen would later recall that at this point the men had lost so much weight that one could easily count their ribs. "We thought about food," Nielsen said, "we talked about it, we dreamed about it, but we didn't eat it. We mentally planned the meals we would eat when we got out—big juicy steaks with plenty of pie and ice cream."

Then one day, to the men's surprise and delight, instead of their usual fare of rice and tea, big trays of food were passed through the hole in their cell door. They would later learn that the Shanghai Municipal Police, Englishmen mostly who were allowed to remain on duty in that international city to provide law and order among the civilian population, was behind it all. They would take up collections to purchase food for the English and American prisoners held by the Japanese.

Subsequently, for the next fourteen days, once a day, the men were treated to fresh corn, deviled eggs, fried beef, dessert, and hot coffee. It was not until years later that Hite, Nielsen, and the others learned who their great benefactors had been. They remain most appreciative.

This fare continued every day for the next two weeks, then it ceased just as suddenly as it had begun, causing the men's morale to sag once again.

Several weeks following the end of this godsend, as Farrow and his fellow airmen sat around pondering their ultimate fate, Farrow suddenly had a brainstorm. Could these guards be bribed with American money?

Strangely enough, Farrow and his fellow airmen had been allowed to keep the money Colonel Doolittle had issued to them before they began their flight to Japan. The Japanese had confiscated everything else—their watches, including the gold Bulova watch that Farrow's Aunt Margaret had given him for his twenty-first birthday in 1939, rings, and wallets—back when they were first captured, but had allowed them to keep their paper money.)

So there they were, ragged, dirty, half-starved, sitting in a jail cell in Shanghai, China, with approximately five hundred dollars in American money in their pockets. The men looked at one another and grinned. Heck, it was worth a try.

Two weeks later, a guard who spoke broken English agreed to see if he could exchange American dollars on the Shanghai black market. The men prayed that he would come through. And, finally, he did.

The men told the guard they wanted meat, sweets, haircuts, a bath, a shave, and clean clothes. Miracle of miracles, they received all they asked for. The food didn't last long, but the sweets and candy bars lasted them for weeks. Bob Hite later recalled the rest of their deliverance:

> I don't think any of us will ever forget the thrill of that first bath, the first in over 120 days. We were taken one at a time up to a fourth-floor hotel room and allowed to stay as long as we wanted. As I remember, I used a cake and a half of soap, and I don't remember a kinder feeling than the soothing, wet warmth of that tub. I changed the water two or three times, and still when I got out there was a thick scum on the top and the tub was black with lice.
>
> They clipped our beards that day, too, and shaved our heads. We got a change of clothes and felt like new men. That afternoon, we got the thing we had sought—a real feed. There was steak, fresh vegetables, strawberry jam, and French bread. The sheer joy of spreading that strawberry jam on that bread will remain with me always.

In the midst of their delight, just a few hours after their great repast, Dean Hallmark suddenly complained of stomach pains. His temperature shot up to dangerous levels, and he developed a terrible case of dysentery. He was overcome with bouts of vomiting during the night, and at one point fell headlong into the open toilet. The other airmen, now terribly alarmed, took turns looking after Hallmark throughout the night. By morning he couldn't stand. His joints ached, and he began to faint at frequent intervals.

Since there were no blankets in the cell, the other men made a pallet for him from their flight jackets. They took turns talking to him and trying to rouse him from his lethargy. But he got no better. Indeed, after three days of being practically comatose, Hallmark began to resemble a skeleton more than a man.

Hallmark would never recover from his strange illness.

By now it was August 28, a day the men would never forget. On this day they were taken from their cell and loaded in the back of a Japanese truck. A stretcher was brought for Hallmark, and Farrow and Hite carried the stretcher to the truck. Then they were driven to another jail, Kiangwan Military Prison, in the civic center area just outside the Shanghai city limits

Unknown to the airmen, they were to be the first Americans tried under a law just passed to cover their war crimes against the Japanese people. The Japanese Ministry of War had passed this law just the past week, and now it was to be applied *ex post facto*, after the fact or retroactively.

Indeed, more than a week earlier the military court had already reached both a verdict and a sentence for the downed Doolittle Raiders. Such war criminals, the military court decided, should definitely be taken out and executed.

The "confessions" the men had signed for the Kempei Tai back on June 15 had been studied by the Japanese minister of war. Some seven weeks later, on July 28, 1942, the vice minister of war, Heitaro Kimura, sent Military Secret Order No. 2190 to army headquarters in Tokyo directing that "[a]n enemy warplane crew who did not violate wartime international law, shall be treated as prisoners of war, and one who acted against the said law shall be punished as a wartime capital criminal."

This directive was immediately sent on to Gen. Sunao Ushiromiya, chief of staff of the Expeditionary Army in China.

General Ushiromiya then appended a memo to this directive (Staff Document No. 383-1) which proves that the fate of the eight American airmen had been decided long before they were placed on trial:

> In regard to Military Secret Order No. 2190 concerning the disposition of the captured enemy airmen, request that action be deferred (probably until the middle of August) pending

proclamation of the military law and its official announcement, and the scheduling of the date of execution of the American airmen.

This directive was referred to as the Enemy Airmen's Act. And it carried the following provisions:

This military law shall apply to all enemy airmen who raid the Japanese homeland, Manchukuo, and the Japanese zones of military occupations, and who come within the areas under the jurisdiction of the China Expeditionary Force.

Any individual who commits any or all of the following acts shall be subject to military punishment.

Sec. 1. This military law shall apply to all enemy airmen who raid the Japanese homeland, Manchukuo, and the Japanese zones of military operations, and who come within the areas under the jurisdiction of the China Expeditionary Force.

Sec. 2. The bombing, strafing or otherwise attacking of private properties whatsoever, with the objectives of destroying or damaging same.

Sec. 3. The bombing, strafing or otherwise attacking of objectives, other than those of military nature, except in those cases where such an act is unavoidable.

Sec. 4. In addition to those acts covered in the preceding three sections, all other acts violating the provisions of International Law governing warfare.

This law shall apply to those individuals who raid Japan proper, Manchukuo, and the Japanese zones of military occupation with the intent of committing such acts, and who prior to accomplishing their objective come within the jurisdiction of the China Expeditionary Force.

Art. III. Military punishment shall be the death penalty, provided however, should the circumstances warrant, this sentence may be commuted to life imprisonment, or a term of imprisonment for not less than ten years.

Art. IV. The death penalty shall be executed by a firing squad. Imprisonment shall be in confinement in a penitentiary for the term of sentence.

Art. V. Under extraordinary circumstances military punishment may be waived.

Art. VI. In regard to the imprisonment, in addition to the stipulation prescribed under this military law, the rules and regulations of penal law shall also apply. This military law shall be effective as of 13 August 1942.

This military law shall be applicable to all acts committed prior to the date of its approval.

Now, thanks to this latest law, which would be applied *ex post facto,* General Sugiyama and the Japanese High Command would be totally justified in executing those American flyers who had earlier participated in the raid on Japan. Revenge for Sugiyama, who had been humiliated before the emperor and the entire Japanese nation, would be sweet. He only wished that he could execute the flyers himself. Their deaths would be neither quick nor painless.

The flyers' trial itself was a mockery of justice, since the court judges had already decided that they were guilty of war crimes and that they should pay the ultimate penalty—death by firing squad. Now the court judges would simply go through the formality of hearing their cases.

Following the war Chase Nielsen, who was totally unforgiving in his attitude toward the airmen's Japanese captors, would write an article that appeared in newspapers across America, describing the trial during which he and his comrades were tried and convicted. Forced into a small room that would serve as their courtroom, the Americans were shoved before five officers seated behind a table on a dais. The prisoners were all in horrible physical condition, but Dean Hallmark was so weak that he had to be carried into the courtroom on a stretcher, oblivious to the flies that buzzed about him.

As the ailing soldiers were coldly scrutinized by guards, officers, and the five judges, George Barr grew so weak he was unable to stand and "keeled over." Though he was given a chair to sit on, the rest of the men were forced to remain standing. However, they somehow managed to stay on their swaying feet while the room swam in front of their eyes.

The chief judge, a bald man with glasses on the end of his nose, began a long recitation in Japanese. No one bothered to interpret for the American soldiers. When the judge finished, someone stepped forward from the side of the room and in English told the men to provide a brief history of their lives, starting with high school. Each man, except Hallmark, mumbled something about his life, but their voices were so low and weak that they had to repeat their stories many times. As none of the Japanese wrote anything down, what the men said obviously was unimportant to the judges. While the interpreter translated the words of the men, the judges simply stared.

Nielsen relates, "I don't know what they expected from us, but most of us told the truth about ourselves until we got to our military service. We double-talked and lied but it didn't seem to make any difference. The judges were obviously disinterested and couldn't have cared less." They were never questioned about their roles in the raid.

After the seven prisoners had provided their histories, the judge read in Japanese a long statement—the verdict and corresponding sentences. Nielsen had no illusions about the verdict reached, but he did ask about the sentencing. The interpreter "only smirked and said the judge had ordered that we not be told."

Farrow and his fellow airmen were then led outside to an adjoining building where they were placed in single cells. Hallmark was taken back to the Bridge House where he was thrown back into cell #6 along with twenty Chinese prisoners. His condition continued to worsen, but the Japanese paid no attention to him. He just lay there, slowly dying.

There at Kiangwan Military Prison, Farrow and his comrades were kept in solitary confinement for a period of twenty long, mind-numbing days, until September 7, 1942. During that time Bill Farrow saw not another living soul, except when the Japanese guards came by three times a day to bring his meals—a glob of dirty rice and a cup of unsweetened tea.

Thus lying on the filthy cement floor, he saw no one, he spoke to no one, and he heard not another human voice. Indeed, to pass the time he could only stare at the whitewashed walls or try to sleep. Likely, he often times prayed that God would deliver him and his comrades out of bondage—if it was God's will. Certainly he must have thought of Lib Sims and tried to imagine just what she might be doing at that very moment. Was she teaching school? Was she still living in Columbia? Did she ever think of him?

And his mother. It broke his heart to think of what his mother must be going through.

He doubtlessly spent much time recalling the events of his past life, and trying to trace the strange links in that chain of cause and effect that had led him from his wonderful home in Darlington to this hellhole halfway around the world.

How strange, how incredibly strange, that he, Bill Farrow, a quiet, country boy who would walk a mile out of his way to avoid trouble, should somehow wind up a star player in this most unlikely drama, a wild adventure story set in Shanghai, China, of all places. It was all just too bizarre. Certainly his story would never sell as fiction. No one would believe it.

He was a young man of a deeply philosophical nature with an IQ of 140, who had found high school and college a breeze. Such being the case, he now felt that if he really set his mind to it, if he truly concentrated, he could somehow find a path through that dark maze set before him. He could somehow separate the numerous strands of that intricate knot known as destiny. He could somehow derive an answer to those overwhelming questions: Just what am I doing here? How did I get here? Why am I here?

Was it fate? Destiny? Predestination? God? Or a combination of all four? Perhaps God, that ultimate determining force, had preordained that his feet would follow this path, that he would be led to make those choices that had guided him to this fate and destiny. But why had God done so? For that, no amount of concentration could furnish him an answer.

On August 7, after twenty days in solitary confinement, Farrow and his fellow airmen were finally allowed out of their cells, one at a time, to exercise for thirty minutes per day. It wasn't much, but after endless days staring at those four blank walls, just to walk outside and see the blue sky and bright sunshine was a blessing beyond description.

On September 24, it occurred to Farrow that it was his birthday. Today he was twenty-four years old. He took some comfort in knowing that on this day of all days his loved ones would surely be thinking of him. Then he remembered the big birthday party held for him by his relatives at the McFall Hotel in Darlington back on September 24, 1941. Was that only one year ago? How happy they had all been. His future back then had appeared so bright and promising. But now, sitting alone in his grim cell, his past life was nothing more than a dream, like something that had happened to someone else in a previous life. His only reality now was hardship and starvation suffered at the hands of people who hated him.

Once their trial ended, Col. Toyama Nakajo, the chief judge, signed the trial record which stated that Farrow and the others "have been found guilty as charged, and are hereby sentenced to death."

But then, on October 10, 1942, the chief of the Imperial General Staff sent the following telegram to the commanding general of the China Expeditionary Force:

> THE VERDICT BY THE MILITARY TRIBUNAL CONCERN-
> ING THE PUNISHMENT OF THE AMERICAN AIRMEN
> WHO RAIDED THE JAPANESE HOMELAND IS CONSID-
> ERED TO BE FAIR AND JUST.
> HOWEVER, UPON REVIEW WE BELIEVE THAT WITH
> THE EXCEPTION OF BOTH PILOTS AND THE GUNNER
> SPATZ, THE DEATH SENTENCE SHOULD BE COMMUTED.
> IT IS RECOMMENDED THAT THE DEATH SENTENCES OF
> THE MEN BE COMMUTED TO LIFE IMPRISONMENT.

A telegram from General Sugiyama accompanied the above message in which he directed that the executions of Bill Farrow, Dean Hallmark, and Harold Spatz should be carried out on October 15, 1942. It further stipulated that the other five prisoners were declared war criminals and should receive no considerations as prisoners of war.

And all this was based on the false statements the Kempei Tai had forced the American airmen to sign in Toyko back in June 1942.

Once the directive from headquarters ordering the executions of Farrow, Hallmark, and Spatz had been received, the Japanese military had only to obey that directive. Thus, on the afternoon of October 14, Dean Hallmark was returned to Kiangwan Military Prison and placed in a cell. By some miracle, he had recovered somewhat from his previous condition, or at least he was conscious.

Later that evening, Farrow, Hallmark, and Spatz were taken one at a time to a large storeroom and seated at a long desk. A Japanese officer informed them that they had been sentenced to death and would be executed the following day. They were then given sheets of paper and pencils and introduced to an interpreter, a Portuguese-Japanese named Caesar Luis dos Remedios. He informed the Americans that they could write last letters to friends and relatives back in America and that the International Red Cross would see that those letters were delivered.

Following the war, during the War Crimes Trial of 1946, Remedios described this grim scene for American authorities:

> On October 14, 1942, I was instructed by Captain Sotojiro Tatsuta, the prison warden, to have Lt. Farrow, Lt. Hallmark, and Sgt. Spatz sign their names on two blank sheets of white paper. One page was signed by each of them in the middle of the sheet, and the other page was signed by each at the bottom. They asked me why they were made to sign these papers. Captain Tatsuta told me that they were signing these as a receipt for their belongings and that he would fill the rest in Japanese later on.
>
> Later Tatsuta gave each two sheets of paper, one on which to write a letter to their family, which he said he would send through the Red Cross; and the other sheet was to be used to describe the treatment they received from the Japanese while they were confined. At that time I didn't know what the Japanese were going to do with these three airmen. The fliers asked me what they should write. My opinion was to give a little "top hat" for the Japanese, so that they would be given good treatment later on. I didn't read the letters, but gave them to Captain Tatsuta early the next morning.

One can only imagine the mental agony Farrow and his comrades must have endured at that time, knowing for a fact that their lives would be blotted out so senselessly the next day. One at a time, the three of them sat down and wrote poignant last letters home to their loved ones.

Harold Spatz, who had just turned twenty and was therefore not even old enough to vote back home, wrote a brief note to his widowed father back in Lebo, Kansas:

> I don't own anything except my clothes. These I leave to you. I want you to know, Dad, that I died fighting for my country like a soldier.

He also wrote brief notes to both his brother, Robert, Jr., and to his girlfriend. To his sister, Reba, he wrote:

I will say my last goodbye to you and may you live a happy life and God bless you.

As for Dean "Jungle Jim" Hallmark, he was as feisty as ever despite his illness, and his bitterness shows through his last letter to his mother, father, and sister back in Dallas:

> I hardly know what to say. They have just told me that I am liable to execution. I can hardly believe it. I am a prisoner of war and I thought I would be taken care of until the end of the war. I did everything the Japanese asked me to do and tried to cooperate with them because I knew that my part in the war was over.
>
> I have a heart and I didn't ever want anyone to die because of me, so that is why I always have been against war. I wish there was some way that war could be avoided and peace be everlasting in the world. I had wanted to become a commercial pilot and would have if it hadn't been for this war.
>
> As for you, Mother, try to stand up under this and pray.

Bill Farrow, to whom deep thinking and good writing came almost without effort, sat down at the long table, picked up his pencil, and decided he would write four letters home: one to his old friend from his Pendleton Field days, Ivan Ferguson; one to his Aunt Margaret; one to his mother Jessie Stem Farrow; and, finally, one to the great love of his life, Lib Sims.

At that point, despite the emotional turmoil raging within him, despite knowing that he was on the eve of a violent death, he began to write. Shortly thereafter he composed the following heart-rending letters, final messages that reflect his concern not with himself but with the people he loved, the people he was leaving behind. To Ivan Ferguson, his old friend from Camp Pendleton, he wrote:

> Dear Ivan:
>
> Hello, old boy. How's life treating you? You have certainly been my best friend, with whom I have shared some of the richest experiences of my life.
>
> Remember those days at Kelly Field with Rose, R. B. Brown and the rest? Those were the days, weren't they? Please remember me to Brown and Angela. Theirs was the best marriage of two young folks that I know. Let's hope they will be together again to enjoy such complete happiness as they had with each other.

I can see their Christmas together at Pendleton—the little tree and the fun we had in the snow and what we said about a place full of so much that is good and beautiful and what it's worth to us. And Crater Lake, Oregon Coves, and the giant sequoias, the Golden Gate. How splendid they were. And the thrill of flying. That we experienced together, too. It was the most wonderful part of my career.

So keep 'em flying, Fergie, and remember me to all the guys in the squadron.

Please write to my mother. She will need your sympathy.

Best luck, pal.

Then, to his Aunt Margaret, who had given him her unstinting support during his early years, he wrote:

Well, here we've come to a parting of the ways for the present. But you have helped give me faith to go forward with a steadfast heart, and I've built my house upon a rock. That we will meet again, I am sure, that I have failed to carry forward your ideal for me I am sorry.

You told me once you wanted me to complete the good life that you started, as a missionary, that you wanted me to do good through Christian ideals; well, unfortunately, I'm unable to do so. However, you have done and are doing so much good—keep up the good work, and all will be right in the end.

You have always been an inspiration to me—you, Pee Wee, and Aunt Mary. I am thankful for having known and loved you all.

Remember me to the folks in Darlington. There are so many fine ones.

So goodbye to you all. I am sorry it had to happen this way. Chin up, and help Mom, will you?

Then he paused. Next he would write a special letter to his mother and one to Lib Sims.

Dearest Mother,

Here's wishing Marge, all the family, and Lib a most happy future. Please carry on for me, and don't let this get you down. Just remember that God will make everything right and that I will see you all again in the hereafter.

We've had some good times together, all of us. Life has

treated us well as a whole and we have much to be thankful for. You are, all of you, splendid Christians and knowing you and loving you has meant much in my life. So for me, and for America, be brave and live a full rich life, pray to God, and do your best.

So, to you Mother for sacrificing so much in making me, I hope, a fine son; to you, Aunt Marge, for helping me through school and holding up a fine ideal to me; to you, Aunt Mary, for being so very helpful and understanding of me; to you, Uncle Fred, for being like another father to me, like taking me hunting, and Uncle Mac [McFall] for helping Mother and me, looking after us; to Pie and Bess, for sincere interest and help; to Pep and Nancy for two fine friends; to Helen and Ivan Ferguson, for my two best friends with whom I have shared some swell times; to Mimi, for being a good cousin to me; and to Lib, for bringing to my life a deep rich love for a fine girl—to each of you I give my most heart-felt thanks—may God treat you kindly and reward you all richly.

Goodbye and thanks again to each of you.

I know, Mom, that this is going to hit you hard because I was the biggest thing in your life. I am sorry not to have treated you with more love and devotion, for not giving you all that I could and will you please forgive me? It is usually too late that we realize these things. If I only could in many small ways have made your life more rich and full, how thankful I would be.

You have given so much, so much more to me than I have returned, but such is the Christian way. Let me say this, that you are, I realize now, the best mother in the world, that your every action was bent towards making me happy, that you are, and always will be, an angel.

So let me implore you to keep your chin up. Be brave and strong for my sake. I love you, Mom, from the depths of a full heart.

Your son,
Bill

P.S. My insurance policy is in my bag that was in the small tent at Columbia. Read "Thanatopsis" by Bryant if you want to know how I'm taking this. My faith in God is complete, so I am unafraid.

As Farrow finished his letter, the words of William Cullen Bryant's "Thanatopsis" echoed in his mind:

> So live, that when thy summons comes to join
> The innumerable caravan which moves
> To that mysterious realm, where each shall take
> His chamber in the silent halls of death,
> Thou go not like the quarry-slave at night
> Scourged to his dungeon, but sustained and soothed
> By an unfaltering trust, approach thy grave
> Like one who wraps the drapery of his couch
> About him, and lies down to pleasant dreams.

Following this heartbreaking letter to his mother, Farrow then took a deep breath and began composing what was doubtlessly the saddest message of his young life, his final letter to his fiancée, Lib Sims, who was living a life of dark worry back in Columbia, South Carolina. Little did Farrow know that it would be another three years before Lib Sims, his mother, his Aunt Margaret, or anyone else back home would even be made aware that the Japanese had executed him on October 15, 1942. This was a matter that the Japanese kept beneath a veil of the deepest secrecy, afraid of world opinion should their cruelty be made public.

Certainly they did not notify the United States War Department of the executions, and Farrow's mother knew only what the War Department knew, and that was very little. Her son was a prisoner of the Imperial Japanese Army and would doubtlessly remain so for the duration of the war.

To Lib Sims, Farrow wrote:

> Dearest Lib:
>
> To me you are the only girl who would have meant the completion of my life. It is a pity we were born in this day and age. At least we had part of that happiness.
>
> I go over each time we were together with each other, the lovely nights at your home before the open fireplace; the never-to-be-forgotten weekend spent at Caroline's together; the walks in the woods, enjoying the fresh air and the smell of growing things; all these times were the greatest pleasure to me.

Please write and comfort Mom for she will need you—she loves you and thinks you a fine girl. Give my best to your mother.

Find yourself the good man you deserve, Lib, because you have so much to give the right one.

Goodbye and may God be with you.

In these simple yet eloquent words young Farrow confirmed his faith, his patriotism, and his deep love for those dearest to him. Indeed, these last letters attest to the fact that he was far more concerned with how his death would affect his loved ones than with how death would prove the end of Bill Farrow.

Despite Japanese promises that these letters would be turned over to the Red Cross for immediate delivery to the condemned flyers' loved ones, such was not to be. In fact, American authorities discovered these last letters on file in the Japanese War Ministry Building in September of 1945. They had been placed together in a neat stack, bound together with string, and labeled *Top Secret*. They were immediately delivered to their intended recipients, almost three years after the fact.

How Farrow, Hallmark, and Spatz spent their final hours from midnight until three the next afternoon, a period of some sixteen hours, in their filthy cell, the world will never know. Likely, knowing Bill Farrow's philosophical bent, he must have pondered why his life was ending so senselessly. All his fine dreams and his great plans for the future now lay shattered before him. He must have remembered all the wonderful training he had received at the hands of his mother and his Aunt Margaret, and the teachings he had received at church and school, and wondered why it had all led to this one senseless moment in time. Why had God allowed him to strive and struggle for excellence throughout his life, only to have it end so senselessly here?

Still, it seems reasonable that he found solace in prayer. It was God's way, he likely told himself. Truly, he did not understand, but he knew that God often worked in strange ways, and he trusted God's judgment. On this night of all nights, his faith became his only salvation, his belief in God his only comfort.

He and Harold Spatz noted that Dean Hallmark, the heroic pilot of the *Green Hornet*, was only semi-conscious and far too ill to understand that he was now living his final hours on earth. As for Harold Spatz, the gunner aboard Farrow's plane, the *Bat Out of Hell,* he was little more than a boy, having turned twenty only weeks before. Back home in Lebo, Kansas, he was still too young to vote. But now, here in this miserable Japanese prison, he was coping with his impending death in a most stoic and admirable manner.

At twenty-four, Bill Farrow was four years Spatz's senior and college educated. Truly, Spatz admired the older and better-educated officer and trusted his word in all matters, including religion. He knew that Farrow was deeply devoted to his Southern Baptist faith, and had even carried a small Bible in his jacket pocket until it was discovered and confiscated by a cruel Japanese guard.

And now, as they lay side by side on that cold cement floor on that dreary October afternoon, it seems likely that young Spatz might have whiled away his final hours discussing the meaning of death. Possibly he might have asked Farrow what it would be like at the moment those big slugs splattered their brains.

"But Lieutenant, at the very second that those Jap bullets crash into our heads, what will it be like? I mean, how long will it take us to pass from life into death? And how painful will it be?"

Farrow desperately searched his memory in hopes of coming up with satisfactory answers to Spatz's questions, questions that he had already asked himself a thousand times. More than anything he wanted to put Spatz's mind at ease as they awaited the arrival of their Japanese guards.

Finally, he may have simply repeated what he had always been taught by his own mother. "Harold, take my word for it, less than a second will pass between life and death. But Christians don't call it death. We call it everlasting life. In other words, if you believe in Jesus, that Jesus is our Lord and Savior, then there will be no death. We just pass from our brief life here on earth to an everlasting life with God in heaven."

"And you're convinced that there really is a God? Are you sure?"

Farrow forced himself to speak with authority. "I know there is a God, Harold. I am as convinced of it as I am that you and I are lying here on this floor at this very moment. I have no doubts, and you don't need to doubt either. Just put your mind at ease."

"But if there is a God, then why does He let terrible things happen to people like us? We're Americans, and we've never harmed anyone. Why would God let us come to such a sad ending?"

Farrow shook his head. "That I can't answer, Harold. Just believe that God has a master plan for all of us. We don't know what His plan is or where we fit into that plan. But believe me, there is a reason for everything He does."

"And what about heaven? You really believe we'll go to heaven when we die?"

"No doubt whatsoever, Harold, no doubt whatsoever. You know God's Son, Jesus Christ, died on the cross so that we can all go to heaven. Do you accept Jesus as your Lord and Savior?"

"I do now, Lieutenant. I haven't always felt that way, mainly because I didn't know anything about Jesus. But now I believe everything you've told me. I do believe in Jesus."

"Then believe that you'll pass from life on this earth to an everlasting life in less than a second." Farrow snapped his fingers. "Just like that. Just that fast. You have nothing to fear."

Spatz sighed and nodded his head. "And what will heaven be like, do you think? We won't really have wings and fly around like a flock of birds, will we?"

"No, I don't think so, Harold. I think we'll look very much as we do here on earth. But in heaven we'll be reunited with all our loved ones who've gone on before us. I think it'll be a wonderful time. And it'll last forever and ever. There'll be no sadness, no troubles in heaven, and we'll live forever and ever."

"My mom died when I was little, but I've never forgotten her."

"And I know she's never forgotten you either. In fact, I'll bet she's waiting to see you right now. It's like she's looking down from heaven, and she knows what's going on down here right now."

In such a way Farrow, Spatz, and Hallmark could have passed their final hours in that small grim cell. Then at precisely 3:30 P.M., they were startled as their cell door was suddenly kicked open and four Japanese guards stormed noisily inside. Farrow and Spatz were hauled to their feet, handcuffed, blindfolded, and roughly shoved from their cell. As for the semi-conscious Dean Hallmark, he was rolled onto a stretcher and carried out to a truck waiting just outside the prison's front entrance. Farrow and Spatz placed their feet upon the truck's rear bumper and attempted to lift themselves aboard, but they moved too slowly for the guards who prodded the emaciated prisoners with the sharp tips of their bayonets. Yes, they bled a little. But what did it matter? They were facing immediate execution anyway.

Back home in Columbia, South Carolina, it was now Thursday, October 15, a pleasant autumn afternoon, and those who sat down and opened *The State* newspaper while having lunch that day found plenty of news concerning America's advances on all fronts. The legendary German general, Field Marshal Erwin Rommel, known as the Desert Fox, was on the run in North Africa, and the Japanese offensive in the Pacific, so successful earlier in the war, had now ground to a halt.

Then, flipping over to the sports section, citizens could read that the Carolina Gamecocks and the Clemson Tigers had open dates on the upcoming Saturday as they prepared to battle each other on Big Thursday, October 22, during State Fair Week. Carolina had lost to West Virginia 13-0 the previous Saturday, while Clemson had lost to Boston College 14-7. So fans from both institutions felt they had something to prove come Big Thursday.

As for entertainment, Columbians could drive downtown to the Carolina Theater that evening and pay forty cents to watch Lionel Barrymore and Donna Reed star in *Calling Doctor Gillespie.* Or, should they prefer something a little lighter, they could attend the 5-Points Theater where Mickey Rooney and Judy Garland were delighting audiences in *The Courtship of Andy Hardy.*

As for lunch  the next day, Columbians could visit Walgreen's drugstore where, for forty-five cents, they could get sugar-cured ham, candied yams, corn, applesauce, rolls, and coffee. A lot to pay for lunch, yes. But what the heck, you only live once, and with this darned war going on . . .

All in all, it looked like a great week for Columbians.

Halfway around the world, however, in Shanghai's Kiangway Military Prison, Bill Farrow, Dean Hallmark, and Harold Spatz were facing the darkest moments of their young lives.

The morning of October 15, 1942, dawned cloudy and cold. But at first light the Japanese began making preparations for the executions that would take place at Public Cemetery No. 1 near Kiangwan Airdrome, north of Shanghai, at 4:30 that afternoon. Japanese soldiers were dispatched there to cut the grass and set up a long table to be used as a ceremonial altar for the Japanese officers who would officiate during the execution ceremony. These officers were Knights of the Bushido, and everything had to be carried out according to traditions begun a thousand years earlier.

Sergeant Tomoicha Yoneya was responsible for erecting three small crosses some thirty feet to the front of the long table. There the condemned airmen would be bound to the crosses, blindfolded, and then shot by the firing squad. Sergeant Yoneya also brought three rough wooden caskets in which the bodies of the airmen would be placed following their executions.

At precisely four o'clock that afternoon Farrow, Spatz, and Hallmark arrived at the cemetery. They were then pulled from the truck, their bodies shaking with fear and anxiety. Farrow and Spatz shot quick glances at one another. Perhaps if they bolted they could make their way out of the cemetery and outrun their captors in a mad dash for freedom. But that was a vain thought, and they knew it. After six months of starvation and cruel tortures they were so weak that they could hardly stand. There was no way they could run away or attempt any sort of escape. Besides, where would they go?

Maybe this was only another fake execution. But no, Farrow's intuition told him this was the real thing, that an hour from now he would be as dead as he would ever be. His thoughts raced back home, halfway around the world, to his mother, Jesse Stem Farrow, and his fiancée, Lib Sims. He knew now that he would never see them again. Not on this earth anyway. He silently prayed that the Japanese would send home the last letters he had written the previous night. At least his family and friends would know what had happened to him and where his body was located. At this point, that was all he could hope for.

Suddenly an unusually tall Japanese officer gave a command, and the guards took the prisoners by the arm and led them up a small hill to the three crosses in the execution area. Each American was halted before a cross and forced to kneel down.

Farrow's place was the middle cross, between Spatz and Hallmark. The guards tied their wrists to the crossbars, then looped a length of rope around their necks to keep their heads in an upright position.

At the War Crimes Trial held in Shanghai in March of 1946, Sgt. Shigetsu Mayama testified that he helped tie the three Americans to their crosses. Then a white cloth was wound around each Raider's head. A black spot was dabbed in the middle of their foreheads.

While this was being done, a nine-man firing squad under the command of Lt. Goro Tashida arrived on the scene. They were armed with high-powered military rifles. He posted three of the men around the area as security guards and then marched the other six into a double rank about twenty feet in front of the Americans.

Three of the Japanese knelt there, while the other three stood behind them. Those kneeling would be the primary executioners, but should they miss or have a misfire, the men standing to their rear would fire.

At this point, with thunder appropriately rumbling overhead, four Japanese officers, the Knights of the Bushido, arrived and took their places behind the long table. There was also present a medical officer and an interpreter. Captain Sotojiro Tatsuta, the prison warden, took his place to the rear of the table. Major Itsuro Hata, who had prosecuted the airmen at their mock trial, lit incense on the altar-like table, and the Japanese officers all removed their caps and bowed their heads in prayer.

Major Hata read a statement condemning the men to death, which was interpreted. Then he made a deep bow and turned to the prison warden, Captain Tatsuta, and motioned for him to come forward and say a few words. During the War Crimes Trial, Tatsuta would offer the following testimony about his part in the execution:

> I told the flyers, "I do not know what relation I had with you in the previous life but we have been living together under the same roof and on this day you are going to be executed, but I feel sorry for you. Your lives were very short but your names will remain everlastingly." I do not remember if this was Lieutenant

*The very grim Public Cemetery No. 1 on the outskirts of Shanghai where the three American airmen were so brutally executed on the afternoon of October 15, 1942. Here, Hallmark, Farrow, and Spatz were bound to the three small crosses erected for that purpose, and then shot. This image was photographed by American authorities at war's end and used as evidence at the War Crimes Trial of 1946.* (Photo courtesy of the U.S. Army Archives)

Farrow but one of them said, "Thank you very much for all the trouble you have taken while we were in your confinement, but please tell the folks at home that we died very bravely." And I told them, "Your ashes will be sent through the International Red Cross to your homes."

I told them that Christ was born and died on the cross and you on your part must die on the cross but when you are executed—when you die on the cross you will be honored as Gods, and I told them to pray and they made a sign which resembled the sign of the cross and they prayed. I told them "You will soon be bound to the crosses and when this is done it is a fact that it is a form that man's faith and cross shall be united. Therefore, have faith." Then they smiled and said they understood very well. Then I asked them if they had any more to say and they said they had nothing more to say.

Then, at a signal from Major Hata, Captain Tatsuta approached the kneeling airmen and told them, as he would later testify at the War Crimes Trial, "You have lived as heroes. Now it is time to die as heroes."

At that point, testified Tatsuta, Farrow raised his eyes to the warden and said, "Captain, would you see to it that our loved ones back home are told that we died bravely?"

"And I am happy to state," concluded Tatsuta to the court, "that they all met death as only true warriors can do."

Then Lieutenant Tashida called his firing squad to attention. As for Bill Farrow, it seems most likely that he followed his strong spiritual inclinations at this point and began to pray—not only for himself but for his comrades as well.

Very possibly he spoke aloud to young Harold Spatz: "Pray with me, Harold. Our Father which art in heaven . . ."

Spatz joined his leader in prayer.

"Face the target!" Tashida commanded. The six Japanese soldiers turned to face the American airmen.

"Thy kindgom come, Thy will be done. . . ."

Tashida withdrew his saber. "Prepare!" he shouted, and the three kneeling soldiers in the front rank raised their rifles, snapped the bolts in place, and took aim at the black spots on the blindfolds.

Tashida raised his arm.

". . . and forgive us our trespasses, as we forgive those who trespass against us. . . ."

In the tradition of the Bushido, Tashida paused and waited until Farrow had finished his prayer. At last he heard the word "Amen," and his arm snapped down.

"Fire!"

There was an ear-splitting explosion, and the heads of the three airmen snapped back simultaneously as the heavy slugs smashed into their skulls. Then their bodies slumped forward, hanging by the ropes from the crosses. Blood gushed from their head wounds to the ground. Obviously no second shots would be necessary.

Whatever dreams and ambitions young Bill Farrow might have had ended at that moment.

The Japanese medical officer stepped forward and after a brief examination verified that the airmen were indeed dead.

Lieutenant Tashida called the firing squad to attention, then marched them away. Other Japanese soldiers loosed the airmen's bodies from their crosses and placed them in the crude wooden coffins. They were then carried to the long table where the incense was burning. There, the Japanese officers, in the tradition of the Bushido, stood with eyes closed, praying for the spirits of the departed airmen. Then they bowed low, replaced their caps, and departed.

The whole procedure had taken only thirty minutes. At last the Japanese High Command had exacted their revenge.

The bodies of the airmen were then placed in a truck and taken to Shanghai, to the Japanese Resident's Association Crematorium, and immediately cremated. The ashes were placed in small boxes, which were tagged and brought back to the waiting room outside the main office of Kiangwan Prison.

Later, again in the tradition of the Bushido, the airmen's ashes were taken to the prison chapel and placed on an altar. Incense burners were lit and placed in front of them.

The airmen had been promised that their ashes, along with the letters written on the eve of their executions, would be sent home via the International Red Cross. But in point of fact, almost three years would elapse before American authorities would discover the urns containing their ashes at the International Funeral Home in downtown Shanghai. They had been hidden there by Japanese warlords who feared reprisals from American investigators, and now American authorities found them simply by accident.

Now, too, their final letters home were at last delivered.

It was then, for the first time, that anyone learned the fate of Farrow, Hallmark, and Spatz. Indeed, throughout these long months during the war, their families had continued to write them letters, to send them packages through the Red Cross, and to pray for their safe return. And even their fellow airmen, though they entertained deep suspicions, would not learn of the executions until August of 1945. The Japanese had kept their revenge a heavily guarded secret.

Indeed, Chase Nielsen would later write that on October 16, the day following the sudden disappearance of Farrow, Hallmark, and Spatz, the other airmen were marched into the courtroom at the prison and told that their lives had been spared, thanks to the tender mercy of Emperor Hirohito. Now, instead of being shot, they would serve life in prison. They were then allowed to shower and shave, and the prison barber cut their hair, and they were given clean clothing, which was a great boost to their morale.

Then, to their total surprise, they were marched back to a cell and their belongings were returned to them, belongings they had not seen in months. They noticed that the flight jackets and personal effects of Farrow, Hallmark, and Spatz were among the belongings, and the others wondered where their three companions might be. Where were they? What had happened to them?

Bob Hite would later recall, "It was obvious to each of us that they had been killed, but we didn't dare let each other down. In the few minutes we had together we managed to whisper some theories as to what had happened to them without mentioning our greatest fears. We all knew in our hearts they were gone, but we knew it didn't help our morale a bit to admit it."

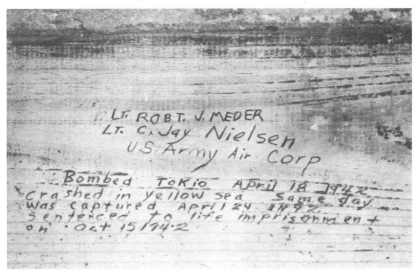

*On October 15, 1942, hours following the executions of Farrow, Spatz, and Hallmark, Chase Nielsen suspected that he and the others would also be taken out and murdered. Yet he wanted to leave some record that they had once been imprisoned there. Thus he took a nail and scratched his name and Bob Meder's on a section of his cell floor. Following the war, American authorities took this piece of flooring and used it as evidence during the Japanese War Crime Trials of 1946. (Photo courtesy of the U.S. Army Archives)*

*On January 19, 1949, last rites were conducted for Lieutenants Bob Meder, Dean Hallmark, and Bill Farrow at Arlington National Cemetery. Corporal Harold Spatz's remains are interred in the National Cemetery in Hawaii.* (Photo courtesy of the U.S. Army Archives)

They were indeed gone, executed senselessly and without reason, their young lives snuffed out long before their time. Indeed, had they managed to survive those terrible years in a Japanese prison, they could very well be alive today.

The war had been over for four long years before the remains of Farrow, Spatz, and Hallmark were returned to the United States. Then, on January 19, 1949, a bitterly cold day in Washington, DC, grieving parents and friends of the fallen airmen were all in attendance when services were conducted at Arlington National Cemetery.

Another great tribute was paid to Farrow in the fall of 1955 when the Air Force ROTC unit at his beloved University of South Carolina was officially named the William Glover Farrow Air Force ROTC Squadron.

A month later homage was again paid to Farrow when James. H. McKinney, writing in the February 1955 issue of *Veterans Magazine*, quoted Farrow's creed that had received so much publicity back in 1943, and then went on to say:

> Bill Farrow was following his creed when he volunteered for the unknown suicide mission which became the Tokyo raid. That

creed was fulfilled when his bombardier cried "Bombs away."
Bill Farrow then had completed his life's mission.

There is no medal high enough to cover Bill Farrow's gift to
America in the form of his creed, which his life and death
proved to be a worthy guide for any man.

His life and his creed serve as a model for any American. The
victory was won by men who followed Bill Farrow's self-proven
creed for victory. Now that creed can become a creed for everlasting peace.

Truly, we can only wonder what Bill Farrow, that magnificent
young man, might have done with his life had he survived the
war. Through constant struggle and hard work, he somehow over-
came the Great Depression and poverty and went on to become
an excellent student at the University of South Carolina, and
then finally he earned the the gold bar of a second lieutenant in
the United States Army Air Corps and the silver wings of an Air
Corps pilot. His future seemed assured. But at approximately
4:30 P.M. on Thursday, October 15, 1942, a Japanese officer yelled
"Fire," and Farrow's dreams, his aspirations and ambitions, whatever they might have been, vanished in an instant.

Today we have only his memory, a memory of one of the
greatest heroes ever to wear the uniform of the U.S. Army.

# Epilogue

Following the executions of Bill Farrow, Dean Hallmark, and Harold Spatz, the surviving five captured airmen—Bob Hite, Jake DeShazer, George Barr, Chase Nielsen, and Bob Meder—tried to get on as best they could with their miserable lives. As they had for the past six months, they struggled each day simply to stay alive. Pain and fear were their constant companions

They remained at Kiangwan Prison for another six months, until April 17, 1943. On that day they were awakened before daylight, then handcuffed, blindfolded, and led outside the prison to a waiting truck. By then spring was in the air, but the Raiders were in no mood for smelling roses.

They were only too aware that the next day would be the one-year anniversary of their famous raid on Japan, and they feared that the Japanese might be planning to execute them as a special anniversary gift to General Sugiyama. But such was not to be. The emperor had spoken, and now these poor unfortunates, these so-called war criminals, would spend the rest of their miserable lives in a Japanese prison.

They had spent many months of captivity at Kiangwan, and certainly they did not wish to begin life all over again in a new prison. Indeed, by that time they had gotten to know many of the guards at Kiangwan and were beginning to receive fairly humane treatment. Now, as their truck roared down the highway, they looked forward to their new home in Nanking with a great deal of trepidation. And it was well deserved.

Back home in Darlington, Bill Farrow's Aunt Margaret Stem sat listening to the news on her radio. It was April 12, 1943, and President Roosevelt was due to make a public address at noon. His words would shatter not only her life but the lives of all those who loved Bill Farrow. For within minutes Roosevelt would announce that the Japanese had executed several members of Doolittle's Raiders:

> Almost a year ago, the crews of two American bombers were captured by the Japanese. On October 19, 1942, this government learned from Japanese radio broadcasts of the capture, trial and severe punishment of those Americans. It was not until March 12, 1943, that the American Government received the communication given by the Japanese Government stating that these Americans had in fact been tried and the death penalty had been pronounced against them. It was further stated that the death penalty was commuted for some but that the sentence of death had been applied to others.

Margaret began weeping uncontrollably when she heard the news. No one had to explain the implications to her. Bill had been the pilot and in command of his plane. Thus it only made sense that the Japanese would have executed him if they were going to execute anyone.

Margaret's elderly mother who had also listened to the broadcast, patted her arm in an attempt to console her. "It's true," her mother said, "and you might as well accept it now. At least we know that Bill is at peace."

Later Margaret would write, "Yes, she was right—it was better to know, so we could not picture all kinds of torture for him. The death knell had rung, and even though our hearts bled, it was a relief in a way. Bill was the pilot, and certainly he stood in line for death."

In Washington, DC, Bill's mother was devastated by news of her son's very possible execution. She seemed to hold up well when in the presence of others, but in the loneliness of her solitary room, she suffered the agony of the damned. Almost immediately she phoned Margaret and asked her to please come up for a few days so that they could try and reason things out. Margaret would later recall:

I went to be with her for a short while. Jessie and I sat and talked in my little basement room there at her boarding place. We had much to say about what happened and about Bill. We had a devotional period, reading passages from "The Upper Room" and prayer. The writer for the day, to whom I will always be grateful, wrote that God did answer Jesus' prayer in Gethsemane by giving Him strength to carry through His mission, and that God was with all mothers' sons who had gone off into unknown lands to sacrifice, if need arose, their very lives in the cause of right and freedom.

Later, though still racked by sorrow, Jessie did manage to come to grips with her grief, as parents all over the world have done since time immemorial. Soon she requested a transfer from Washington to Cleveland, Ohio, where her daughter Margie, now married, was living. There on Mother's Day, May 9, 1943, she was asked to make a national radio broadcast sponsored by the *New York Journal-American*. This was a weekly broadcast and known throughout the country as *Mothers Courageous*. Swallowing her sadness for the moment, she explained that her son had served a purpose in the war and fearlessly paid the price for that service, sacrificing his educational dreams to become a pilot for the military. She recalled:

> He wrote then [upon deciding to join the military], "Fear nothing, be it sickness or failure; fear not the future, build on each day as though the future for me is a certainty. If I die tomorrow, that is too bad, but I will have done today's work."

But that which gave her the most comfort were words he had relayed to her before he had left for his mission:

> "Stay close to God. Do His will and commandments. He is my friend and protector. Believe in Him, and trust in His ways."

As for Farrow's younger sister, Margie, by 1943 she was twenty, married, and working in an aircraft factory in Cleveland, Ohio. His cousin, Peppy Stem, who had been Farrow's frequent companion when growing up, was unable to enlist for military service because of a physical disability, so he had joined the merchant marines instead. On one convoy trip to England, a German U-boat sent his ship to the bottom of the dark gray Atlantic, and

Peppy was left adrift, floating about in the ocean with nothing but a life preserver between him and sudden death. He was picked up after two days, and later wrote to his Aunt Margaret that he credited his years of experience swimming with Bill in Black Creek with having helped save his life.

. As for the surviving Raiders, they had now departed Kiangwan Military Prison and were being held in a jail in Nanking, China. If they had hoped for better treatment there, they were sorely disappointed. In fact, the next two years in Nanking, as Bob Hite recalled, "would be hell."

At this point, following the sudden disappearance of Dean Hallmark, the leadership role among the men shifted to Lt. Bob Meder, a man famous for his sharp wit and keen sense of humor. No matter how dark the situation, Meder could always find a bright side and a way to lift his comrades' spirits.

Unfortunately, toward the end of September 1943, Meder developed a severe case of dysentery, and his condition worsened as the days progressed. Like the others, he was terribly underweight, and as a result of his illness he lost even more pounds. After two weeks he became so weak that he could no longer exercise, though he did go outside each morning and talk with his fellow airmen. Yet through it all, Meder maintained his sense of humor and refused to let the others see how miserable he felt.

Toward the end of November his legs began to swell, which is the first symptom of beriberi. At that point he must have known that without proper medical treatment he could not survive.

During one exercise period at that time he very pointedly reminded Chase Nielsen that they had all agreed to visit the family of any member who failed to survive the war. Nielsen later said that he was alarmed to hear the normally cheerful Meder speak so darkly. "I remember, we were outside, and Bob was sitting on the back steps," Nielsen recalled. "I had just filled a bucket with water when he called me over. He gripped my hand, looked me square in the eye, and asked me to pray for him. I didn't like the sound of that. It scared me because we'd all come to depend on Bob's sense of humor to see us through our bad situations."

It was then that a typically bad situation was about to develop.

A sadistic Japanese guard yelled for Nielsen to stop talking with Meder, but Nielsen, aware that his companion was terribly ill, paid no attention. The more the Japanese guard yelled, the faster Nielsen talked. Finally, the guard's fist lashed out, catching Nielsen on the right cheek. He was staggered by the blow but managed to keep his feet. Then he very calmly set down his bucket, looked at the guard, and gave a deep bow. Then, as he straightened, he brought up his right fist from knee level and caught the guard squarely on the jaw, knocking him to the ground. Stunned and humiliated, the guard quickly withdrew, and Nielsen was led back to his cell by three grinning guards. Following that episode, says Nielsen, whenever a guard pushed or shoved him, he had only to drop into a fighting crouch, and the guard would make a hasty retreat.

On the evening of December 1, 1943, Bob Meder was found dead in his cell. He had died of starvation and neglect. He became the sixth member of Doolittle's crews to die as a result of the raid on Japan.

Left now were Bob Hite, George Barr, Chase Nielsen, and Jake DeShazer. The next day they heard hammering coming from Meder's cell. Later they were led there to visit him for the last time. They found him lying in a crude coffin the Japanese had made for him. On his chest were flowers placed there by the guards. This was just another tradition of the Knights of the Bushido. Meder was being honored as an enemy warrior who had served his country honorably to the end. His body was later cremated.

At war's end two years later, Meder's parents would finally learn of his death. At that time they opened a letter that Bob had left with them soon after he joined the Air Corps the day Pearl Harbor was bombed on December 7, 1941. It was to be opened only in the event that Bob died during the war. It read:

Dear Mother, Dad and Doris-Mae,

I am writing this letter on December 7, 1941—that fateful day when the Japanese started the spark of this conflagration. As it had been the will of God I have answered my country's call and I pray that whatever efforts I may have exerted have been to some avail.

The main purpose of this letter to you is to try at this very last minute to comfort you. During this time of strife for all, those of you that have had to sacrifice loved ones are the real heroes of any struggle. The word hero is truly inadequate. Just remember, therefore, that the soul of a person is greater than his own physical body; therefore, you have not lost me, my spirit shall ever be with you, watching, and aiding if possible from wherever the "Great Beyond" may be. Be brave, not bitter; be determined, not overcome. That is the job of those of you that I love most dearly. Democracy shall continue. It is our sacrifice for that cause.

I bless and love you all very dearly; some day I feel certain that we shall all be united in a happier life in the life ahead. God bless and protect you. Keep up your courage! Your loving son,

Bob

By January of 1944 the Japanese were fighting a defensive battle on every front, and it was obvious that they were losing the war. Fearing that he might later be held accountable to American authorities, the warden at the jail in Nanking ordered that books should be brought for Doolittle's flyers. An orderly thus visited a bookstore in the city and returned with five religious books written in English: Karl Adams's *The Spirit of Catholicism* and *The Son of God*; Alfred Noyes's *The Unknown God*; and William Scott's *The Hand of God*. The fifth book delighted the men beyond their wildest dreams. It was a Bible written in English.

Bob Hite and Jake DeShazer would later remember that over the coming weeks the men almost memorized those works as they read them repeatedly, hungrily devouring them word by word. After two years of staring silently at blank walls, they were at last able to fight back against the terrible boredom that was devastating their lives, and they would pass those books back and forth via the guards and read them until the material had become deeply ingrained in their minds.

Indeed, those religious books would have a profound inspirational effect on the surviving airmen's lives, and enable them to develop their own religious beliefs, ideas that would sustain them during the darkest days that still lay ahead. They knew that God worked in strange ways, but was their capture and imprisonment just a small part of His overall grand plan for them? If so, what was His grand plan? Was all this simply a part of His grand plan for their salvation? This was a matter they began to discuss with wonder every morning during their exercise periods.

For Jake DeShazer the Bible and the other religious works took on special meaning. The others said he had become a changed man. He not only read the Bible, he literally memorized it, and recited the verses over and over to himself. In time the words assumed special meaning, and he began to lose his hatred for his sadistic guards. He would later recall that he experienced a "revelation" in which he believed that the Lord spoke to him and urged him to show "faith as a grain of mustard seed."

> You see, [said DeShazer years later,] the Japanese deprived us of everything that made us feel human. It was their goal to make us feel like beaten dogs. But we had the one thing that they could not take away, and that was our faith in God. We knew that we were God's children, and that God loved us. And that is the one thing that we clung to—the way a drowning man clings to a life jacket. That is the one thing that sustained us and constantly reassured us that we were quite human after all.

Soon the men made a startling discovery. They were not alone in the prison at Nanking. There were other Americans there also. From a friendly guard they learned that Cdr. W. S. Cunningham, who had commanded Marine troops on Wake Island, and four other Marines were also imprisoned there. They had earlier escaped from a jail in Shanghai, been recaptured, and now, as punishment, were locked safely away in Nanking.

The months passed, and the airmen experienced the terrible heat of summer and the bitter cold of winter locked away in their solitary cells in Nanking. Then on June 12, 1945, with the war's end finally at hand, they were all blindfolded, handcuffed, taken downtown, and loaded aboard a train. Then they sat, handcuffed and blindfolded, for three days and three nights as the train rumbled ever northward through the countryside, deeper into the interior of China. The American army was drawing nearer, and the Japanese wanted to make sure that their captives were not rescued any time soon. They knew too much.

Finally, they arrived at the ancient city of Peking and were driven to a large military prison some four miles outside the city on North Hatoman Road. They were then marched inside and led down numerous hallways and past dozens of cells until they were deep inside the grim belly of the prison. During the days to come they would find that their treatment here was even worse than in Nanking. For twelve to fourteen hours a day they were forced to sit on little stools eight inches wide and face the wall three feet away. Such treatment was very cleverly designed to drive the men insane.

At night they had only a straw mat to lie on, and their food diminished to almost nothing. After only a few days in Peking, dangerously depressed and totally malnourished, they became so weak that they could hardly remain upright on their stools.

And what made it all worse, of course, was the fact that no one even knew that they were there. They could be taken out and murdered at any time, and no one would ever know. No one.

Jake DeShazer became extremely ill, with huge boils erupting all over his body. The next day he became delirious and couldn't sit on his stool. Then he lapsed into unconsciousness. At that point a Japanese medical officer was finally called in and gave him vitamin shots until he gradually recovered.

DeShazer would later write that some two months later, on August 9, 1945, he awakened to a voice telling him to "start praying." DeShazer, startled at this clear voice speaking to him, asked the voice:

> What shall I pray about? "Pray for peace and pray without ceasing," I was told. I had prayed about peace but very little, if at all, before that time, as it seemed useless. I thought God could stop the war any time with the power which He had manifested.
>
> About seven o'clock in the morning I began to pray. It seemed very easy to pray on the subject of peace. I prayed that God would put a great desire in the hearts of the Japanese leaders for peace. I thought about the days of peace that would follow. Japanese people would no doubt be discouraged, and I felt sympathetic toward them. I prayed that God would not allow them to fall into persecution by the victorious armies.
>
> At two o'clock in the afternoon the Holy Spirit told me, "You don't need to pray any more. The victory is won." I was amazed. I thought this was better and quicker than the regular method

of receiving world news. Probably this news broadcast had not come over the radio to America as yet. I thought I would just wait and see what happened.

DeShazer had no way of knowing that August 9, 1945, the day he experienced his first vision, was the day that America dropped the second atomic bomb on a Japanese city or that the Japanese were negotiating a complete and unconditional surrender.

Jake DeShazer would further write that, locked away in solitary confinement as he had been for many weeks, he had no way of receiving any news from the outside world. But that voice that called to him on August 9 was as clear as a bell and totally filled his small cell. "I heard it just as clear as I hear you right now [he told me], maybe clearer. And I somehow knew it was a voice from God. I had not the least doubt."

He sat pondering what he had just heard, and he wondered what would happen to the Japanese now that their evil war was over. Then it came to him: If the Japanese people learned about Jesus, their military defeat would prove a blessing and a great victory for succeeding generations.

Then, eleven days later, on August 20, 1945, DeShazer had a second vision. He wrote that he awakened that morning to a blinding light. And then the same voice he had heard a few days earlier said to him:

> Your travail will soon be over and you will be free. You will return to your loved ones and rejoice once more. But you are called to return to the Japanese people and teach them the way of the Lord.

Unknown to DeShazer and the others, at that very moment American authorities, fearing for the lives of the Doolittle Raiders and other prisoners of war being held in Peking, had taken steps to insure their safe release. To that end, American planes had flown over the city dropping thousands of leaflets announcing that the war had ended. Then, once the Japanese had been given time to absorb that startling bit of information, it was decided that a six-man team of agents from the Office of Strategic Services (the OSS), led by Maj. Ray Nichol, would parachute into the prison area and demand the release of all American prisoners of war.

These six heroic agents strongly suspected that the Japanese would murder them once they reached the ground, but such was not to be. Instead, Japanese officers greeted them as victors and immediately obeyed their orders. Within hours after their arrival, the four survivors of the raid on Japan were led outside the prison walls. Also freed that day were Col. William Devereux and Cdr. Winfield Scott Cunningham who had commanded American troops on Wake Island. They had been held in captivity since their surrender in December of 1941.

(A member of the OSS team that parachuted in that day was radio operator and translator Dick Hamada, with whom the Raiders would have a wonderful reunion in 2001, some fifty-six years following their initial introduction.)

Later that afternoon a prison guard threw open the door to DeShazer's cell. The guard bowed low. "You come out now," he said. "War over. You go home now."

DeShazer was then reunited in the hallway outside his cell with Bob Hite and Chase Nielsen. He was told that George Barr was too ill to be moved and was being cared for in an American military hospital there in Peking. Smiling Japanese guards then led them to the washroom, and they were given shaves and a bucket of water for washing. Then to their amazement, the Japanese handed them their old Air Corps uniforms, the ones they were wearing the day they bombed Japan more than three years earlier. They were told simply that the war was over.

Jake DeShazer was not surprised.

That evening they were met by jubilant American authorities who led them to a waiting C-47. They were then flown to an air base in Chungking where more American authorities were awaiting their arrival. They were treated as great celebrities and spent the night in a beautiful home owned by the prime minister of China and given new clothing and toilet articles. As for food, for the first two days they were fed a mild concoction that strongly resembled eggnog, but after their stomachs again became accustomed to solid food, they had only to ask for whatever delicacy they could dream up. Bob Hite remembers with relish that they were fed an endless stream of steaks, french-fried potatoes, and chocolate pie.

*It was August 20, 1945, the day of the airmen's release from a Japanese prison in Peking, and here they are waiting to board a plane for Chungking. They had then been incarcerated three years and four months. It should be noted that they are wearing the same uniforms they had worn when captured back in April 1942. (L-R): Cpl. Jake DeShazer, Lt. Bob Hite, and Lt. Chase Nielsen. (Lt. George Barr was too ill to travel and was taken to an American military hospital in Peking.)* (Photo courtesy of the U.S. Army Archives)

The next day the airmen again were put aboard a C-47 to begin their long trek home. They arrived in Washington on September 5, and were immediately taken to Walter Reed Hospital for extensive treatment. This was the first time they had touched American soil since April 11, 1942. At that time George Barr was still hospitalized in Peking.

*Mrs. James Doolittle greets three of the Raiders in September of '45. (L-R): Bob Hite, Mrs. Doolittle, Jake DeShazer, and Chase Nielsen. It should be noted that the Raiders all received promotions during their three years and four months of imprisonment: Hite and Nielsen are now both captains, while Jake DeShazer is wearing the three stripes of an Air Corps sergeant.* (Photo courtesy of Bob Hite)

Some five months later in February 1946, the day these airmen had so long awaited, the beginning of the War Crimes Trial of their Japanese tormentors finally got underway in Nanking, China. Surprisingly, only four Japanese officers would be brought to trial: Lt. Gen. Shigeru Sawada, commanding general of the Japanese Imperial Expeditionary Thirteenth Army; Capt. Ryuhei Okada, a member of the mock court that tried the eight airmen in August 1942; Lt. Yusei Wako, prosecutor during the mock trial; and Capt. Sotojira Tatsuta, the warden at Kiangwan Military Prison and the official executioner of Dean Hallmark, Bill Farrow, and Harold Spatz.

Other Japanese war criminals had died over the succeeding months, and still others were being held in Tokyo by the International War Crimes Commission. The commission refused to release these officers for trial in China.

On February 27, 1946, the four Japanese officers—Sawada, Okada, Wako, and Tatsuta—were arraigned before the American Military Commission. Their trial actually began on March 18, 1946. And it was conducted in Shanghai, the site of the infamous Bridge House jail where the American airmen had been held during their initial months of imprisonment.

The first witness for the prosecution was none other than the unsinkable Chase Nielsen, who had sworn on numerous occasions that some day he would return to China and make his tormentors pay for their terrible crimes.

Nielsen was seen by his comrades as a man who would always fight back, a man who would risk death rather than face humiliation at the hands of his Japanese captors. In Bob Hite's own words, Nielsen was "one more tough cookie." He was also extremely intelligent and articulate, and upon his return home he wrote a series of articles concerning his experiences at the hands of the Japanese that was syndicated in dozens of newspapers across America.

And now he was back to face those who had starved and tortured him and his comrades for three years and four months.

In fact, Nielsen was the first witness called to the stand to testify for the prosecution. Over the next two days, then, he spoke very forcefully and without any prompting from the prosecutor. He knew the story by heart, and he didn't mince words when relating it to the court.

Had his crew bombed any civilian targets? Absolutely not, Nielsen said. General Doolittle had stressed that the airmen were under strict orders to confine their bombing to military targets only.

Had they machine-gunned any civilian targets? No, said Nielsen. In fact, they had not even fired their machine guns from the time they left the *Hornet* until they crashed off the coast of China late that night.

At the end of his first day of testimony, Nielsen stood and gazed in the direction of the four Japanese officers on trial for war crimes now standing with their defense attorneys. Those officers noticed Nielsen's baleful glare and quickly hustled around behind their attorneys for protection. Nielsen simply grinned and walked away.

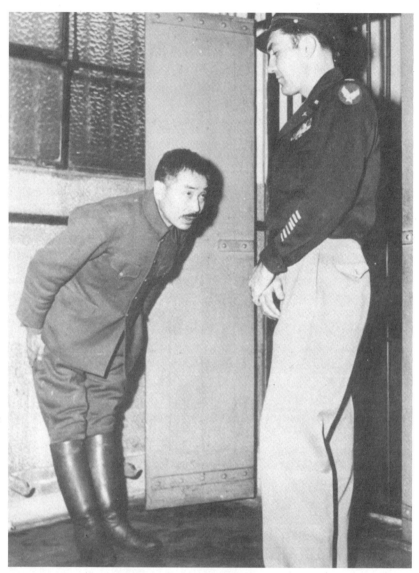

*Captain Sotojiro Tatsuta, charged with the executions of Bill Farrow, Dean Hallmark, and Harold Spatz, bows low to Capt. Chase Nielsen during the War Crimes Trial of 1946. Tatsuta was given a minimum sentence of only five years at hard labor.* (Photo courtesy of the U.S. Army Archives)

Following Nielsen's testimony, written depositions from George Barr, Bob Hite, and Jake DeShazer were admitted into evidence. They matched Nielsen's testimony in every detail.

At the conclusion of the trial the four Japanese defendants were found guilty on all counts. To the surprise of the audience, as well as the defendants, the sentences were extremely light, considering that they were directly responsible for the deaths of four of the Raiders, three by execution and one from mistreatment and neglect.

Sawada, Okada, and Tatsuta were each sentenced to five years imprisonment. Wako, a trained lawyer who should have known that the trial of the airmen was illegal, was sentenced to nine years' imprisonment. All four of the defendants, who had been expecting to be taken out and shot, burst into tears of gratitude when the sentences were read.

General Albert C. Wedemeyer, commander of American forces in China, reviewed the trial and sentences in August, and declared that the court "by awarding such extremely lenient and inadequate penalties committed a serious error of judgment."

And reaction in America was immediate and heated. Citizens throughout the country were outraged. How could these sadistic murderers be let off with a few years of imprisonment when they obviously deserved to be executed? After all, at the war crimes trials in Germany then in progress, war criminals were being taken out and hanged left and right.

The families of Bill Farrow, Dean Hallmark, Harold Spatz, and Bob Meder were especially bitter. And certainly no one can blame them.

But it must be remembered that immediately following the war there was a great fear in Washington that Japan might well follow the nations of Eastern Europe and go Communist. Thus President Harry Truman and the American government were doing everything in their power to placate the Japanese, which included letting off their war criminals with a mere slap on the wrist. After all, many of these high-ranking war criminals held tremendous political power in Japan, and American officials felt they had to show them that democracy and not Communism was the best route to take. The prevailing sentiment seemed to be: "We must not make them angry."

For many years following their release from Japanese jails, the four survivors of Doolittle's Raid still bore the scars of their imprisonment. The physical scars from years of torture and malnutrition finally healed, yes, but the captured Raiders carried their mental and emotional scars far longer.

# Update

As incredible as it may seem, as of this writing (August 2006) eighteen of Doolittle's original eighty airmen, better than 20 percent, are still among the living. For whatever reasons, whether genetic or environmental, these doughty heroes have far exceeded the life expectancy of the average citizen and are looking forward to the future with confidence and enthusiasm. Indeed they can hardly wait to attend their next annual convention, this time in San Antonio, Texas, on April 18, 2007.

It might also be pointed out that of the eighty airmen who participated in the raid on Japan back in April 1942, fifty-two were officers and twenty-eight were enlisted men. Of those still living (including Chase Nielsen and Bob Hite), fourteen are former officers (27 percent), while only four (including Jake DeShazer) are former enlisted men (14 percent). The author feels that these are interesting statistics, though he isn't quite sure what to make of them.

The survivors are:

**William L. Birch:** Born in Calexico, California, in 1917, he entered the Army Air Corps in 1939 and served as the bombardier on plane #11 during the raid on Japan. He received his pilot's wings in 1943 and left the service following the war. Today, at the age of eighty-nine, he lives in Santa Ana, California, with his wife Barbara.

**William M. Bower:** Born in Revenna, Ohio, in 1917, he entered the Army Air Corps in 1939 and served as the pilot aboard plane #12 during the raid on Japan. He retired from the Air Force as a colonel in 1966. Today, at the age of eighty-nine, he and his wife Lorraine live in Boulder, Colorado.

**Richard E. Cole:** Born in Dayton, Ohio, in 1915, he received his pilot's wings in 1941 and served as the copilot aboard plane #1 (Col. Jimmy Doolittle was his pilot) during the raid on Japan. He retired from the Air Force as a colonel in 1967. Today, at the age of ninety-one, he and his wife Martha live in San Antonio, Texas.

**Horace Ellis Crouch:** Born in Columbia, South Carolina, in 1918, he entered the Air Corps in 1941 and served as the navigator aboard plane #10 during the raid on Japan. He retired from the Air Force as a colonel in 1962. Today, at the age of eighty-eight, he and his wife Mary live in Columbia, South Carolina.

**Thomas Carson Griffin:** Born in Green Bay, Wisconsin, in 1916, he entered the Air Corps in 1940 and served as the navigator aboard plane #9 during the raid on Japan. He was later captured in North Africa and spent the rest of the war in a German prisoner of war camp. Today, at the age of eighty-eight, he and his wife Esther live in Cincinnati, Ohio.

**Nolan Anderson Herndon:** Born in Greenville, Texas, in 1918, he entered the Air Corps in 1940 and served as the navigator-bombardier aboard plane #8. It was his plane, piloted by Capt. Edward J. York, that was forced to land on the coast of Siberia, where the crew members were imprisoned by the Russians until their escape in June 1943. Following the war he returned to civilian life. Today, at the age of ninety, he and his wife Julia make their home in Edgefield, South Carolina.

**Edwin Weston Horton, Jr.:** Born in North Eastham, Massachusetts, in 1916, he entered the Air Corps in 1935 and served as the gunner aboard plane #10 during the raid on Japan. Following the war he returned to civilian life. Today, at the age of ninety, he and his wife Monta live in Fort Walton Beach, Florida.

**Aden Earl Jones:** Born in Flint, Michigan, in 1920, he entered the Air Corps in 1939 and served as the bombardier aboard plane #3 during the raid on Japan. Today, at the age of eighty-six, he and his wife Doris live in Pomona, California.

**David M. Jones:** Born in Marshfield, Oregon, in 1913, he received his pilot's wings in 1938 and served as the pilot aboard plane #5 during the raid on Japan. He was captured in North Africa in December 1942 and spent the rest of the war in a German prisoner of war camp. Following the war he served as commander of the Air Force Eastern Test Range in Florida for Manned Space Flights until his retirement as a major general in 1973. Today, at the age of ninety-three, he and his wife Anita live in Indialantic, Florida.

**Frank Albert Kappeler:** Born in San Francisco, California, in 1914, he entered the military service in 1936 and served as the navigator aboard plane #11 during the raid on Japan. He retired as a colonel from the Air Force in 1966. Today, at the age of ninety-two, he and his wife Betty live in Santa Rosa, California.

**James Herbert Macia:** Born in Tombstone, Arizona, in 1916, he entered the Air Corps in 1941 and served as the navigator-bombardier aboard plane #14 during the raid on Japan. He retired as a colonel from the Air Force in 1973, the last Raider to retire from the service. Today, at the age of ninety, he and his wife Mary Alice live in San Antonio, Texas.

**Charles John Ozuk:** Born in Vesta Heights, Pennsylvania, in 1916, he entered the Air Corps in 1940 and served as the navigator aboard plane #3 during the raid on Japan. Today, at the age of ninety, he and his wife Georgia live in Mundelein, Illinois.

**Edward Joseph Saylor:** Born in Brussett, Montana, in 1920, he entered the Air Corps in 1939 and served as the flight engineer aboard plane #15 during the raid on Japan. In 1967, after twenty-eight years of service, he retired as a major. Today, at the age of eighty-six, he and his wife Lorraine live in Graham, Washington.

**Jack A. Sims:** Born in Kalamazoo, Michigan, in 1921, he entered the Air Corps in 1940 and served as the bombardier aboard plane #10 during the raid on Japan. He retired as a colonel from the Air Force in 1965. Today, at the age of eighty-five, he and his wife Lee live in Naples, Florida.

**David J. Thatcher:** Born in Bridger, Montana, in 1921, he entered the Air Corps in 1941 and served as the gunner aboard plane #7 during the raid on Japan. He left the service at war's end, and today, at the age of eighty-five, he and his wife Dawn live in Missoula, Montana.

As for the four Raiders who survived three years and four months in various Japanese prisons, George Barr is now deceased, *but three are still living:*

*Miracle of miracles, they survived four years and three months of torture, starvation, and mistreatment in various Japanese prisons. Here they are gathered for a Doolittle's Raiders reunion in 1967. (L-R): Chase Nielsen, Jake DeShazer, Bob Hite, and George Barr. Americans everywhere owe them and all the other heroic Raiders a deep debt of gratitude.* (Photo courtesy of Bob and Dorothy Hite)

**George "Red" Barr:** His condition was so grave in August 1945 that he spent months in various military hospitals in China and the United States before being allowed to return home in December 1946. It was obvious that had his liberation come just a few days later, he would never have survived. He retired from the Air Corps in 1947 because of physical disabilities. He had been an outstanding basketball player at Northland College in Wisconsin, and his ambition had been to become a high school teacher and

*The three surviving Raiders gather for their annual reunion in Fresno in 2001. (L-R): Jake DeShazer, Bob Hite, Dick Hamada, and Chase Nielsen. Dick Hamada was the radioman and interpreter with the OSS team that parachuted into the Japanese POW camp in Peking on August 21, 1945. He is a resident of Honolulu.* (Photo courtesy of Chase and Phyllis Nielsen)

coach. But due to the scars he bore from years of torture and malnutrition, he decided instead to become a management analyst for the U.S. Army. He died in 1972 at the age of fifty-four.

**Bob Hite:** Born in Odell, Texas, in 1920, Bob Hite remained in the Air Corps until 1947. Then he resigned and returned to civilian life. But then came 1950 and the Korean War, and, believe it or not, he was recalled to active duty as a bomber pilot. He resigned from active duty in the Air Force in 1954, though he remained in the reserves, retiring as a colonel in 1960. Then he chose to pursue a career in hotel management. He and his wife Dorothy later retired to Camden, Arkansas, where they live today and still devote much of their time to church work. In fact, during a recent interview, Bob said that he is convinced that it is only his firm faith in God that has allowed him to live to the ripe old age of eighty-six.

**Chase Nielsen:** Born in Hyrum, Utah, in 1917, Chase Nielsen chose the Air Force as a career following his release from captivity, retiring finally in 1962 as a colonel after more than twenty-two

*Bob Hite and his wife Dorothy were married in 1999 and for years now have made their home in Camden, Arkansas. Bob credits God with helping to pull him through all the rough days in captivity, and says that religious activities still make up a large part of his and Dorothy's lives. He too is one of America's greatest heroes, and we owe him a deep debt of gratitude. (He and DeShazer and Nielsen still maintain close contact and phone each other at least once a month.)* (Photo courtesy of Bob and Dorothy Hite)

*Chase Nielsen, wife Phyllis, and a friend, Sgt. Rob Gordon, at the Raiders 61st reunion at Travis AFB in 2003. America owes Chase, and so many others like him, a deep debt of gratitude. We will always remember their daring deed and the price they paid afterward.* (Photo courtesy of Chase and Phyllis Nielsen)

years of active duty. Then he and his wife moved to Brigham City, Utah, where he took a job as a management engineer at nearby Hill Air Force Base. While serving all those years in solitary confinement in various Japanese prisons, he said, he dreamed of being free in the great outdoors, and now at last in the state of Utah he has found the freedom he had so long yearned for. He has not wasted a minute of it. At the age of eighty-nine Chase, accompanied by his dear wife Phyllis, is still going strong. He too experienced a deep religious awakening during his imprisonment and has devoted much of his time to church work since his release. He does have one complaint, however. He says that he wishes that everyone would stop refighting World War II and put it behind them. He was extremely angry at the Japanese during his imprisonment, he says, but he got most of that anger out of his system when he returned to Japan to testify at the War Crimes Trial of 1946. Since then, as a Christian (he is a devoted Mormon), he

*It was September 1945 and Hyrum, Utah, held a giant welcome home party for their favorite son, Capt. Chase Nielsen, in appreciation for the tremendous sacrifices he had made for his country over the past four years. In attendance that day were Governor Herbert Snow and other dignitaries. It was a day that Nielsen still remembers.* (Photo courtesy of Chase and Phyllis Nielsen)

has meditated on numerous occasions in an effort to understand and forgive the Japanese for treating him and the others so harshly. During a recent conversation with the author, Chase said, "I can forgive all the rest, but it's still hard to forgive them for executing Farrow, Hallmark, and Spatz. That was really unnecessary."

**Jacob DeShazer:** Born in West Stayton, Oregon, in 1912, Jake DeShazer is, and has been for most of his life, quite a man. The son of a Christian minister, he experienced a deep religious conversion while in prison and vowed that some day he would return to Japan as a missionary and convert the people to Christianity. That was not just "jailhouse" talk. DeShazer kept his word. He

*Jake DeShazer experienced a deep religious conversion while in a Japanese prison. He had several visions in which a voice told him that the war had ended and that he must return to Japan some day to preach Christianity to the people. He lived up to those commands, and following the war he completed seminary training in Seattle and returned to Japan as a Christian missionary. Here he is preaching in Nagoya, the city he and his crewmates bombed in April 1942. (Today, at the age of ninety-four, DeShazer is the oldest surviving member of Doolittle's famous raid on Japan. Long may he live!)* (Photo courtesy of Jacob and Florence DeShazer)

*The four survivors at the Raiders' annual reunion on April 18, 1970, this time in Los Angeles. George Barr would die at the age of fifty-two soon after this photo was taken. (L-R): Chase Nielsen, George Barr, Jacob DeShazer, and Bob Hite.* (Photo courtesy Bob and Dorothy Hite)

earned his degree in theology at Seattle Pacific College in 1948, became a missionary, and in 1949 he and his wife returned to Japan. Among his thousands of converts, there was a Capt. Mitsuo Fuchida, a former Japanese Air Force pilot, who accepted Jesus Christ as his Lord and Savior, and was baptized by DeShazer. It was a conversion that won headlines in newspapers around the world, for it was he, Capt. Mitsuo Fuchida, who led the Japanese attack on Pearl Harbor on December 7, 1941. To DeShazer this was living proof of God's miracles promised in the pages of that poor ragged Bible he read while in prison.

DeShazer remained in Japan for sixteen years, until his church called him home to go on a national speaking tour. Later, he was assigned a church of his own in Salem, Oregon. (Today Jake and his wife Florence continue to make their home in Salem.) At the age of ninety-four, he is the oldest of all the surviving Raiders,

*The Reverend Jacob DeShazer in 2004.* (Photo courtesy of Jacob and Florence DeShazer)

and in rather poor health. But now he looks back, he says, and it is obvious to him that God had a purpose in putting him and his fellow airmen through such hardships at the hands of the Japanese. They all became devout Christians as a result of their imprisonment, while he himself became a missionary and brought many souls to Christ. He recalls those who died at the hands of the Japanese with a great deal of sadness, but he knows that they too were devout Christians and are with God in heaven.

True, DeShazer alone of the four survivors decided to go into the ministry. But all of them eagerly agree that the Bible they were given immediately following Bob Meder's death had a profound effect on their attitudes toward religion and life and death. Their spiritual outlooks, they say, were profoundly changed forever.

As for the six Raiders who died in the service of their country as a result of Doolittle's famous Raid on Tokyo—Bill Farrow, Dean Hallmark, Harold Spatz, Donald Fitzmaurice, Robert Meder, and William Dieter—they were all brave men, the bravest of the brave, and our country indeed owes them a deep debt of gratitude. May we hold them in our memory forever.

*Bill Farrow*

*Harold Spatz*

*Donald Fitzmaurice*

*Robert Meder*

*Dean Hallmark*

*William Dieter*
(Photos courtesy U.S.
Army Archives)

# An Intriguing Mystery

After all is said and done, there remains one final bizarre twist to the tragic story of Bill Farrow, a mystery that would test the skills of Sherlock Holmes.

In 1998 a farmer named Michael Buckmaster was walking a recently plowed field on his farm in Suffolk County, England. It was in the fall of the year, and the leaves had all fallen from the trees, and their limbs were bare. It was while gazing at his trees that he noticed something hanging from a small limb nearby, something metallic. Intrigued, Buckmaster walked over and lifted the object from the limb. Now he could see that it was a South Carolina driver's license, and there were several keys attached by a small chain.

The license was in the name of Bill Farrow of Darlington, South Carolina. The expiration date on the license was July 1941.

Buckmaster would later explain: "It was hanging in plain sight, yet I'd never noticed it before. Obviously someone had found it lying in my field, picked it up, and hung it on the limb."

Intrigued, Buckmaster began an investigation. He suspected that the license belonged to an American soldier stationed in England during World War II. But a thorough investigation on his part turned up nothing. Adding to the mystery, Buckmaster also found an American Army issue dog tag attached to Farrow's license in the name of Eugene E. Metz.

Finally, after his investigations had led nowhere, he phoned the sheriff of Darlington County, Glenn Campbell. Campbell in turn advised him to call Darlington historian, Horace Rudisill. But Rudisill was as mystified as everyone else. He was quoted in the local newspaper as saying, "When that guy called me and told me what he found, I almost dropped the phone."

Buckmaster then mailed Farrow's driver's license to Rudisill and made an appointment to meet with him in Darlington. Subsequent to their meeting, Rudisill joined in the investigation. How did Farrow's license wind up in a tree in Suffolk County, England, and just who in blazes was Eugene E. Metz, and what was he doing with Bill Farrow's driver's license in Suffolk County, England?

To date neither Buckmaster nor Rudisill has been able to trace a Eugene E. Metz in U.S. Army records.

Many years have now elapsed since this bizarre mystery began. But to date no one is any closer to the truth than they were in 1998. Perhaps time will furnish the answers. Until then we can only scratch our heads and wonder.

*Bill Farrow's South Carolina driver's license was found in a tree on a farm in Suffolk County, England, in 1998. How this invaluable artifact wound up in England remains one of the mysteries of World War II.* (Photo courtesy of the Darlington County Historical Society)

# Index

263

## I



## J



## K



## L



## M

## R



## S



## T

## U



## V



## W



## Y